Frauds and Financial Crimes

This edited volume provides a contemporary overview of major issues and control strategies associated with frauds and financial crimes, including prevention, public ethics, compliance mechanisms, and law enforcement in England and Wales.

The UK – and in particular, England and Wales – has had a number of public strategies and plans to address frauds and financial crimes, beginning (in this edited volume) with the 2009 National Fraud Strategy and now including, most recently, the 2020 Local Government Fraud and Corruption strategy, the 2019 Economic Crime Plan and National Fraud Policing Strategy, the 2018 Serious and Organised Crime Strategy, and the 2017 Anti-Corruption Plan. All, together with a number of past, existing, reconfigured and new institutions and procedures, reflect a continuing collective response to emerging issues and themes in frauds and financial crimes.

Frauds and Financial Crimes: Trends, Strategic Responses, and Implementation Issues in England and Wales contributes insights about the continuing interplay of strategic responses, priorities, and implementation in an era of budget reductions, competing local and national agendas, and a continuing absence of joined-up oversight and ownership. Drawing on both academic and practitioner experts, the book seeks to explore a range of important themes, including: the gaps between strategic intentions and practice on the ground; different approaches to the same issue; labelling of crimes as 'organised' and/or 'economic'; collaborative public–private and inter-agency approaches and problem ownership; the role of prevention; and the translation of experience upwards and policy downwards in development and implementation. In doing so, it seeks to inform better strategic responses to frauds and financial crimes.

The chapters in this book were originally published in the journal *Public Money & Management*.

Alan Doig is currently Visiting Professor, Newcastle Business School, Northumbria University. He developed the first MA in Fraud Management for UK police, public and private sector investigators, and investigation managers. He is author and editor of practitioner and academic reports, articles and books on fraud, financial crime, and public ethics; the books include *Corruption and Misconduct in Contemporary British Politics*, *Fraud*, and *Fraud: The Counter-fraud Practitioners Handbook*. He was the Council of Europe's full-time Resident Advisor in Turkey for a public ethics and prevention of corruption project and a resident UNODC UNCAC mentor to Thailand. Since then he has worked for various organisations, including the World Bank, OECD, Council of Europe, and the UNDP.

Michael Levi is Professor of Criminology at Cardiff University. He has an international reputation in academic and policy-oriented research on money laundering, corruption, cybercrimes, transnational organised crime, and white-collar crimes. He has been advisor to the European Commission and Parliament, Europol, Council of Europe, UN, and World Economic Forum, and UK government departments. His books include *The Phantom Capitalists* and *Regulating Fraud*. He has received major research prizes from the British and American Societies of Criminology, the first lifetime Tackling Economic Crime Award in the UK in 2019, and the Al Thani Rule of Law Committee/UNODC Corruption Research and Education prize in 2020.

Frauds and Financial Crimes

Trends, Strategic Responses, and Implementation Issues in England and Wales

Edited by
Alan Doig and Michael Levi

Routledge
Taylor & Francis Group

LONDON AND NEW YORK

First published 2022
by Routledge
2 Park Square, Milton Park, Abingdon, Oxon OX14 4RN

and by Routledge
605 Third Avenue, New York, NY 10158

Routledge is an imprint of the Taylor & Francis Group, an informa business

© 2022 Taylor & Francis

British Library Cataloguing in Publication Data
A catalogue record for this book is available from the British Library

ISBN: 978-1-032-01532-3 (hbk)
ISBN: 978-1-032-01533-0 (pbk)
ISBN: 978-1-003-17898-9 (ebk)

DOI: 10.4324/9781003178989

Typeset in Baskerville MT Std
by Newgen Publishing UK

Publisher's Note

The publisher accepts responsibility for any inconsistencies that may have arisen during the conversion of this book from journal articles to book chapters, namely the inclusion of journal terminology.

Disclaimer

Every effort has been made to contact copyright holders for their permission to reprint material in this book. The publishers would be grateful to hear from any copyright holder who is not here acknowledged and will undertake to rectify any errors or omissions in future editions of this book.

Contents

Citation Information

The following chapters were originally published in different issues of the journal *Public Money & Management*. When citing this material, please use the original citations and page numbering for each article, as follows:

Chapter 2

A case of arrested development? Delivering the UK National Fraud Strategy within competing policing policy priorities
Alan Doig and Michael Levi
Public Money & Management, volume 33, issue 2 (2013), pp. 145–152

Chapter 3

Understanding the police response to fraud: the challenges in configuring a response to a low-priority crime on the rise
Michael Skidmore, Janice Goldstraw-White and Martin Gill
Public Money & Management, volume 40, issue 5 (2020), pp. 369–379

Chapter 4

When opportunity knocks: mobilizing capabilities on serious organized economic crime
Kenneth Murray
Public Money & Management, volume 40, issue 5 (2020), pp. 397–406

Chapter 5

For fraud, look under 'serious and organized crime'
Simon Avery
Public Money & Management, volume 40, issue 5 (2020), pp. 407–414

Chapter 6

Implementing a divergent response? The UK approach to bribery in international and domestic contexts
Nicholas Lord, Alan Doig, Michael Levi, Karin van Wingerde and Katie Benson
Public Money & Management, volume 40, issue 5 (2020), pp. 349–359

Chapter 7

Tracking the international proceeds of corruption and the challenges of national boundaries and national agencies: the UK example
Jackie Harvey
Public Money & Management, volume 40, issue 5 (2020), pp. 360–368

Chapter 8

Estate agents' perspectives of anti-money laundering compliance—four key issues in the UK property market
Ilaria Zavoli and Colin King
Public Money & Management, volume 40, issue 5 (2020), pp. 415–419

Chapter 9

Forensic accounting services in English local government and the counter-fraud agenda
Mohd Hadafi Sahdan, Christopher J. Cowton and Julie E. Drake
Public Money & Management, volume 40, issue 5 (2020), pp. 380–389

For any permission-related enquiries please visit:
www.tandfonline.com/page/help/permissions

Notes on Contributors

Simon Avery is Researcher and Dawes Scholar at Cardiff University. His research interests include criminal governance, the policing of organised crime, and the sociology of organised crime groups.

Katie Benson is Lecturer in Criminology at Lancaster University, where she teaches and conducts research in the areas of organised, financial, and white-collar crimes. Her primary area of research is money laundering and its control.

Colin Copus is Emeritus Professor of local politics at De Montfort University and a Visiting Professor at the University of Ghent. His academic interests are central-local relationships and the constitutional status of local government, devolution, localism, local party politics, local political leadership, and the changing role of the councillor.

Christopher J. Cowton is Emeritus Professor at Huddersfield Business School, University of Huddersfield. He is also Visiting Professor at the University of Leeds and the University of the Basque Country, Bilbao, Spain; and Associate Director (Research) at the London-based Institute of Business Ethics. He is a Chartered Governance Professional.

Alan Doig is currently Visiting Professor, Newcastle Business School, Northumbria University. His research focuses on corruption, financial crime, and public ethics. He has undertaken anti-corruption work for various organisations, including the Council of Europe, the UK DFID, OECD, Transparency International, UNDP, UNODC, and the World Bank.

Julie E. Drake is Subject Group Leader in the Department of Accounting, Finance and Economics at Huddersfield Business School, University of Huddersfield. She is a Chartered Accountant and is actively involved in governance through audit committees.

Martin Gill is Criminologist and Director of Perpetuity Research. He holds honorary/visiting Chairs at the Universities of Leicester and London. Martin has been actively involved in a range of studies relating to fraud and dishonesty offences. In 2016 ASIS International awarded him a Presidential Order of Merit for distinguished service.

Janice Goldstraw-White is an independent criminologist running her own management and research consultancy, Goldstraw-White Associates, working with academic, private, not-for-profit, and public sector organisations. As a former accountant, she has expertise in the areas of counter fraud, governance, audit, risk management, and security.

Jackie Harvey is Professor of Financial Management and Director of Business Research at Newcastle Business School. The primary focus of her research is anti-money laundering policy and asset recovery; the second focus is anti-corruption.

Colin King is Reader in Law at the Institute of Advanced Legal Studies, University of London.

Michael Levi is Professor of Criminology at Cardiff University. His academic and policy-oriented research has been on fraud, money laundering, corruption, cybercrimes, transnational organised crime, and white-collar crimes. He has been advisor to the European Commission and Parliament, Europol, Council of Europe, UN and World Economic Forum, and UK government departments.

Nicholas Lord is Professor of Criminology in the School of Social Sciences at the University of Manchester. He has research interests in corruption, white-collar crime, financial crime, and organised crime.

Kenneth Murray is Chartered Accountant and Head of Forensic Accountancy at Police Scotland.

Jonathan Rose is Associate Professor in Politics and Research Methods at De Montfort University, and a member of the University's Local Governance Research Centre. His research focuses on issues of corruption and integrity in public life.

Mohd Hadafi Sahdan is Senior Lecturer in Accounting at Universiti Utara Malaysia. He undertook his doctoral research at the University of Huddersfield in the UK.

Michael Skidmore is Organisational Lead for serious and organised crime at the Police Foundation. Areas of research have included fraud, child sexual abuse and exploitation, modern slavery, and organised crime offenders. Previously he has worked at the Home Office and Ministry of Justice.

Karin van Wingerde is Professor of Corporate Crime and Governance at Erasmus School of Law, Erasmus University Rotterdam, the Netherlands. Her research focuses on the interplay between regulatory governance and corporate crime.

Ilaria Zavoli is Lecturer in Law at the School of Law of the University of Leeds and a qualified lawyer in Italy. Her research interests lie in the areas of money laundering, cryptocurrencies, and International Criminal Law.

Dedication

ALAN DOIG

To Ann, Chris, Natalie, Chloe and Jack for what they have brought – and bring – to my world away from frauds and financial crimes.

MICHAEL LEVI

Many thanks to my family, our horses, dogs and cats, who have endured and/or enjoyed my absence during this, previous and hopefully future research and writing projects.

Introduction

Alan Doig and Michael Levi

The focus of this book[1] is on current approaches and perspectives on contemporary UK frauds and financial crimes.[2] It begins with the formal recognition by the UK government in the early 2000s that fraud was an emerging significant public problem (though not yet a national security problem). The first response was the 2009 national fraud strategy, 'developed with organisations across the private and public sectors, to a crime that affects every business, public organisation and person in the country' (National Fraud Strategic Authority [NFSA], 2009, p. 1). The strategy was allowed to lapse formally in 2014 when the government announced its intention to close the National Fraud Authority (NFA), as the National Fraud Strategic Authority had been renamed, and 'realign its responsibilities', including strategic development, to continue its response to fraud through other strategies, plans and organisations. The response is currently part of the 2019 Economic Crime Plan, which states that HM Government is working with public and private sectors 'to jointly deliver a holistic plan that defends the UK against economic crime,[3] prevents harm to society and individuals, protects the integrity of the UK economy, and supports legitimate growth and prosperity' (HM Government and UK Finance, 2019, p. 9). Work on delivering that plan continues with a February 2021 agreement 'to further develop an ambitious vision that would deliver a comprehensive economic crime response' (HM Government and UK Finance, 2021, p. 5).

Successive governments have sought to address frauds and financial crimes through strategies and plans and we have long been aware that the search for more effective, and more *cost*-effective responses is neither new nor yet fully resolved. Failings in components of a policy or strategy are, however, often a consequence of other, more complex and continuing issues, not the least in seeking how best to respond to the continuing evolution of frauds and other financial crimes within the constraint of existing resources and institutions and within the remit of other strategies and plans. This is why, when we planned the special issue of *Public Money and Management*[4] on which this book is largely based, we wished to address from various perspectives the issue of – to what problems are the range of responses a 'solution'? We are aware that there needs to be a much more proactive and flexible approach to make strategies or plans work

in practice, and we wish to bring to both an academic and a practitioner readership the importance of drawing upon current research from experienced academics, practitioners, and researchers.

The book sets out to do this by looking at the national strategic responses in the past two decades in Chapter 1, followed by a range of contemporary issues and practical perspectives from Chapters 2 to 11. It concludes with Chapter 12, which on the basis of a regional case study, argued that the strategic approaches so far have not been fully reflected in terms of practice on the ground but represent a work in progress. They provide guidance rather than an enduring framework, with different sectors and organisations still adopting specific components or approaches for specific purposes, rather than using strategic frameworks for a holistic, joined-up, and coherent approach to frauds and financial crimes. To provide an overview for this argument, Chapter 1 also seeks to bring together the narrative of the policy and strategic approaches to frauds and financial crimes in order to learn from the current research what may be the inhibitors and facilitators of more effective responses.

The structure of the book is as follows:

Overview
Chapter 1 [*Frauds and financial crimes: national strategic responses*]. This chapter provides a narrative from the 2006 Fraud Review, through the 2009 National Fraud strategy to the 2019–22 Economic Crime Plan, as well as an assessment of implementation of national strategic responses in order to illuminate some issues that should be addressed in the future to secure more impactful strategic responses.

Context: Early Days
Chapter 2 [*A case of arrested development? Delivering the UK national fraud strategy within competing policing policy priorities*]. This chapter begins by noting that the UK government had been developing a strategic response to fraud since 2006 as a consequence of the recognition of its cost, as well as its presence in many other areas of criminality, from identity theft to organised crime. The chapter focuses on the police dimension of the UK's strategic response, and its assimilation and implementation in the context of other policies and priorities.

Contemporary Practice on the Ground: Issues and Perspectives

Policing

Chapter 3 [*Understanding the police response to fraud: the challenges in configuring a response to a low-priority crime on the rise*]. This chapter argues that, on the one hand, there is still a lack of priority in tackling fraud, despite there being much more clarity that it is a volume crime[5] which is sometimes linked to organised offending and frequently overlaps with cybercrime. On the other, the newly introduced national approaches, intended in part to overcome the limitations of the local response, have added a complication in divorcing the national and local responses.

Organised Crime

Chapter 4 [*When opportunity knocks: mobilizing capabilities on serious organized economic crime*]. The chapter makes a persuasive case based on real investigations that, either directly or through criminal network connections, organised crime groups (OCGs) have access to the relevant technology and to the necessary professional expertise that enables them both to perpetrate the crime of fraud and do it in such a way that secures its proceeds.

Chapter 5 [*For fraud, look under 'serious and organized crime'*]. The chapter argues that the UK government's response to fraud is entangled in its broader 'serious and organised crime' (SOC) strategy which effectively imposes one homogenous strategy onto an eclectic jumble of criminal activities and has also proven to be highly invasive when it comes to local policing. The chapter proposes that fraud needs to be 'rescued' from the broader SOC strategy in order to develop targeted intervention strategies with a more bottom-up problem-oriented policing approach.

Corruption

Chapter 6 [*Implementing a divergent response? The UK approach to bribery in international and domestic contexts*]. From empirical research into UK domestic corruption cases, the chapter draws attention to the paradox of scrutiny from inter/nongovernmental organisations of UK governments' efforts to stop UK businesses from bribing officials abroad which has led to an improved response for the international context, but an unintended consequence is that bribery in the domestic context has been left in the political and enforcement cold.

Chapter 7 [*Tracking the international proceeds of corruption and the challenges of national boundaries and national agencies: the UK example*]. In terms of international corruption, the chapter argues that the relationship between the International Corruption Unit and the Department for International Development (DFID) has been innovative

as a way of tackling overseas corruption, but short political and organisational time frames and the need to be able to demonstrate both action and value for money may adversely affect its future.

Money Laundering Compliance

Chapter 8 [*Estate agents' perspectives of anti-money laundering compliance—four key issues in the UK property market responding to public sector priorities*]. In terms of the practice on the ground and the sometimes-modest engagement of policymakers with those being asked to implement their (often top-down) policies and strategies, the chapter looks at a specific sector and the impact of a specific policy – estate agents and their role in Anti-Money Laundering (AML). Its conclusions reflect a number of general truths in that those involved in implementation would like to see a more tailored approach to AML obligations, one that takes account of sector-specific circumstances and the lived-reality of AML in the real estate sector.

Local Government

Chapter 9 [*Forensic accounting services in English local government and the counter-fraud agenda*]. The chapters in this section also take a bottom-up view of implementation from both compliance and prevention perspectives. This chapter describes how local government has been subject to budget cuts, wholesale loss of fraud investigators to the Department of Work and Pensions, and of the loss of oversight by the abolished Audit Commission, which has seen the existing fraud capacity limited to a compliance response where the majority of councils have not accessed specialist forensic accountancy services necessary to address current patterns and trends of fraud.

Chapter 10 [*Local government ethics in England: how is local ownership working?*]. With the abolition of the Audit Commission and the Standards Board for England, and the emphasis in the Localism Act 2011 on local ownership in England for standards, this chapter uses a regional case study to assess councils' legislative compliance arrangements and the development of organisational ethical cultures. The research argues that the delivery of the former is a work in progress and that there is little evidence of the latter.

Chapter 11 [*Councillor's ethics: a review of the Committee on Standards in Public Life's 'Local Government Ethical Standards'*]. The chapter argues that policymakers and practitioners are often faced with difficult choices concerning ethical regulation, and attempts to improve ethical regulations can sometimes cause new and unexpected problems. The authors review the Committee on Standards in Public Life's report on Local Government Ethical

Standards, placing the ethical challenges and opportunities for unintended consequences into a values-vs-compliance framework.

Strategic Intentions

Chapter 12 [*Fraud: from national strategies to practice on the ground—a regional case study*]. Focusing on one region, this chapter reviewed the intentions of a number of national strategies and other initiatives to address fraud. It concludes that the interplay between national strategies and organisational priorities, within a context of budget reductions and other, often competing, agendas, remains an unending story. Both the rhetoric and the recommendations of the strategies in place may be – or are – required, but there are not yet the necessary or sufficient conditions for effective operational implementation. It notes that the situation is exacerbated by the absence of additional resources, and of national leadership or oversight on rolling out good practice, as well as a lack of progress ensuring the more cultural and governance arrangements to facilitate anti-fraud organisational environments.

Chapters 2 and 12 provide the substantive research and analysis which offer insights into current approaches and perspectives on contemporary UK frauds and financial crimes. First, Chapter 1 provides the overview in assessing how the national strategic responses to frauds and financial crimes have developed in England and Wales and – where the writ of devolved governments does not run – in the UK as a whole.

Notes

1 We would very much like to thank our colleagues and contributors – who represent some of the most engaged and informed academics and practitioners from a broad range of perspectives and disciplines relating to frauds and financial crimes in the UK – for their involvement in both the journal Special Issue and this book.

2 Our working definition of fraud for this book is the loss of income or funds as a result of internal or external perpetrators accessing services, resources or functions through a variety of illicit means, including abuse of trust, deception, misappropriation, or misrepresentation. For the purposes of this book, other relevant areas of financial crime include money laundering (concealing and/ or moving the proceeds of frauds and other crimes) and bribery.

3 The 2019–2022 Economic Crime Plan defines economic crime as a broad category of activity involving money, finance, or assets, the purpose of which is to unlawfully obtain a profit or advantage for the perpetrator or cause loss to others, including fraud against the individual, the private sector, and the public sector; terrorist financing; sanctions contravention; market abuse (encompassing the criminal offences of insider dealing, making misleading statements, and making misleading impressions); corruption and bribery; and the laundering of proceeds of all crimes.

4 *Public Money & Management*, 40 (5); 2020. Theme: *Fraud and financial crime in the public sector*.

5 Terminology is important here because the distinctions between types, causes, processes, and perpetrators may be contestable, including the serial nature of offending, involvement of the internet, and the role of networks and enablers. Levels of OCG engagement also may not necessarily indicate greater harm, loss or number of victims, bearing in mind the effects of the cost to, and numbers of, those adversely affected by various investment schemes, or banking activities, that have been or are now the subject of various ongoing inquiries (see, for example, Cranston, 2019, and Gloster, 2020). In looking at, for example, fraud as a national public problem (and in terms of areas or issues covered by this book), we note that fraud often crosses sectors and types of criminality. We also should indicate that much fraud is outside the remit of the Action Fraud crime reporting mechanism and general law enforcement because it is primarily dealt with in-house by agencies such as the Department of Work and Pensions (benefits fraud) and HM Revenue and Customs (including tax, tax credits, and customs frauds). Further it may not be formally defined as fraud at all but is handled – if at all – by financial or other business regulators or by the Insolvency Service.

References

Cranston. (2019). *The Cranston Review*. Accessed at www.cranstonreview.com.

Gloster, E. (2020). *Report of the Independent Investigation into the Financial Conduct Authority's Regulation of London Capital & Finance plc*. Presented to Parliament pursuant to section 82 of the Financial Services Act 2012. London: Financial Conduct Authority.

HM Government and UK Finance. (2019). *Economic Crime Plan 2019–22*. London: HM Government.

HM Government and UK Finance. (2021). *Economic Crime Plan: Statement of Progress*. London: HM Government.

National Fraud Strategic Authority. (2009). *The National Fraud Strategy. A New Approach to Combating Fraud*. London: National Strategic Fraud Authority.

Frauds and financial crimes: national strategic responses

Alan Doig and Michael Levi

Introduction

The use of strategic planning to shape and deliver policy issues by governments and public sector organisations has 'become ubiquitous' (Poister, 2010, p. 246); 'to be without a strategy is to appear direction-less and incompetent' (Bovaird, 2003, p. 55). Strategies offer a flexible means to address longstanding public problems across sectors and institutions; 'when the task is to rationalize a set of steering principles for managing uncertainty and complexity, a *strategic* response is appropriate' (Andrews, 2007, p. 168; emphasis in original). On the other hand, strategies are not self-implementing; there is 'an increasing awareness that policies do not succeed or fail on their own merits; rather their progress is dependent upon the process of implementation' (Hudson et al., 2019, p. 1).

British governments have increasingly used strategies as a basis for the delivery of national public policy objectives in relation to, for example, public health (see Pencheon, 2006) or addressing the emerging public problem of cybercrime which 'requires a broad-based strategy that recognises the diversity of offences, actors and motivations' (Saunders, 2017, p. 4). The recommendation for a national strategy for fraud followed the Attorney-General Peter Goldsmith's proposal for a national policy review – the Fraud Review – to the UK Government's Cabinet: 'the Fraud Review wasn't at the top of anyone else's agenda, but generally the Cabinet was supportive' (Fraud Advisory Panel, 2016, p. 3).

Following the publication of the Fraud Review's Final Report, the UK Attorney General's Office announced in 2007 that the proposal for a national fraud strategy was 'the key Fraud Review recommendation' (Attorney-General's Office, 2007, p. 3). Another Fraud Review proposal was the allocation of responsibility for the strategy's design and implementation to a National Strategic Fraud Authority (NFSA; renamed shortly after as the National Fraud Authority [NFA]). The NFSA issued the national strategy in 2009 (NSFA, 2009). The strategy was revised in 2011 through a national 'strategic plan' (NFA, 2011).

In 2013 the government announced the closure of the NFA; the 'strategic plan' was allowed to lapse. Nevertheless, other agencies took on a number of NFA responsibilities while other strategies continued to address fraud. In 2019, echoing many of the issues and themes that lay behind the earlier national fraud strategy, the Economic Crime Plan again proposed a national response. It argued that there had been insufficient coordination and cooperation both within and between the public and private sectors, as well as no clear sense of prioritisation. Albeit positioning fraud as a component of economic crime, the Economic Crime Plan – reflecting the 2009 national fraud strategy's language[1] of partnerships, coordination and information-sharing – set out new strategic objectives for another holistic, national response.

Drawing on the contributions to the book, the specific focus of this first chapter is on national strategic responses to fraud, beginning with an overview of the Fraud Review and other legislative and institutional reforms. It considers what happened to the national fraud strategy and, after it was allowed to lapse formally, what happened to fraud as a public problem in terms of continuing policy and strategic responses. It then assesses variables influencing implementation. While the chapter reprises past and existing plans and strategies, we wish to be more forward-looking in terms of what the current evidence from the book's contributors tells us about issues to be addressed in the future to enhance and sustain better strategic responses. We thus wish to emphasise importance of using current research to inform and underpin future responses, including their formulation and implementation.

In relation to strategy implementation we note that, despite the widespread fashion for strategies by governments and the periodic follow up action reports, 'research on the dynamics of strategy implementation in the public sector is still in its infancy' (Andrews et al., 2017, p. 1). Further, there are 'few studies that actually examine the antecedents of successful strategy implementation in public service organizations..., with little systematic investigation of any of the major themes relating to implementation success' (Elbanna et al., 2016, p. 1018). Given that the strategic responses to frauds and financial crimes involve a complex and continuing public problem across a range of political, public and private sector actors, we also want to explore the responses in terms of the 'alignment across strategy, process, structure, and environment' (Walker, 2013, p. 682). In a modest way we wish to explore strategy implementation, as the chapter – and the book – seek to 'contribute to a better insight into and a more efficient use of policies: the intention is to improve policy in an instrumental sense' (van Thiel, 2014, p. 6).

First, however, we take a narrative overview of national responses[2] to fraud from 2000 onwards up to the abolition of the NFA, and afterwards to the publication of the 2019 Economic Crime Plan.

Fraud: From Public Policy Problem through a National Fraud Strategy to an Economic Crime Plan

2000–2014

With some rare exceptions, fraud had never been an important component of national security, or of the politics of law and order, though there have been periodic concerns about the ways that criminal justice copes with it (see, for example, Levi, 1993). Nevertheless government-funded research was published in 2000 which identified that the cost of fraud was high and rising (National Economic Research Associates, 2000). Fraud was also considered a funder of other crimes, such as terrorism, while new opportunities for fraud were increasingly opened up by new technology, for example the growth in identity and internet fraud. One consequence was that, by 2003, fraud was ranked as one of seven significant threats facing the UK public and private sector (see National Criminal Intelligence Service, 2003); another was the 2005 announcement of a review by the Government.[3]

The Fraud Review itself was undertaken by government, prosecutorial, and law enforcement personnel working in the area of criminal justice and fraud; consultations also took place with organisations ranging from banks to public sector auditors. It was unusual that a non-departmental minister should lead the Review, especially the senior Law Officer, but (now Lord) Peter Goldsmith had a strong personal interest and intellectual grasp, and the Home Office and the Chancellor of the Exchequer were more interested in other issues. The 'emerging findings' of the Interim Report (Fraud Review, 2006a) were that: information on fraud was poor, there was no national policy on fraud, police resources had dwindled to the point where low- or medium-value private sector fraud was unlikely to be investigated, and fraud investigative capacity was spread across organisations, often in ways that were uncoordinated, not cost-effective, and not using the full range of methods or sanctions. Lengthy fraud trials were 'a heavy burden' and penalties were low even when convictions occurred.

In developing its response to the findings, the final Fraud Review report (Fraud Review, 2006b) took a primarily but by no means exclusively criminal justice approach, making a range of thematic and institutional recommendations which fitted into the Crime Reduction model (see, for example, Bullock and Tilley, 2009). These included: a comprehensive measurement of fraud; a National Fraud Reporting Centre (later renamed Action Fraud) to which businesses and individuals nationwide would report fraud; a police-based intelligence resource (now the National Fraud Intelligence Bureau [NFIB]); a national lead police force to house the NFIB and become centre of excellence for other fraud squads, disseminating best practice and giving advice on or leading complex enquiries; promotion of good practice in terms of prevention; reforming the trial process including the use of plea bargaining and of a specialised 'financial' court; more innovative sanctions; and more public–private partnerships.

In addition to the national fraud strategy and the NFSA, many other Fraud Review recommendations were approved by government; the NFSA housed Action Fraud and undertook an annual measurement of fraud. The designated National Lead Force for fraud was the City of London Police (CoLP) which, smaller than the Metropolitan Police and located within London's traditional financial centre, was seen as having less diverse national responsibilities and was viewed as more likely to retain a focus on fraud. CoLP housed the NFIB – which analysed Action Fraud reports for dissemination to police forces – and begun to develop a capability for national police fraud training. Around £29 million in total was allocated for the various reforms.

After issuing the national fraud strategy in 2009 the rebadged NFA published an overarching national 'strategic plan' – *Fighting Fraud Together* – in 2011 to revise and refresh it. The reasons for this were based on a review of current issues and post-Fraud Review responses, and an analysis of factors inhibiting the implementation of the existing strategy. One area, for example, not covered by the 2009 strategy was the fraud opportunities and threats posed by cybercrime; as the strategic plan noted, 'we need to find new approaches to new threats such as those posed by the increased use of, and dependence on, technology' (NFA, 2011, p. 6). The strategic plan also noted that it was 'closely linked with a number of major Government strategies and programmes which themselves involve partnership working with private sector and voluntary organisations'. These in turn would require stronger strategic collaboration in order to make better 'collective and individual, sector-specific choices which will have the most impact' within 'significant financial and budgetary challenges' (NFA 2011, p. 26).

There would be a governance structure that would have a 'strong role' in improving collaboration, removing blockages to progress, measuring performance, and mediating with other, related, strategies. The NFA would lead 'the development of a new strategic approach to tackling fraud across the public, private and non-profit sectors' (NFA, 2011, pp. 22, 27; see also Cabinet Office 2012, p. 2). In the same year, the NFA also issued a fraud strategy for local government in conjunction with the Fighting Fraud Locally Oversight Board (FFL Board; an advisory committee comprising mainly local government officials); this gave a much greater role to one of the Fraud Review's proposals in advocating a focus on prevention and anti-fraud organisational cultures.

In 2012 the Home Office issued a framework agreement for the NFA's role to lead and co-ordinate partnership working across all sectors to prevent fraud and improve the enforcement response. In 2013, the NFA had also noted that CoLP were leading a project intended to implement an enhanced, co-ordinated national policing response to economic crime in order to meet the Home Office Strategic Policing Requirement (SPR[4]). In 2015 CoLP's National Police Coordinator for Economic Crime issued a draft National Policing Fraud Strategy that was designed to support chief officers in meeting economic crime aspects of the SPR and their own local priorities. A draft National Policing Fraud 'Protect' strategy was also launched to support police forces delivering crime prevention aimed at reducing the impact of fraud in their communities. Progress updates were issued by the NFA in 2013.

In 2019, Her Majesty's Inspectorate of Constabulary and Fire and Rescue Services (HMICFRS) retrospectively noted that:

> In 2014, the National Fraud Authority was closed and its responsibilities shared across government agencies. Responsibility for setting the national response to fraud transferred to the newly established National Crime Agency and responsibility for Action Fraud transferred to City of London Police. Following this, the notion of a single national fraud strategy such as Fighting Fraud Together was largely forgotten.
>
> In 2015, City of London Police circulated a draft National Policing Fraud Strategy. This document was intended to provide guidance and support to police forces. However, we did not find any evidence of general awareness of the document, or that it had ever been formally adopted by police forces.
>
> The net result of all these changes is that there is no current government or national policing strategy for tackling fraud.
>
> (HMICFRS, 2019a, pp. 30–31)

2014–2019

In 2019 the National Crime Agency (NCA) stated that the public problem that had generated the government response in 2005 was still serious: 'fraud remains the most commonly experienced crime in the UK, with an estimated overall cost of £190 billion. It covers a wide range of activity, with fraudsters targeting individuals, businesses, charities and the public sector through a range of criminal techniques' (NCA, 2019a,

p. 42). In the same year, the government's recognition of the problem and the continuing need for a policy commitment was acknowledged in the 2019 Economic Crime Plan which, the Home Secretary and Chancellor of the Exchequer stated, 'sets out our commitment to improving our response to fraud' (Economic Crime Plan, 2019, p. 3). However, the apparent disjuncture between the continuing, even increased, challenge posed by fraud, the announced abolition of the institution tasked to draft the strategy and manage its implementation in 2013, and allowing the national fraud strategy and the national policing fraud strategies[5] to lapse (although a national strategy for local government fraud continued) highlights a number of issues about strategic responses and strategy implementation.

Unsurprisingly, however, there was a continuing response in terms of how best to address fraud as a national public problem after the NFA's abolition. The government professed that, while the NFA had been successful in raising awareness of fraud and improving co-ordination, its closure was presented[6] as 'part of the Government's reforms to policing and the fight against serious and organised crime' and a focus on 'cutting economic crime'. In the written statement the Home Secretary announced that she would 'close the National Fraud Authority and realign its responsibilities to reflect the creation of the National Crime Agency'; the NCA had taken over and in some respects widened the role of SOCA to fight serious and organised crime, following the publication of the 2013 Serious and Organised Crime (SOC) strategy. With its Economic Crime Command (EEC), the NCA would, it was claimed, 'bring a single national focus to cutting economic crime and will lead and co-ordinate the national fight against fraud, working with law enforcement agencies, regulators, Government and the public, private and voluntary sectors'.[7]

In terms of reallocation of NFA roles and responsibilities, the written statement and a limited Home Office notice indicated that the NCA's EEC was to be responsible for strategic development and threat analysis. Action Fraud was relocated to CoLP, which already housed the NFIB. At central government level, the Home Office would work on raising awareness of fraud, including some aspects of cybercrime. Elsewhere it was noted that the Cabinet Office was to be the policy lead for fraud at central government level while the Department for Communities and Local Government (DCLG; now the Ministry for Housing, Communities and Local Government [DHCLG]) would support counter-fraud work at local government level. A professional body, the Chartered Institute of Public Finance and Accountancy (CIPFA, whose primary role was the provision of qualifications and standards for public sector auditors) set up a Counter Fraud Centre. This included responsibility for the local government strategy, in conjunction with the (renamed) Fighting Fraud and Corruption Locally Board (FFCL Board). The strategy was revised and reissued in 2016 (FFCL Board, 2016).

Between 2015 and 2019, central government and law enforcement reviews prompted further responses which had implications for fraud. In 2016 HM Treasury and the Cabinet Office issued a national Cyber Security Strategy with significant resources for law enforcement and other areas. The strategy was to be the responsibility of the National Cyber Security Centre which was created from a number of existing organisations and located in GCHQ to provide a unified national response to cyber threats.[8] The Cabinet Office's Anti-Corruption Plan, first published in 2014, was updated in 2017 to a five-year anti-corruption strategy with both domestic and international perspectives. In 2016, the Home Secretary set up the Joint Fraud Taskforce; this was a partnership between banks, law enforcement and government to deal with fraud and to focus on issues that have been considered too difficult for a single organisation to manage alone. Though it has been reconstituted somewhat since,[9] its last formal published minutes in 2018 noted that work tackling fraud would come within the scope of a new Economic Crime Delivery Board and a new National Economic Crime Centre (NECC).

The NECC was set up in 2018 within the NCA. Its role was to set threat priorities to inform operational coordination between its collaborating agencies, jointly identify and prioritise the most appropriate type of investigations to ensure maximum impact, and facilitate the exchange of data and intelligence between the public and private sectors in relation to serious and organised economic crime. Its strategic and operational responsibilities, and a number of other sectors and agencies, came within the 2019 Economic Crime Plan. The Plan 'builds on the commitments made in the UK's 2016 Anti-Money Laundering and Counter-Terrorist Financing Action Plan, 2017 Anti-Corruption Strategy and 2018 Serious and Organised Crime Strategy to provide a collective articulation of the action being taken by the public and private sectors to ensure that the UK cannot be abused for economic crime' (HM Government and UK Finance, 2019, p. 2). To oversee the Economic Crime Plan, an Economic Crime Strategic Board (ECSB) is chaired by the Home Secretary and the Chancellor of the Exchequer, sets strategic priorities, and provides oversight and evaluation. An Economic Crime Delivery Board oversees the priorities for the public sector and a Private Sector Steering Group focuses on developing shared strategic priorities with the private sector.

The Cabinet Office was identified in the Economic Crime Plan as leading the public sector response to fraud. This includes the development of what the Cabinet has described as a Counter Fraud Function Strategy, led by a Counter Fraud Centre of Expertise whose work includes a Functional Standard, promoting data-sharing, and measurement of risk and losses. The development and ownership of the counter-fraud Functional Standard (part of a suite of operational standards that may include both mandatory and advisory elements and which set expectations for management within government) determines competences expected of fraud investigators. This provides the Cabinet Office with a lever through which to measure and report on compliance, with ministerial support for it to apply the Standard in terms of direction and guidance to all government departments and their associated bodies (see Cabinet Office, 2020).

In 2019 a new National Fraud Policing Strategy was launched 'in response to an HMICFRS inspection of the police response which identified the absence of a current national policing strategy for fraud' (National Police Chiefs Council, 2019, p. 2). In 2019, the secretariat for the FFCL Board and its Fighting Fraud and Corruption Locally Good Practice bank of information, was transferred by CIPFA 'on a pro bono basis' to Cifas (a not-for-profit fraud prevention fee-based membership organisation primarily including private sector financial services members, though available for the public sector). In 2020, the third revised local government strategy was issued.

We would like to consider a number of issues and themes relating to this period from the perspectives of both current research and practice but, before we do, we would like to identify the questions within which we wish to shape the consideration of issues and themes relating to implementation of strategies and of strategic responses.

Two Implementation Questions

Fraud as a public problem has been signalled throughout the period since the Fraud Review, as has the need for a national strategic response or responses (usually labelled either as a strategy or as a plan). In 2009, the national fraud strategy was announced as a key element in the Government's response to fraud, and part of its commitment to deliver key recommendations of the recent Fraud Review. The 2011 strategic plan called for the fight against fraud to be re-energised, with the need to be absolutely clear on the strategic direction and priorities. In 2019 the Economic Crime Plan proposed an ambitious agenda to strengthen the UK's whole-system response to economic crime – a flexible construct – and to ensure a proper strategic approach for tackling it. In relation to the Plan, 'at the February 2021 ECSB, Board members agreed the need to further develop an ambitious vision that would deliver a comprehensive economic crime response' (HM Government and UK Finance, 2021, p. 5). The practice over this period has, however, revealed a significant fraud dynamic within national strategic responses, whether relating to the particular strategy – or strategies – seeking to address fraud, the focus or emphasis of these strategies, and the institutional and other configurations to implement them. From the literature we posit two questions about the implementation of the national strategic responses that we would like to address later.

Given the approach of the national strategic responses, the first question involves the dynamics and complexities of implementation: those variables that may affect or influence the implementation of a strategic response in practice, particularly which are 'the defining variables and how it might best influence them to arrive at the desired results' (Brynard, 2005, p. 663; see also Hill and Hupe, 2003). Complex national public problems and the involvement of several actors or layers of government increase the numbers and effect of 'intermediary variables between government intentions and governmental performance' (Hupe, 2011, p. 63; see also Saetren, 2014). There is also a recognition of 'the dimensions of variety in institutional settings and other contextual aspects' (Hupe, 2011, p. 76), where the relationships between layers is not 'a simple and uniform phenomenon that can be expected to have similar characteristics in dissimilar situations' (Hill and Hupe, 2003, p. 487). Further, implementation may be, and need to be, influenced, altered, and revised as a consequence of being 'contingent on *both* the nature of the organisation…*and* its external environment' (McKevitt, 1992, p. 35; emphases in original).

The second question relates to the issue of responsibility for implementation (including, as the 2009 national strategy recognised, facilitating engagement and information-sharing; managing delivery performance; co-ordinating and delivering a range of activities to strengthen the national counter-fraud infrastructure). To adapt Mintzberg and Waters, a government that cannot be close enough to a situation, or to know enough about the implementation issues relating to a national strategic response, may choose 'to surrender control to those who have the information current and detailed enough to shape and implement realistic strategies…for collective action and convergent behaviour' (Mintzberg and Waters, 1985, p. 271). Certainly, the 'alternative to "top-down" policy making is not simply relinquishing all responsibility for public outcomes. Too much faith in self-organisation too soon may lead to problems: there is still a role for an overarching perspective and a capacity for steering…' (Hallsworth, 2011, p. 29). Here the steering, stewardship, or 'surrender' of control may be to an agency with responsibility for implementing the strategy, tasked with 'serving collective interests or act as stewards to the

interests of their principals' (Schillemans, 2013, p. 544). However, responsibility – whether ownership, management, or stewardship – may in in itself be ineffective without means or levers of control intended to 'improve…strategic implementation capabilities when used in concert' (Sheehan, 2006, p. 56), securing consistency of purpose, accommodating adaptation, and maintaining and measuring progress as a consequence of experience during implementation (see Tessier and Otley, 2012; Simon, 1994).

In the next section we also want to seek to summarise a number of contemporary issues from practice on the ground from contributions to the book to help answer these questions.

Current Research and Practice on the Ground: the Book Contributions

Fraud as a continuing (and growing) public problem, the continuing use of national strategic responses (often reflecting similar intentions and language), but with changes in strategic emphasis, sectoral approaches and institutional arrangements suggest that, at a national level at least, the most effective strategic implementation approach may not yet be achieved. Between policy intention and practice on the ground, further, it is recognised that 'there is no single best implementation strategy, that the appropriate strategy is very much contextual in terms of what are the contingencies surrounding the policy issues and how they can best be addressed in terms of implementation' (deLeon and deLeon 2002, p. 471). We now draw on what we perceive to be important perspectives from our contributors that contribute to the discourse on national strategic responses.

Although we should avoid mythologizing a past Golden Age of Fraud Policing – which never existed – cuts in general police, Home Office and Ministry of Justice funding in the past decade continue to restrict the scope for serious action against frauds and financial crimes, forcing periodic requests for private sector funding. Even when funds were more plentiful, however, fraud got very little of them, despite its growth in profile in survey-based crime statistics, both individual and business. It is and remains only lightly embedded in policing. In Chapter 2 we noted that neither the NFA nor the National Lead Force had formal authority to require adherence to either strategy, nor resources for staffing and other initiatives. We drew attention to a shift in policing priorities and resources toward complex, sophisticated, and enduring patterns of criminal activity, which looked at fraud principally as a medium of exploitation by those already engaged in ongoing criminality.[10] This was in part because of government intentions but also because organised crime offenders were seen as a bigger social threat than the policing of one-off or low-value frauds, or those frauds committed by managers, staff, customers, contractors, or clients of public or private sector organisations. Between the 'high policing' of serious or complex fraud by the Serious Fraud Office and the policing of fraud committed by organised crime groups (OCG), there was a large hinterland of fraud, from non-trivial through 'organised' but non-OCG, to volume or lower-value fraud that might still cause serious distress, that did not appear to be anyone's specified business (or, when it was, could still end up being filtered and then prioritised as serious, complex fraud [see, for example, King and Doig, 2016]).

Such trends and tensions are continuing. Chapter 3 (*Understanding the police response to fraud: the challenges in configuring a response to a low-priority crime on the rise*) reports that there is still a lack of priority in tackling fraud holistically and that artificial boundaries between what the police classify as volume fraud and what is 'serious and complex' fraud may push the specialist resources toward the latter category. We note here that the 2019 National Fraud Policing Strategy is infused with the language of organised fraud and organised crime – indeed, two of the three strategic objectives mention organised fraud and organised crime – and has still to clarify this issue in suggesting that 'the understanding of the link between organised crime and volume fraud is under developed. They can be one and the same' (National Police Chiefs Council, 2019, p. 5). Of course these may be merely pragmatic appeals to government priorities, but that understanding may need to be resolved, as Chapter 3 notes, to avoid a substantive rift between what is known about fraud at the national level, and what is done about it on the ground. A coherent, evidence-based approach to integrating fraud into decision-making frameworks that are central to configuring local service delivery – threat, harm, risk, and vulnerability – would be, the chapter argues, one step for introducing more consistent, rationalized decision-making in the police.

Addressing fraud as an organised crime issue raises questions about the proper labelling of financial crimes, and whether different aspects should receive different or integrated responses. Chapter 4 (*When opportunity knocks: mobilizing capabilities on serious organized economic crime*) makes a persuasive case drawn from real investigations that either directly, or through criminal network connections, OCGs have access to the relevant technology and to the necessary professional expertise that enables them both to perpetrate fraud and to do it in such a way that secures its proceeds from enforcement interventions. In terms of responses, the chapter suggests a significant collective effort involving all facets of the domestic regulatory culture affected should be involved. It adds that until the tackling of financial crime is accepted as an issue

of national priority, the chances of sufficient will and resolve being applied to prevent these kinds of consequences remain modest.

On the other hand, conflating fraud with organised crime is challenged in Chapter 5 (*For fraud, look under 'serious and organized crime'*). The chapter argues that the UK government's response to fraud is firmly entangled in its broader 'serious and organised crime' (SOC) strategy, and is now labelled as a form of SOC alongside drug-dealing, modern slavery, and human trafficking as part of a broader threat to national security. The chapter proposes that the notion of an overarching SOC policy effectively imposes one homogenous strategy onto an eclectic jumble of criminal activities and has also proven to be highly invasive when it comes to local policing. The chapter argues that fraud needs to be 'rescued' from the broader SOC strategy. Doing so would provide greater autonomy for those charged with tackling fraud and allow specific fraud problems to be mapped-out and situated within broader social or economic systems.

To explore another aspect of policing frauds and financial crimes two chapters look at the impact of the implementation of parallel agendas for bribery in international and domestic contexts in terms of delivering strategic objectives through variations in policy, institutional, and resourcing approaches. In the 2014 UK Anti-Corruption Plan, the NCA was tasked with leading, coordinating, and supporting the operational response to serious and organised crime, including economic crime, and overseeing the law enforcement response to bribery and corruption. For the English domestic context, and unlike Scotland which had set up a dedicated Public Sector Counter Corruption Unit to prevent and investigate corruption across the public sector, no institutional arrangements were made. This is in contrast to the international context where, to boost capacity to investigate cases of international corruption and act as a centre of excellence, a new central bribery and corruption unit – the International Corruption Unit (ICU) – was created within the NCA by bringing together existing law enforcement units funded by the UK's Department for International Development.

Chapter 6 (*Implementing a divergent response? The UK approach to bribery in international and domestic contexts*) states that, prior to the pressures that led to the Bribery Act 2010, using bribery in foreign countries to further the corporate and UK national interest had been seen as a necessity driven by exploitative foreign public officials and other international businesses in highly competitive export environments, and not an issue for significant government intervention through legislative and institutional reform. Bribery within the UK, on the other hand, particularly bribery of public officials, was increasingly presented as inimical to democracy and the public interest, and generated appropriate legislative and institutional responses. Paradoxically, scrutiny from inter/non-governmental organisations of UK governments' efforts to stop UK businesses from bribing officials abroad has led to an improved response for the international context, but an unintended consequence is that bribery in the domestic context has been left out in the political and enforcement cold.

Chapter 7 (*Tracking the international proceeds of corruption and the challenges of national boundaries and national agencies: the UK example*) describes not only the innovative ring-fenced resourcing relationship between the ICU and the former Department for International Development (DFID; now closed and merged into the Foreign, Commonwealth and Development Office [FCDO]) but also the advantages of mergers which brought together intelligence and information-sharing with investigations; DFID also funded dedicated prosecutors. This has been augmented by the NCA providing an institutional location and taking responsibility for the ICU's administrative arrangements. It also provides several resources to support the ICU's work, from specialist investigative techniques to access to the UK's Financial Intelligence Unit (also located within NCA). On the other hand, wider organisational objectives and the need to be able to demonstrate both action and value for money may affect its future, particularly now the Economic Crime Plan is in place. The Plan has confirmed that UK Aid[11] will pay for increased ICU staffing levels to 2025, but the FCDO also funds a newer International Anti-Corruption Co-ordination Centre within NCA which brings together law enforcement officers from multiple jurisdictions to target high-level corruption and the proceeds of corruption, raising the possibility of internal rationalisation and shared resources.

By way of contrast and in terms of issues raised in the Fraud Review and elsewhere, we would emphasise an old issue of ours – the importance of evidencing practice on the ground and the sometimes-modest engagement of policymakers with those being asked to implement their (often top-down) policies, strategies, and strategic plans. Chapter 8 (*Estate agents' perspectives of anti-money laundering compliance—four key issues in the UK property market*) looks at a specific sector and the impact of a specific policy – real estate agents and their role in anti-money laundering (the 2019 Economic Crime Plan notes that 'money laundering enables criminals to profit from some of the most damaging crimes' while the 2019 Asset Recovery Action Plan was published alongside the Plan). We suggest that the chapter's conclusions reflect a number of general propositions, including the value of a more partnership enforcement approach based on practice on the ground which should be part of improved responses when it states that the chapter's aim is:

…simply intended to present the (often) overlooked perspective of those involved in the buying and selling of domestic property in the UK. It was clear from the interviews that participants would like to see a more tailored approach to AML obligations—one that takes account of sector-specific circumstances and the lived reality of AML in the real estate sector. Instead, however, the current regime demonstrates a gap between policy-makers' and others' perceptions and the reality of how the sector operates; failure to consider this gap is likely to lead to continued lingering discontent in the sector.

From another perspective, we turn to the question of focus or emphasis in strategy implementation. The general use of the four Ps (Prevent, Pursue, Protect and Prepare) in a number of fraud-related strategies or plans may offer not only limited scope for variation and interpretation but also choices over emphasis and the synergy between them. The concepts[12] were introduced in the national counter-terrorism strategy (CONTEST) and are now used in the national serious organised crime, anti-corruption, and cyber security strategies. Interestingly none seek to explain how these concepts are to be integrated or mutually supportive nor, indeed, how organisations should approach their use collectively, know how to seek the balance between each, or deliver or resource them.[13] In terms of public integrity or prevention, the 2019 Economic Crime Plan makes only limited mention of either (and that only in the context of business and the international markets). In relation to prevention of corruption, the 2017 UK Anti-Corruption strategy talks of 'strengthening professional integrity. We will promote professional standards and ethical personal behaviour in both the public and private sectors through training and education' (HM Government, 2017, p. 28) but provides little or no detail of how this was to be implemented, and by whom.

Indeed, in terms of practice on the ground outside the law enforcement context, the emphasis that could or should be accorded to prevention now plays out more prominently in both central government – where a Cabinet Office-sponsored guide states that 'prevention is the most effective way to address fraud and corruption' (International Public Sector Fraud Forum, 2019, p. 7) – and more explicitly in the context of local government.[14] The second iteration of the local government strategy in 2016 noted the importance of organisational culture which 'fundamentally affects all elements of counter fraud and corruption activity: prevention, detection, deterrence, investigation, sanctions and redress' (FFCL Board, 2106, p. 21). Chapter 9 (*Forensic accounting services in English local government and the counter-fraud agenda*) describes how local government has been subject to budget cuts, wholesale loss of local government fraud investigators transferring to the Department for Work and Pensions and the irony of the loss of oversight by the abolished Audit Commission, the public external auditor (and likely steward of the 2011 Fighting Fraud Locally strategy). The chapter notes in relation to investigation and compliance that existing fraud capacity continues to be a limited response and that, in the absence of funding, the majority of local government areas have not accessed the specialist forensic accountancy services necessary to investigate current patterns and trends of fraud as well as reinforce compliance.

Similarly, Chapter 10 (*Local government ethics in England: how is local ownership working?*) demonstrates from a regional case study, the current emphasis remains grounded in arrangements based on compliance with required legislation and related regulations rather than promoting public ethics and ethical organisational cultures. Further, as Chapter 11 (*Councillor ethics: a review of the Committee on Standards in Public Life's 'Local Government Ethical Standards'*) notes, addressing public ethics at local level is not easy and there are many potential pitfalls. This is partially because of the challenges of positioning ethical regulations where, as the chapter points out, encouraging pro-integrity values or banning corrupt behaviour has different benefits and limitations, and there are substantive questions about which approach is better. The chapter notes that even the Committee on Standards in Public Life's report continues to reinforce a legalistic approach, recommending introducing important rule-based standards where compliance will be assured through sanctions, rather than attempting to reinforce a value-based system within which councillors should operate.

Finally, Chapter 12 returns to the overall issue of strategy and strategy implementation. It notes that integral to the approach was the strategic response that integrates, among other things, the roles of the four Ps. The strategic response, the 2006 Fraud Review argued:

> should take a 'holistic' approach, focusing efforts and resources where they are likely to be most effective rather than most attention grabbing, and focusing on the causes of fraud as well as dealing with the effects. The strategy will not replace existing strategies but rather will help co-ordinate ongoing efforts. Such an approach is likely to emphasise upstream action to prevent and deter fraud, such as educating consumers and businesses on how to avoid becoming victims. Despite these efforts fraud will still happen and the strategy will have to set priorities for downstream

investigations and effective ways of punishing fraudsters and obtaining justice for victims.
> (Fraud Review, 2006b, p. 6)

Chapter 12 concludes by asking a number of questions concerning strategies and practice, including why there appears to have been little progress on the recommendations of past strategies and initiatives and why generally there is a gap between strategic objectives and the practice on the ground. Having considered the contributions, we now turn to similar issues through a discussion of our two questions concerning those variables that have affected the implementation of the strategic responses, and ownership or stewardship. The chapter's summary considers current developments and how far they may begin to address the issues raised in order to achieve a more impactful strategic and implementation response in the future.

Implementation and Answering Our Questions
Question 1: Variables

Fraud is a significant public problem that continues to benefit from the formal engagement of government. It is now included in a number of strategies and plans, in areas such as the investigation or prevention of organised crime and cybercrime which have received dedicated strategic, institutional, and resourcing arrangements. Other areas have not and the first – and general – variable affecting implementation is: *the absence of appropriate or commensurate resourcing to facilitate implementation.* For example, for law enforcement and local government, budget cuts and staffing reductions remain within the overarching government austerity programme that begun in 2009. Though more resources have since been allocated and promised by the present Government, in 2018/19, £13.3 billion was spent on the police in England and Wales, excluding capital spending; this was 16% less in real terms than in 2009/10 while local authority 'spending power' – that is, the amount of money local authorities have to spend from government grants, council tax, and business rates – had fallen by 18% since 2010 (Institute of Government, 2019). This has meant decisions on whether to engage in additional expenditure or prioritisation of existing resources.

Chapter 3 notes that in the case of fraud, structural reform at a national level has not been mirrored by reform at the local level, with most police forces managing the influx of so-called 'new' demand with resources that are relatively unchanged. It reports that a lack of prioritisation and resources are the most common barriers described by practitioners interviewed, influencing not just preliminary decisions about cases, but also the subsequent quality of investigations. Chapter 6 argues that raising of public awareness of SOC-sponsored companies operating in legitimate commercial and public markets requires sustained institutional effort and commitment, involving suitable resource. For local government, the last additional resource provided by central government was a Ministry of Housing, Communities and Local Government ad-hoc competitive fund in 2014, with only a minority of councils receiving any allocation. Currently where new funds are sought for economic crime, these are for specific, nationally-determined purposes, rather than driven by the requirements as seen by those on the ground. The proposals for an Economic Crime Levy on the regulated sector in 2020–2021, for example, are aimed more at financing changes to the UK Financial Intelligence Unit's money laundering reporting processing capabilities than spending on fraud reduction or significant enhancements of the policing of frauds of any kind – whether elite, volume, and/or 'organised'.

While recognising continuing efforts to address fraud to reflect sector or organisational contexts, we would argue that a national policy requires a national framework – the umbrella that provides for collective action and convergent behaviour – because, as a second variable, *lapsing a national strategy may have adverse consequences for expectations that the policy response will be maintained through a disaggregated approach.* As Chapter 3 notes for the police, where there was an absence of national direction in the form of a specific strategy for tackling fraud, then even with coverage incorporated into related strategies these may be insufficiently specific to drive a common standard. The NCA was the agency supposed to lead and co-ordinate the fight against fraud, working with the public, private, and voluntary sectors on fraud but, as the 2016 HM Inspector of Constabulary (HMIC) review noted when it 'looked very closely at the quality of the strategic action plans' produced by the NCA and its 'efforts to improve them', the NCA had not provided any plans for public sector fraud (HMIC, 2016, p. 24). In 2019 the NCA and the NECC published an ECSB-commissioned update of 'key' economic crime threats; this did not mention either public sector or voluntary sector fraud (National Crime Agency, 2019b).

The National Audit Office published a report in 2016 on fraud in relation to central government, concluding that levels of fraud were unknown, that in the absence of incentives or resources there was poor reporting with gaps and inconsistencies in information collection, that departments were relied on to manage fraud but had mixed capacity and capability to do so. This was in part because 'fraud appears to be a low priority' and 'increasing cost pressures mean that longer-term savings from fraud can lose out against shorter-term objectives to reduce costs and staff'. There was also an absence of 'mechanisms for holding departments to account for performance' and that there were limited means to evaluate 'success' (National Audit Office, 2016, pp. 32, 37, 6). At local level, and although the second iteration of the Fighting Fraud strategy was issued in 2016 the preparation work noted that CIPFA had stated that 'many of the challenges from 2011 had not been resolved' and that many council leaders were not championing the strategy[15] and that 'senior managers were finding it difficult to dedicate sufficient time to demonstrate their support for counter fraud activities due to the focus being on other priorities' and that counter fraud work had a low profile and its benefits were not 'fully appreciated' (FFCL Board, 2016, p. 15).

We have noted that strategic responses to fraud have continued once the national fraud strategy was allowed to lapse but our third variable concerns *what happens to fraud when subsumed within related strategies or their prioritisation.* The 2011 strategic plan had noted that one of the two factors affecting the future trajectory of the fraud threat was likely to be linked to organised crime (see NFA 2011, p. 11), a trajectory confirmed both in the reasons given to the abolition of the NFA and the current trends described in Chapter 4. This thread runs through much of current UK government thinking about fraud and its attractiveness to OCGs (and their underlying management of risk in law enforcement [MoRiLE] methodology [Home Office, 2018]) as a metric of harm and threat. The UK response is also general among other Western states, reflecting the work one of us undertook many years ago about the way frauds committed by those 'organised criminals' were treated far more seriously than the same sorts of frauds done by individuals or networks that did not do 'other crime' (Levi, 2008; originally 1981) and work by the other on the impact this labelling has had on the law enforcement response, particularly where OCGs are not involved (Gannon and Doig 2010; King and Doig 2016).

We agree that the level of conscious harmful intent is relevant to prioritisation, but these assumptions about relative threats and dangerousness of different frauds and fraud actors generally need to be re-examined both in policy and law enforcement terms. The 2011 strategic plan had already warned that cumulatively, the financial cost of non-OCG frauds to society 'is greater than that perpetrated by organised criminal gangs, though the number of offenders and victims is higher (and therefore more challenging to tackle) and the size of individual losses is lower, meaning that cases may fall below thresholds for detailed investigation' (NFA, 2011, p. 10). We would argue that some repeated insolvency and specialist fraudsters, for example, may be just as 'dangerous' as generalist

OCGs to individual and corporate victims, and to government finances. We are not alleging fraud, but we have only to consider the impact of the collapse of major UK companies into insolvency, to see how mismanagement and recklessness – or 'bandit capitalism' – can lead to massive harms and losses (see, for example, Wylie, 2020). As Chapter 7 asks (and we think correctly), if fraud, particularly non-OCG fraud, *is* significantly different from drug-dealing, modern slavery, and other SOC activities, is it best dealt with through a very broad definition of economic crime and any strategy involving elements of Pursue, Prevent, Protect, and Prepare?

This takes us to the fourth variable: *whether the core priorities of other strategies or plans may distort approaches to addressing fraud holistically?* There is an ongoing tension over where and whether law enforcement investigative responses are the most appropriate or the most effective, although the SOC strategy is largely shaped by the 'Pursue' component within the four 'Ps' framework, to the extent that this is the component most controllable by government. This in turn drives the consequential allocation of the respective emphases, resources and initiatives between and across each 'P'. At a strategic and practical level, whatever the symbolic importance of criminal law, responses that are law enforcement-led – especially when enforcement-*only* – are not always the better option: when dealing with many financial crimes in which the private sector holds much of the data and resources for action, reducing crime and scale of crime opportunities by better designed controls could play an important role.[16] Indeed, it is now conventional wisdom in law enforcement and policy circles, internationally as well as (particularly) domestically, that we cannot prosecute our way out of cybercrime generally or fraud in particular, although we recognise that there are social legitimacy as well as deterrent arguments to the effect that *some* fraud victims deserve justice outcomes, unless justice is to be abandoned generally as a policy goal.

Further, we would also draw attention to the lack of focus on or prioritisation of prevention, relevant at public sector, central, and local government levels[17] (and one of the four priorities of the 2009 national fraud strategy which was to improve the nation's long-term capability to prevent fraud). At a central government level, the National Audit Office reported in 2016 that 'there is a reactive rather than preventative approach to managing fraud. Resources tend to be focused on investigating fraud after the event, rather than earlier in the process. Small pockets of experience exist in prevention and detection but they are not widespread' (NAO, 2016, p. 33). In terms of local government, the 2016 FFCL strategy called for 'a greater emphasis on prevention' (FFCL Board, 2016, p. 19) while the 2020 FFCL strategy

proposes councils should 'demonstrate the culture and commitment to preventing fraud' (FFCL Board, 2020, p. 22), although local government has been shown to be unlikely to invest in specialist resources in Chapter 8 or move beyond compliance with legislative and other requirements to any notion of ethical organisational cultures, as noted in Chapters 10 and 11.

Indeed, such perspectives are the basis for the fifth variable: *the importance of informing or revising strategies from evidence about perspectives and practice on the ground.* If strategies are to gain traction, and reflecting some of the issues raised in Chapter 8, then, if not at the start, a mechanism is needed to review and revise the strategy using evidence gathered during implementation. In 2016, for example and on the basis of very limited information from practice on the ground but already identified as an issue in the 2013 SOC strategy, the Home Office sent to all English local councils a report highlighting risks associated with threat from serious and organised crime to publicly procured services in local government. The report provided guidance both on the issue and how it should be addressed; the less-than-enthusiastic response was in part a consequence of 'addressing an issue identified at the national level without an assessment of the circumstances at the local level and susceptibility to countervailing influences, from resourcing to access to relevant information, for comprehensive and continuing implementation. There is a continuing absence of oversight and coordination between reforms at central/local levels' (Doig and Sproat, 2020, p. 88).

Chapter 3 also explains that, in the context of a national response model, and unless that response is shaped by local concerns, reflecting localised resources, structures, and priorities, the strategy and policy intentions will be ignored or will deliver variations in implementation across different jurisdictions and often leads to an uncoordinated, disjointed, and often ineffective response. As some chapters note, many of the current strategic responses put policy and strategy first and then seek to apply them to different environments while one of the consequences is, conversely, that practice on the ground may then not benefit from reflecting good practice elsewhere without an *appropriate* strategic response. As two 2019 HMICFRS reports have noted:

> There is no national strategy for tackling fraud. Police forces have therefore developed a range of different responses. We found some examples of good practice but, taken as a whole and given the scale of fraud, not enough is being done. When it exists, good practice is not always disseminated or widely adopted.
>
> (HMICFRS, 2019a, p. 7)

The national strategy for tackling cyber-dependent crime is well established but, outside national agencies, its relevance is limited. Within police forces, the threat from cyber-dependent crime is often not fully understood and is rarely seen as a priority. Knowledge about good practice isn't shared in a structured way, and as a result there is too much variation in the local responses to a national threat.

(HMICFRS, 2019b, p. 7)

Further, as Chapter 5 argues, even where non-OCG and OCG fraud may be superficially similar to each other in their illegality, profit-motive, and degree of organisation, each may have different causal connections in the sorts of social, economic, and cultural factors that actually drive crime problems. Therefore, where it makes far more sense, we might build strategy and policy around specific crime problems – for example, non-OCG fraud – according to both the underlying causes and vulnerabilities that drive the specific public problem, and the organisations involved, so that continuing targeted interventions can be developed or adapted, rather than to group very different things together based on arbitrary similarities or the fact that they all involve offline or online deceptions of some kind. Alternatively, the criteria for defining OCGs may require revisiting.

Question 2: Ownership and Stewardship

Our final variable addresses our second question: *what happens to national strategic responses without ownership or stewardship*. As we warned as early as 2013 – Chapter 2 (*A case of arrested development? Delivering the UK national Fraud Strategy within competing policing responses*) – the interplay between government policy initiatives, policing priorities, and an emphasis on budget reductions, targets, and performance remained fluid from the outset. As we stated:

> Significant progress has been made in defining the issues and reshaping responses at a strategic level but the NFA - now currently part of the Home Office – will need to ensure that any hard-won reforms are on-going in order to avoid the development of a uniform and enduring fraud strategy being downplayed or arrested before the commitment, resources and processes necessary to achieve its 2015 objectives are agreed, available and in place.

Without the NFA we have seen the above variables come into play. These have both affected the pursuit of the public policy response to fraud implemented through other strategies and plans. We have noted

previously that the response to fraud has reflected a general identifiable dis-connectedness and potential dysfunctionality at national level as a consequence of the absence of resources, clarity of priorities and leadership, or oversight that could be translated into institutional, procedural, and resourcing implementation. That perception continues with a recent think tank report arguing that there is 'a systemic "responsibility vacuum" in the UK government response to fraud, with ownership of the problem fragmented across different government departments and law enforcement and criminal justice agencies. With fraud continuing to be everybody's problem but nobody's priority, the UK has emerged as a low-risk/high-reward jurisdiction for fraudsters' (Wood et al., 2021, p. 5).

Chapter 12 (*Fraud: from national strategies to practice on the ground—a regional case study*) noted the value of the NFA not only in setting strategic objectives but also with the role to review and report at six-monthly intervals on activities and the progress made against the strategic priorities, adapting the strategy to meet emerging challenges and evolving threats, to measure and analyse the national incidence and impact of fraud to help to shape initiatives and measure success, and – crucially – providing continuing (and informed) oversight at national level. Much of the NFA's responsibility lay in coordinating and using evidence to promote collaboration between other agencies implementing the strategy.[18] With responsibility for both the national and local strategy and supporting a central government and law enforcement Counter Fraud Strategy Forum, intended 'to strengthen senior strategic oversight of national fraud enforcement activity' (NFA, 2010, p. 5), the NFA was also in a position to mediate between approaches across sectors and partners, thereby generating greater consistency and impact.

We would argue for the primacy of the ownership or stewardship variable to manage not only the issues relating to implementation but also the influence of the owners or stewards of other strategies that then fill the vacuum. In 2018 the Police Foundation, a policing-focussed think tank, reported on the impact of competing policy agendas on the police:

> the last national strategy for tackling fraud was published in 2011 by an agency that no longer exists…and we found few practitioners at any level made reference to it. Instead, strategic direction is derived to some extent from the Modern Crime Prevention Strategy…, but more prominently from broader strategies to tackle serious and organised crime… where other problems with a higher profile and stronger intelligence base (for example, drug offences) gain greater priority and

attract more resources…More recently there has been a greater national strategic focus on cybercrime. There is now a national agency, the National Cyber Security Centre, which helps to coordinate efforts to improve cyber security.

(Police Foundation, 2018, p. 67)

At local level the third iteration of the strategy, while supported by a secretariat within Cifas, makes a virtue that 'it is not "owned" by any one organisation but by the local authorities who have given time and support to develop it' (FFCL Board, 2020, p. 6). On the other hand, that lack of ownership or stewardship has meant that the problems identified in the 2016 review were still in place in 2020 (see FFCL Board, 2020, p. 18). Interestingly, and only six years after the government abolished the Audit Commission because of its perceived prescriptive, costly, and centralised roles as the national external audit body for local government, a 2020 Ministry of Housing, Communities and Local Government report into the oversight of local audit argued, in terms of the standards required for effective local audit arrangements, 'the evidence is compelling to suggest that the current audit service does not meet those standards… A single body would embrace all aspects of local audit incorporating procurement, contract management, the code of local audit practice, accountability for performance, oversight and regulation' (Ministry of Housing, Communities and Local Government, 2020, pp. 72, 73).

One further aspect of ownership and stewardship is the availability of levers or influence. Two reviews by the National Audit Office have noted what happens when these were not in place (although in the case of the Cabinet Office, as noted above, this is changing). In terms of responsibility for fraud at central government level, it reported that the Cabinet Office

has tried to raise the profile of counter fraud activity and has taken steps to improve understanding of the cross-government picture by collecting data and surveying department's counter fraud capacity. In the absence of firm levers, it has tried to improve aspects of governmental capability through influence, and promote collaboration between departments. However, some areas of its work have less defined plans for achieving the government's ambitions to reduce fraud and there is a need for clearer measures of success to assess progress and the impact of central initiatives.

(National Audit Office, 2016, p. 6)

In 2017 the NAO also published a report on online fraud, in which it reviewed the work of the Joint Fraud Taskforce. It noted that the Home Office had set up the Joint Fraud Taskforce in 2016 as a strategic commitment to fraud. In practice the NAO found that the work of the Taskforce relied on voluntary participation of those involved and that 'without clear indicators of the positive impact of the Taskforce, there is a risk that partners may be less willing to engage, especially since engagement relies on their goodwill'. In particular the NAO noted that the Home Office lacked 'formal legal or contractual levers' and that 'there is no senior responsible owner' (NAO, 2017, pp. 32, 34). The Taskforce's own management board was to acknowledge, two years after its creation, that it had not clarified its objectives, its resource requirements, its place within the wider economic crime reform landscape, and how to drive the fraud agenda forward.

Interestingly, the importance of ownership, stewardship, and clarity of vision has been underlined by the creation of the 2019 Economic Crime Plan and the Economic Crime Strategic Board. The Plan (HM Government and UK Finance, 2019) notes the need to identify strategic priorities, sector and organisational implementers, information-sharing, and partnership working, as well as clarifying and complementing rather than duplicating other strategies and responsibilities 'aimed at targeting economic crime holistically' (p. 17). While it also talks of resources and addressing all four Ps,[19] the Plan's main thrust lies in its proposed governance framework, with ownership through the Boards and stewardship through strategic priorities and monitoring. This is intended to 'ensure that it effectively implements the actions outlined in this plan and addresses new threats as they emerge' (p. 65). In particular, the Economic Crime Strategic Board:

drives the public and private sector response to economic crime by setting shared strategic priorities for tackling economic crime and ensuring resources are aligned to deliver these priorities. The Board also holds the economic crime system to account for performance against the strategic priorities. The Board is ultimately the body that is accountable for the development and delivery of this plan.

(HM Government and UK Finance, 2019, p. 65)

Summary: Better Strategic Responses? The Futures for Frauds and Financial Crimes

It is clear that the 2019 Economic Crime Plan and the roles of the Economic Crime Strategic Board and its satellite Boards, as well as that of the NECC (which shared in an additional £48 million provided by the government for law enforcement's capabilities to combat economic crime in 2019–20) within NCA, addresses the need for a national remit and of ownership or stewardship in an approach that echoes that envisaged by the Fraud Review proposals for a national fraud strategy and the NFA as the basis of a better strategic response: 'the government must formulate a national strategy for dealing with fraud… (with) a central strategic "authority"…responsible for identifying, measuring and analysing problems and determining the best way of dealing with them…any oversight body must have the authority to act to fulfil its functions' (Fraud Review, 2006b, pp. 6, 50).

Whether this addresses all the salient issues identified in this chapter and in the contributions to this book – particularly in terms of implementation – is, however, still open to question. It is far from clear how much capacity is 'sufficient' and how we might even have a sensible conversation about the criteria for assessing that, not just as between public and private sectors but also in terms of 'Pursue' versus the other Ps, and what criteria should be employed for prioritising the sorts of fraud that will be pursued and, inevitably, those that will not be, even if we doubled or quadrupled the modest amount of Pursue and other counter-fraud resources currently employed in the public sector. Of course, it is politically easier for these priorities not to be explicit, because there are always reactions to exclusions in the real world of scarcity – but the present mess also is not without risk, and managing expectations is a serious business. This is not thought through in the RUSI report (Wood et al., 2021), since though the engagement of national security with fraud would be welcome, the risk is that this would continue to be trapped in the same sort of SOC/OCG discourse that it has been in the past. 'Threat actors' are not the same as 'harm' for fraud or other crimes. How is alleged influence of the 'chumocracy' – with its implications for legitimacy and faith in government – going to be treated in a prioritisation conflict with Russian and other oligarchs and Bounce Back Loans scams by OCGs, and offline frauds against 'vulnerable persons'; and what is the intellectual or ethical basis for those decisions (see Levi and Smith, 2021 for a review in the context of the pandemic)?

While we acknowledge that the 2019 Economic Crime Plan and the Economic Crime Strategic Board – with the latter offering an answer to our second question about ownership and stewardship – may begin to provide the platform for a better response but for a specific target grouping, we also note that it is too early to see how this addresses the other variables noted above (although some of which have been recognised in the Plan). However, we consider that there has been a very differentiated and uneven approach to addressing some sorts of fraud, aggravated by austerity – for example, the number of police investigations – and the lack of prioritisation

(and resources) for prevention at central and local government levels, both for fraud and the UK anti-corruption strategy. Further, in strategic terms, fraud remains very much part of the organised crime agenda, whether in the Economic Crime Plan or the new National Fraud Policing Strategy.

Addressing the tensions we have noted above has raised the issue of a more thorough strategic response – and one which should address not only those frauds connected to 'organised crime' but also take a more holistic approach to fraud, including those not connected (or not known to be connected) to OCGs as defined by law enforcement protocols. Here we draw attention to the findings of the 2016 Insurance Fraud Taskforce:

> Fraud however exists on a continuum, from application fraud to bogus, fictitious or intentionally inflated claims, right through to sophisticated organised crime. There is also no simple profile of someone who commits insurance fraud, and there are different degrees of criminality and premeditation. Some otherwise honest people commit fraud when the opportunity presents itself; some people commit fraud that is premeditated and some fraud can even be linked to organised crime…The Taskforce is mindful that different types of fraud require different solutions.
> (Insurance Fraud Taskforce, 2016, p. 5)

Acknowledging such perspectives, and while we recognise both the growing sophistication and complexity of OCGs, as well as their appetite for fraud and capacity for exploiting legitimate business and professional enablers, we would argue that, unless there is evidence of which we are unaware, the 2011 strategic plan remains relevant to future strategic responses when it states: 'the majority of frauds are not perpetrated by sophisticated, organised criminal gangs. They are a variety of opportunistic frauds and those which require a degree of sophisticated planning – often coupled with insider knowledge and access but without links to a wider organised criminal enterprise' (NFA, 2011, p. 10). This is the hinterland to which we have already referred and which we consider, alongside other strategies, should now become both more prominent and also someone's specified business. We consider, however, that these perspectives may be beginning to resonate with – if not yet addressed by – the ECSB.

While it may be too early to see how the 2019 Economic Crime Plan addresses all the variables noted in relation to our Question 1 (Variables) above, we note that ECSB has 'agreed that a Fraud Action Plan will be developed by the government, private sector and law enforcement and will be published following the 2021 Spending Review' (HM Government and

UK Finance, 2021, p. 6). The Fraud Action Plan (FAP) will give a central role to the NECC but also relaunch the Joint Fraud Taskforce. It envisages roles for the NCA and the Serious Fraud Office, and it calls for a more coordinated response across law enforcement while enhancing the roles of regional organised units. It proposes the promotion of prevention as well as investigations. As our initial thoughts on the future for frauds and financial crimes – reflecting much of the practice on the ground this book addresses – we ask whether this FAP, and the range of activities discussed in the Economic Crime Plan's Statement of Progress which announced the FAP (HM Government and UK Finance, 2021) will work toward resolving the issues in Questions 1 and 2, and how.

It remains to be seen if these very recent developments will achieve a better and more holistic strategic response to fraud, particularly for non-OCG frauds and with a greater emphasis on prevention, on resourcing and supporting those responsible for implementation, and on using evidence from practice on the ground to revise and adapt the FAP. The strategic responses to fraud following the abolition of the NFA and the side-lining of the national fraud strategy have not shown major benefits to date – hence the need to revisit the responses through the proposed FAP. As discussed above, we would argue that, to be optimal, strategic responses and implementation need to be informed (and revised) according to both the underlying causes and vulnerabilities that drive the specific public problem (s); and the organisations with the capability to counteract them need to be involved so that continuing targeted interventions can be developed or adapted.

A broad-brush, top-down approach through the proposed FAP may turn a policy intention into a strategic response. It will be interesting to see how the two questions we have posed, and the perspectives raised in the chapters in the book, play out in FAP implementation and how far, in terms of implementation, the FAP addresses them, and revises its approach, in order to enhance and sustain the strategic response. It is a huge challenge to provide coherence, structure, and momentum across multiple sectors and society, to (intentionally plural) ensure better strategic responses to frauds and financial crimes. However it is necessary to address this challenge if we are to see further net benefits from counter fraud efforts. Fraud as a public problem will not diminish naturally: it will require control (rather than crime-facilitative) technologies, targeted prevention and enforcement.

Notes

1 For example, the Economic Crime Plan talks (2019, p. 2) of 'harnessing the capabilities, resources, and experience of both the public and private sectors'; the national fraud strategy talked (NFSA, 2009, p. 5) of the need to 'harness the existing work, energy, expertise, resources and opportunities for action provided by our delivery partners across government, business and the voluntary sector'.

2 It should be noted that when we use the term 'national', this needs to take account the peculiar characteristics of devolved powers within the UK. Policing is not currently devolved in Wales, and therefore in a policing context, 'national' refers to England and Wales, but not (in this chapter) to Scotland or Northern Ireland. Some fraud policing functions are carried out by Trading Standards, which are devolved in all the nations of the UK, as is local government. Other policing functions for fraud and money laundering are carried out by HM Revenue and Customs which is not devolved, though there are some additional taxes, for example in Scotland, which are devolved. The UK parliament retains the ability to legislate even in devolved areas of criminal justice, but under the Sewel Convention it does 'not normally' do so without the consent of the relevant devolved legislature.

3 In terms of public policy and criminal justice responses, however, it should be remembered that the 2000 cost of fraud survey and the 2006 Fraud Review were only two initiatives in a decade notable for a range of anti-fraud and financial crime responses at national level. These included: the 2002 Proceeds of Crime Act, setting up the Assets Recovery Agency in 2003, the 2006 Fraud Act, the establishment of the Serious Organised Crime Agency (SOCA) in 2006, a more refined assessment of the cost of fraud in 2007, and the 2010 Bribery Act.

4 The SPR identified national threats and the appropriate national policing capabilities required to counter those threats, including the reduction and prevention of economic crime.

5 The draft National Policing Fraud strategy lapsed almost on inception. In 2015, Her Majesty's Inspectorate of Constabulary (HMIC) reported that in nearly all forces there was 'an absence of strategic leadership', less than half of forces regularly considered 'the impact of fraud in their strategic risk assessments' and nearly two-thirds of forces failed to provide the CoLP Coordinator with a nominated senior officer to oversee the draft strategy (HMIC, 2015, p. 67).

6 https://hansard.parliament.uk/Commons/2013-12-02/debates/1312021000011/NationalFraudAuthority.

7 https://hansard.parliament.uk/Commons/2013-12-02/debates/1312021000011/NationalFraudAuthority.

8 In 2015, but not connected to this development, a report on the implications of economic cybercrime for policing published by the City of London Corporation had noted from an analysis of Action Fraud data that well over half of the reported fraud-related crimes by individuals and businesses were significantly cyber-related (Levi et al., 2015).

9 https://questions-statements.parliament.uk/written-questions/detail/2019-01-22/211121.

10 Apart from organised crime's increasing engagement in fraud, one developing aspect of the law enforcement approach to the investigation of OCGs was pursuit of their fraud schemes or money laundering-related activity because they presented a significant vulnerability to investigation and/or disruption and proceeds of crime confiscation under the relevant legislation and the broadened definition of economic crime.

11 UK Aid is the badge used by the FCDO for any overseas expenditure.

12 The general intention of the concepts is: prosecuting and disrupting people engaged in the criminality (*Pursue*);

preventing people from engaging in this criminality (*Prevent*); increasing protection against this criminality (*Protect*); and prepare for criminality occurring and mitigate its impact (*Prepare*).

13 When looking at the balance and allocation of resources a 2019 House of Commons Committee of Public Accounts report noted that only 4% of the government budget for tackling serious and organised crime was spent on 'Prevent' activities as opposed to 79% on 'Pursue' activities (see House of Commons Committee of Public Accounts, 2019, p. 5).

14 The current Fighting Fraud and Corruption Locally strategy uses Prevent, Pursue, and Protect; it also adds 'Govern' and 'Acknowledge'. It notes that 'for the purposes of this strategy we have retained the terms "fraud" and "corruption" while recognising that they are part of a wider agenda. The strategy has not been re-titled "Economic Crime"' (FFCL Board, 2020, p. 12).

15 Public Sector Executive February 2016; www.publicsectorexecutive.com/Crime-Reduction/a-new-strategy-for-fighting-fraud-and-corruption-locally. Accessed May 2018.

16 We were both involved in a significant – if subsequently largely ignored – project on fraud and cybercrime grounded in Action Fraud data and practitioner interviews where we argued that, even if a significant OCG involvement may be assumed and a 'reasonable' amount of extra resources was available, this would not solve a large proportion of the investigations into economic cybercrime, nor would greater investigative success alone be likely to reduce substantially the levels of such crime (see Levi et al., 2015, 2017).

17 As a footnote on one P – Prevent – we would like to note the absence of any reference in any strategy or strategic plan to the work on public integrity, prevention, and governance arrangements by the Committee on Standards in Public Life (CSPL; a longstanding advisory standing committee with limited resources and influence). The UK now lags behind the initiatives of, for example, the OECD to develop an evidence-based, strategic approach to mitigate domestic public integrity risks (see OECD, 2020).

18 It is interesting to note in relation to one agency – Action Fraud – once located within the NFA that a review commissioned following *The Times'* articles and published in January 2020, succinctly noted that, 'for fraud to be investigated effectively, Action Fraud and the NFIB [National Fraud Intelligence Bureau] need to work seamlessly with the 43 police forces in an assured "end to end" process. However, the reality is that when cases are sent to forces for investigation, they frequently become lost among other priorities; there are disagreements about which force should take responsibility for investigations; and, most importantly of all, rarely are there sufficient detectives available to investigate them' (Mackey and Savill, 2020, p. 3, para 1.5).

19 In 2019 the House of Commons Committee of Public Accounts report identified the government response to serious and organised crime as an area where the effect of similar variables to those discussed in this chapter needed to be addressed (House of Commons Committee of Public Accounts, 2019).

References

Andrews, C. J. (2007). 'Rationality in Policy decision making', in Fischer, F., Miller, G. J. and Sidney, M. S. (eds). *Handbook of Public Policy Analysis*. Boca Raton, Florida: CRC Press. 161–172.

Andrews, R, Benyon, M. J. and Genc, E. (2017). Strategy Implementation Style and Public Service Effectiveness, Efficiency, and Equity. *Administrative Sciences*, 7(4), 1–19.

Attorney-General's Office. (2007). *The Fraud review: progress report July 2007*. London: Attorney-General's Office.

Bovaird, T. (2003). 'Strategic Management in Public Sector Organisations', in Bovaird, T. and Loffler, E. (eds). *Public Management and Governance*. London: Routledge, 55–74.

Brynard, P. (2005). Policy implementation: lessons for service delivery. *Journal of Public Administration*, 40(4.1), 649–664.

Bullock, K. and Tilley, N. (2009). Evidence-Based Policing and Crime Reduction. *Policing: A Journal of Policy and Practice*, 3(4), 381–387.

Cabinet Office. (2012). *Tackling Fraud and Error in Government. A Report of the Fraud, Error and Debt Taskforce*. London: Cabinet Office.

Cabinet Office. (2020). *Cross-Government Fraud Landscape Annual Report 2019*. Cabinet Office.

deLeon, P. and deLeon, L. (2002). What Ever Happened to Policy Implementation? An Alternative Approach. *Journal of Public Administration Research and Theory*, 12(4), 467–492.

Doig, A. and Sproat, P. (2020. Local Responses to a National Initiative on Organised Crime and Local Government Procurement Fraud. *Journal of Financial Crime*, 27(1), 78–91.

Elbanna, S., Andrews, R. and Pollanen, R. (2016). Strategic Planning and Implementation Success in Public Service Organizations: Evidence from Canada. *Public Management Review*, 18(7), 1017–1042.

FFL Board. (2011). *Fighting Fraud Locally. The Local Government Fraud Strategy*. London: FFL Board/National Fraud Authority.

FFCL Board. (2016). *Fighting Fraud Locally. The Local Government Fraud Strategy*. London: FFCL Board/CIPFA.

FFCL Board. (2020). *Fighting Fraud and Corruption Locally. The Local Government Counter Fraud and Corruption Strategy*. London: FFCL Board/Cifas.

Fraud Advisory Panel. (2016). *The Fraud Review: Ten Years On*. London: Fraud Advisory Panel.

Fraud Review Team. (2006a). *Interim Report*. The Legal Secretariat to the Law Officers, London. Available from www.lslo.gov.uk/fraud_review.htm.

Fraud Review Team (2006b), *Report*. The Legal Secretariat to the Law Officers, London. Available from www.lslo.gov.uk/fraud_review.htm.

Gannon, R. and Doig, A. (2010). Ducking the Answer: Fraud Strategies and Police Resources. *Policing and Society*, 20(1), 39–60.

Hallsworth, M. (2011). *System Stewardship. The Future of Policy Making?* London: Institute for Government.

Hill, M. and Hupe, P (2003). The Multi-layer Problem in Implementation Research. *Public Management Review*, 5(4), 471–490.

HM Government. (2017). *UK Anti-Corruption Strategy 2017–2022*. London: HM Government.

HM Government and UK Finance. (2019). *Economic Crime Plan 2019–22*. London: HM Government.

HM Government and UK Finance. (2021). *Economic Crime Plan: Statement of Progress*. London: HM Government.

HMIC. (2015). *Real Lives, Real Crimes. A Study of Digital Crime and Policing*. London: Home Office.

HMIC. (2016). *An Inspection of the National Crime Agency. An Inspection of the National Crime Agency's Progress Against Outstanding Recommendations Made by HMIC and Areas for Improvement*. London: HM Inspectorate of Constabulary.

HMICFRS. (2019a). *Fraud: Time to Choose. An Inspection of the Police Response to Fraud*. London: HMICFRS.

HMICFRS. (2019b). *Cyber: Keep the Light On. An Inspection of the Police Response to Cyber-dependent Crime*. London: HMICFRS.

Home Office. (2018). *Management of Risk in Law Enforcement (MoRiLE) Based Scoring: Standards.* London: Home Office.

House of Commons Committee of Public Accounts. (2019). *Serious and Organised Crime.* 119th Report. HC2049. London: House of Commons Committee of Public Accounts.

Hudson, B., Hunter, D. and Peckham, S. (2019). Policy Failure and the Policy-implementation Gap: Can Policy Support Programs Help? *Policy Design and Practice,* 2(1), 1–14.

Hupe, P. L. (2011). The Thesis of Incongruent Implementation: Revisiting Pressman and Wildavsky", *Public Policy and Administration,* 26(1), 63–80.

Institute of Government, (2019). www.instituteforgovernment. org.uk/publication/performance-tracker-2019/police and www.instituteforgovernment.org.uk/explainers/local-government-funding-england (accessed 03 August 2020).

Insurance Fraud Taskforce. (2016). *Final Report.* London: HM Treasury and Ministry of Justice

International Public Sector Fraud Forum. (2019). *A Guide to Managing Fraud for Public Bodies.* London: International Public Sector Fraud Forum/Cabinet Office.

King, J. and Doig, A. (2016). A Dedicated Place for Volume Fraud within the current UK Economic Crime Agenda? The Greater Manchester Police Case Study. *The Journal of Financial Crime,* 23(4), 902–915.

Levi, M. (1993). *The Investigation, Prosecution, and Trial of Serious Fraud,* Royal Commission on Criminal Justice Research Study No.14. HMSO.

Levi, M. (2008). *The Phantom Capitalists: The Organization and Control of Long-Firm Fraud,* 2nd edition with new introduction/postscript on changes in the organization of fraud and its control. Andover: Ashgate.

Levi, M., Doig, A., Gundur, R., Wall, D. and Williams, M. (2015). *The Implications of Economic Cybercrime for Policing.* City of London Corporation. http://orca-mwe.cf.ac.uk/88156/1/Economic-Cybercrime-FullReport.pdf

Levi, M., Doig, A., Gundur, R. Wall, D. and Williams, M. (2017). Cyberfraud and the Implications for Effective Risk-Based Responses: Themes from UK Research. *Crime, Law and Social Change,* 67(1), 77–96.

Levi, M. and Smith, R. (2021) *Fraud and its Relationship to Pandemics and Economic Crises: From Spanish Flu to COVID-19,* Research Report no. 19, Canberra: Australian Institute of Criminology. www.aic.gov.au/publications/rr/rr19

Mackey, C and Savill, J. (2020). *Fraud: A Review of the National 'Lead Force' Responsibilities of the City of London Police and the Effectiveness of Investigations in the UK.* Accessible at: www.cityoflondon.gov.uk/about-the-city/about-us/Documents/action-fraud-report.pdf

McKevitt, D. (1992). 'Strategic Management in public services', in Willcocks, L. and Harrow, J. (eds). *Rediscovering Public Services Management.* McGraw-Hill, pp. 33–49.

Ministry of Housing, Communities and Local Government. (2020). *Independent Review into the Oversight of Local Audit and the Transparency of Local Authority Financial Reporting.* London: Ministry of Housing, Communities and Local Government.

Mintzberg, H. and Waters, J. A. (1985). Of Strategies, Deliberate and Emergent. *Strategic Management Journal,* 6(3), 257–272.

National Audit Office. (2016), *Fraud Landscape Review HC 850. Session 2015–16.* London: National Audit Office.

National Audit Office. (2017). *Online Fraud.* HC 45. London: National Audit Office.

National Criminal Intelligence Service. (2003). *UK Threat Assessment 2003: The Threat from Serious and Organised Crime.* London: NCIS.

National Economic Research Associates. (2000). *The Economic Cost of Fraud.* London: NERA Associates.

National Police Chiefs Council. (2019). *National Fraud Policing Strategy 2019–2022.* Accessible at www.cityoflondon.police.uk/advice-and-support/Documents/National%20Policing%20Fraud%20Strategy%202019.pdf

NCA. (2019a). *National Strategic Assessment of Serious and Organised Crime.* London: National Crime Agency.

NCA. (2019b). *Public Private Threat Update. Economic Crime. Key Judgements.* London: National Crime Agency.

NFA. (2010). *The Work of the Counter Fraud Strategy Forum 2010.* London: National Fraud Authority.

NFA. (2011). *Fighting Fraud Together.* London: National Fraud Authority.

NFSA. (2009). *The National Fraud Strategy. A New Approach to Combating Fraud.* London: National Strategic Fraud Authority.

OECD. (2020). *Public Integrity Handbook.* Paris: OECD.

Pencheon, D. (2006). 'An Introduction to Health-care Strategy', in Pencheon, D., Guest, C., Melzer, D. and Muir Gray, J. A. (Eds). *Oxford handbook of Public Health Practice.* 2nd edition. Oxford: Oxford University Press. 376–381.

Poister, T. H. (2010). The Future of Strategic Planning in the Public Sector: Linking Strategic Management and Performance. *Public Administration Review,* 70(1), 246–254.

Police Foundation. (2018). *More Than Just a Number: Improving the Police Response to Victims of Fraud.* London: Police Foundation.

Saetren, H. (2014). Implementing the Third Generation Research Paradigm in Policy Implementation Research: An Empirical Assessment. *Public Policy and Administration,* 29(2), 84–105.

Saunders, J. (2017). Tackling Cybercrime – the UK Response. *Journal of Cyber Policy,* 2(1), 4–15.

Schillemans, T. (2013). Moving Beyond the Clash of Interests. *Public Management Review,* 15(4), 541–562.

Sheehan, N. T. (2006). Want to Improve Strategic Execution? Simons Says Levers. *Journal of Business Strategy,* 27(6), 56–64.

Simon, R. (1994). *Levers of Control.* Boston: Harvard Business School Press.

Tessier, S. and Otley, D. (2012). A Conceptual Development of Simons' Levers of Control Framework. *Management Accounting Research,* 23, 171–185.

Van Thiel, S. (2014). *Research Methods in Public Administration and Public Management. An Introduction.* London: Routledge.

Walker, R. M. (2013). Strategic Management and Performance in Public Organizations: Findings from the Miles and Snow Framework. *Public Administration Review,* 73(5), 675–685.

Wood, H., Keatinge, T., Ditcham, K. and Janjeva, A. (2021). *The Silent Threat. The Impact of Fraud on UK National Security.* London: Royal United Services Institute for Defence and Security Studies.

Wylie, B. (2020). *Bandit Capitalism: Carillion and the Corruption of the British State.* Edinburgh: Birlinn Ltd.

A case of arrested development? Delivering the UK National Fraud Strategy within competing policing policy priorities

Alan Doig and Michael Levi

The UK government has been developing strategy on fraud since 2006 looking at its cost to the nation, as well as its presence in many other areas of criminality, from identity theft to organized crime. This article focuses on the police dimension of the UK's fraud strategy, and its assimilation and implementation in the context of other policies and priorities. To avoid being arrested before it achieves anything, the fresh impetus sought by the last of the strategy reviews must take account of the 'facts on the ground', such as diminished police fraud investigation resources resulting from financial cutbacks and other, competing, priorities for these reduced resources.

Introduction: policing and the evolving fraud policy agenda

Fraud in the UK encompasses a variety of offences, perpetrators and victims, ranging from low-value, high-volume benefits fraud to significant corporate losses. The institutional and legislative landscape is fragmented (see Button, 2011; Doig, 2012), with much of the responsibility for addressing fraud resting with public and private sector institutions (Doig and Macaulay, 2008; Brooks *et al.*, 2009). How both sectors address fraud, with what level of resource, however, depends not only on an assessment of the level and extent of the risk but also on the pressures from external scrutiny and from competing priorities and initiatives on delivering the core functions of the institution.

Similar imperatives also apply to the police who, however, face no direct fraud risk but are required to respond to the public, as well as public and private sector institutions, who approach them with allegations of criminal conduct. An awareness of investigation policies and the availability of resources within other institutions and regulators, as well as a requirement to follow a broad range of government-initiated policies, has resulted in the UK police committing fewer resources to high-volume, low-value cases and more resources to élite forms of fraud such as insider trading and corporate accounting frauds (Doig

et al., 2001; Levi and Maguire, 2012).

While the evolving fraud strategy has implications for the general public and for the public and private sectors (see, for example, Tiffen and O'Donnell, 2012), it also has specific implications for the police. This article focuses on these latter implications, and discusses how the police are prioritizing the various policies and initiatives. It concludes that the development of a uniform and comprehensive fraud reduction policy for the police must take account of the 'facts on the ground' and other, competing, priorities if it is to deliver any sustainable and effective impact.

2006 Fraud Review

Despite a number of legislative and institutional changes in the preceding three decades, such as the establishment of the Serious Fraud Office in 1987 and the Fraud Act 2006 (which moved the focus toward specifying areas of actual fraudulent behaviour, rather than the consequences of that behaviour), concerns continued to be expressed over the costs of fraud (see figure 1). These were heightened by perceptions that documentary, financial and other types of fraud were enabling and facilitating other crimes, such as terrorism and organized crime, and that new opportunities for fraud were increasingly opened up by new technology, for example the growth in identity and internet fraud. The then Labour government initiated a review process in 2005 to produce an evidenced strategic response across public and private sectors, and law enforcement.

The 'emerging findings' of an interim report (Fraud Review Team, 2006a) were that:

• Information on fraud was poor.
• There was no national policy on fraud.
• Police resources had dwindled to the point where low- or medium-value private sector fraud was unlikely to be investigated.
• Fraud investigative capacity was spread across organizations, often in ways that were unco-ordinated, not cost-effective and did not use the full range of methods or sanctions.
• Lengthy fraud trials were 'a heavy burden'.
• Penalties were low, even when convictions occurred.

In developing its response to the findings, the final Fraud Review report (Fraud Review Team, 2006b) took a primarily, but not exclusively, criminal justice approach, making a range of thematic and institutional recommendations, including: a comprehensive measurement of fraud; a national strategy for dealing with fraud, together with a national fraud strategic authority (NFSA, later renamed the NFA), a national fraud reporting centre (NFRC, later renamed Action Fraud) to which businesses and individuals nationwide would report fraud; a police-based intelligence resource (now the National Fraud Intelligence Bureau [NFIB]); promotion of prevention good practice; reform to the trial process including the use of plea bargaining and of a specialized 'financial court'; more innovative

sanctions; and more public/private partnerships.

It also proposed that fraud should be a policing priority, with the establishment of regional fraud groups, the promotion of fraud work at divisional detective and uniform levels, the identification of a national lead force (the City of London Police) and the ring-fencing of local police fraud squad resources 'to stop the current practice in many forces of diverting them into other work as soon as the force has a pressure somewhere else' (Fraud Review Team, 2006b, p. 10).

The fraud strategy, updating the strategy and providing the impetus

In the aftermath of the Fraud Review, the newly-created NFSA published a national anti-fraud strategy (NFSA, 2008). This proposed information-sharing and a better understanding of fraud, addressing the most serious and harmful fraud threats, widening the range of investigative and sanctions options, and promoting fraud awareness, prevention and inter-institutional co-operation. The strategy priorities and objectives were supplemented in 2011 by the publication of a detailed programme of activity and information on implementation.

The publication of the strategy was supplemented by further reviews, supported by pilot projects to test the validity of some of the proposals (see Cabinet Office, 2012). Two reports were issued by taskforces looking at both thematic and departmental issues (NFA, 2010a; Cabinet Office/NFA, 2011). These (and the second focused primarily on the public sector) recommended more work on the costs and risks of fraud, collaboration and shared good practice (including those involving the police), greater intelligence and information sharing, a greater focus on prevention, target-hardening and use of technology.

Issued in 2010, the Counter Fraud Strategy Forum's report (NFA, 2010b) was largely focused on law enforcement, arguing for a rationalized counter-fraud landscape where overlaps in roles and responsibilities were removed, including Action Fraud and the NFIB taking on centrally for England and Wales all reports of fraud from individuals and businesses; sharing of criminal data between public and private sectors through the NFIB; improved mechanisms for case allocation across the counter-fraud community; increased partnership with the private sector to improve investigations; a greater emphasis on prevention and disruption activities across the

Figure 1. The costs of fraud.

ough too late for inclusion in the review process, ACPO-sored research (Levi et al., 2007) into the value and sector ibution of fraud estimated the overall cost of fraud in the UK ninimum of £13.9 billion. This contrasts with a 2000 report consultancy, the National Economic Research Associates, for Home Office which (on less developed data) argued that overed fraud could range from £5b–£9 billion and scovered fraud from £5b–£9 billion. Subsequent National d Authority (NFA) cost estimates have been rising over time, £30 billion in 2009 to £73 billion in 2012 (NFA, 2012). ough the quality of the underlying data is variable and cult to verify, this rise also reflects a broadening in the rage of the Annual Fraud Indicator, so year-on-year parisons are not entirely comparing like with like.

counter-fraud community; and quicker prosecutions and use of confiscation to improve sanctions.

The final, over-arching strategy review was published in 2011 (NFA, 2011a) to 'provide fresh impetus in our fight against fraud' (p. 4). Within three general 'strategic objectives' of awareness, prevention and enforcement the report had a significant criminal justice perspective in terms of responding to fraud involving organized crime, organized approaches to fraud, use of technology and professional advisers, and international connections. Of its two main objectives, one involved 'law enforcement and other partners increasing the risk of disruption and punishment to organized and opportunistic fraudsters, thus deterring potential criminal offenders' (p. 17) by increasing knowledge on fraud through a Joint Serious and Organized Crime Assessment Centre, part of the successor to the Serious Organized Crime Agency (SOCA), the National Crime Agency. This new agency would also include an Economic Crime Command which would address constraints on police resources by developing 'innovative, partnership solutions working across police forces, the NCA and its Economic Crime Command, other law enforcement organizations and the public, private and voluntary sectors' (p. 20).

Priorities and other initiatives: influences on strategy implementation

Crime control and the wider policing context

The evolving fraud strategy very much reflects the changes to crime control in the wider policy context. Crime control in the UK was once widely seen as virtually the sole domain and responsibility of law enforcement, but in the past two decades the situation has changed markedly in a number of ways. There is now an emphasis on partnership and information-sharing, and the framing of responses to crime in terms of prioritizing on the basis of harm, disruption, prevention and reduction. There are also explicit and measurable policies, strategies or 'policing plans'—themselves ostensibly the result of analyses of crime patterns and trends, and the application of intelligence-led policing, as well as taking account of the priorities of central and local government, other agencies and local communities (Maguire and John, 2006).

Policing has also been subject to continuing efficiency, devolved budgeting, performance and management approaches and reviews promoted by the Audit Commission, official

inquiries, Home Office consultancies and HM Inspector of Constabulary (HMIC) within the wider new public management agenda (see Doig et al., 2001; Flynn, 2002). Currently they are also subject to central government funding reductions—20% in real terms by 2014/15 (Treasury, 2010, p. 54; HMIC, 2011). They are required to respond to statutory performance indicators and quantitative targets that reflect governments' priorities, including an emphasis on front-line and public-facing services (see, for example, Treasury, 2009).

Competing policy agendas and priorities

A continuing focus in favour of 'front-line policing' has led to forces reviewing the retention of central units, and what level of resource and what type of organizational structures to apply to those that are retained. Both have been influenced by locally-accountable police authorities, by the operational independence of 43 English and Welsh Chief Constables, and by a number of government-initiated national policies. These last include CONTEST, the national counter-terrorism strategy which has imposed a prescriptive and resource-specific requirement on the police (Doig, 2006a; Home Office, 2011).

Another involves organized crime, a long-standing priority for government initiatives and official reviews (Home Office, 2009, 2011). The use of Organized Crime Group Mapping (OCGM)* is only part of the development of an intelligence-led approach which draws heavily on proactive and uniform practices that has been rolled out not only across law enforcement, but also through a lead operational institution—SOCA.

A third concerns the implementation of the Proceeds of Crime Act (POCA), another policy-driven initiative (see Cabinet Office, 2000) to shift the focus of crime control toward both social restitution and financial incapacitation/deterrence and to embed financial investigation as an integral aspect of investigations into acquisitive crime, from

---

*OCGM has been in existence since 2005 and now involves all UK law enforcement agencies. It focuses on serious crime that causes 'significant harm' through financial profit and loss, impact on community safety or well-being, serious violence, corruption and exercise of control. It maps and indexes the presence and methods of those involved in designated organized crime through agency intelligence, arrests, open sources, and then assesses them according to their judged intent and capability.

burglary to drug trafficking. Here there was also a lead operational agency (the Assets Recovery Agency, which was later merged with SOCA). Governments also established targets for recovery while incentivizing the police to achieve them by agreeing to give a percentage share of the monies recovered or seized to the forces involved. This, in turn, has seen the police expand proceeds of crime work across most areas of force criminality, supported by regional asset recovery teams to maximize asset recovery from specific criminal targets (professional or organized criminals, and enablers) where the cross-border or international dimension, time and need for a dedicated resource were not available to individual forces.

Finding a place for fraud?

Even before the development of a fraud strategy, one noticeable consequence of competing agendas, and the emphasis on front-line policing, has been the continuing abolition of police fraud squads (Doig et al., 2001), or their merger with serious crime units or the establishment of economic crime units (ECUs) in order to align existing expertise and resources to address organized crime groups (OCGs), corrupted professionals and asset recovery.

Currently, where the title 'fraud squad' is retained, intake criteria, numbers and types of staff and caseload often reflect the focus on such agendas: 'forces continue to restructure under the "serious and organized" banner and strive towards demonstrating "best value" and where "the investigation of fraud is then purported as being considered in the context of contributing towards 'POCA league tables'", and the dismantling and disruption of OCGs' (Gannon and Doig, 2010, p. 19). Certainly ECUs show 'a shift to units primarily concerned with money laundering legislation and financial investigation towards the confiscation of the proceeds of crime from all levels of criminality, and not necessarily—if at all—as a result of any fraud investigation' (ibid., p. 12).

Assessment: implementing the National Fraud Strategy

Strategy delivered?

The main institutional reforms discussed in the 2006 review, and subsequently, have been established. The NFSA/NFA was set up, work developing knowledge on types and cost of fraud has been undertaken, and a national strategy (and a sub-national strategy for local government) has been published. The national lead force has been expanded, primarily with help from central government. Its Economic Crime Directorate also houses the NFIB (which is funded by the government). Its two main functions are:

- The analysis of fraud data from law enforcement and other sectors, and Action Fraud, for onward distribution as intelligence leads to law enforcement agencies nationally, including the police.
- The analysis of patterns and trends, in terms of volume and value of fraud, and mapping by type, level and victims.

Action Fraud, hosted by the NFA, is extending its role nationally so that all complaints will be made to them (including those initially made to individual police forces) as a central reporting point for fraud from 2013. Central government is also funding for three years a number of regional fraud intelligence and then fraud investigation teams, linked to the national lead force, as a regional resource from 2013.

These, however, are the recommendations over which government has both control and is willing to fund. In practice, even these are developing rather than delivered. The NFA has (and was intended to have) no direct compulsion, operational or resource allocation responsibilities in terms of implementing the strategy. The national lead force does not have a fully-functional national remit, while regionalization may either derive from amalgamating existing resources under local control or centrally-funded teams attracting staff from local forces who are unlikely to be replaced. The Fighting Fraud Together report argued that 'law enforcement capabilities are being strengthened by measures such as the National Fraud Intelligence Bureau receiving and analysing increasing volumes of fraud crime data, with intelligence packages then being disseminated for targeted investigations' (NFIB, 2011a, p. 15). In practice, the impact of Action Fraud and the NFIB, which currently work in a number of pilot areas, has not been fully assessed in terms of either the likely level, volume or geographical distribution of complaints, analysis of patterns and trends or intelligence packages, or the quality or 'usability' of what is to be provided, or the availability of a dedicated police response. The imbalance between the over-supply of 'intelligence packages' and the much more limited operational capacity to act on them is not restricted to fraud, but it is particularly acute there. Although regional fraud analysts and investigators should provide a better bridge between the national and the local, they will not be able to take on many cases and thus cannot substitute for the local police.

Will 'measuring' fraud influence the police response?
A continuing concern has been the declining local force resource, which begs the question as to whether the work of the NFIB or the NFA annual fraud indicator are used to ensure an appropriate force response. As the Financial Service Authority (FSA) has recognized, mapping the cost and main groups of perpetrators has little value unless it is also mapped against the resources, roles and responsibilities within the existing control environment: 'the FSA needs to know which aspects of market failure leading to criminality it can effectively address (where it can make a difference). After all, knowing the scale or impact of various aspects of financial crime, but without knowing which of these the FSA can effectively address, would be unhelpful' (Dorn *et al.*, 2009, p. 5).

Within an estimated figure of £73 billion losses from fraud, the January 2012 annual fraud indicator provided by the NFA, the identification on where fraud occurs, and its perpetrators and its victims, in ways that identify both the responsible institutions and the resources necessary to respond, is, despite disparate sources among consultancy firm surveys, occasional privately funded criminological studies, the Crime Surveys for England and Wales and the NFA itself (NFA, 2011b), a work in progress.

Further, while some may argue for the measurement of fraud is an essential precursor to fraud reduction strategies (see Tunley, 2011; Button *et al.*, 2012), others would stress the irreducibly contested definitional, and data collection, aggregation and interpretative, issues. Empirically and perhaps normatively, the police appear to be more concerned about harm than about direct economic costs; undifferentiated nationally-aggregated data may be seen as insufficiently well-translated to local force agendas. At the same time, insider dealing rings excepted, many kinds of frauds—whether opportunistic or pre-planned—that often fall to be dealt with by the police but which are *not* the product of 'career criminals', such as the malefactions of élites or frauds by senior management or corrupt cartel agreements, do not lend themselves easily to any annualized quantitative assessment or as an evidence base for long-term resource commitment (see Levi and Burrows, 2008).

Indeed, this has been emphasised in terms of the context of the Libor rate-fixing cartel scandal of 2012, where pressure for a criminal inquiry required an investigative team capable of conducing a complex enquiry among élites, with élite suspects, at a time when such a need had not been previously foreseen and expertise was not readily available.

Prioritizing fraud
In support of the original NSFA strategy the Association of Chief Police Officers (ACPO) proposals included integrating new police resources, such as Action Fraud, into national policing structures, promoting and building financial investigation and asset recovery skills so police can track more fraud, and strengthening the relationship between police and businesses to help identify where they need to work together most closely (NFSA, 2008, p. 53).

Outside the national lead force, this has not generally happened, partly because of local force priorities, and partly because competing agendas have captured limited resources. Further, as Levi noted over two decades ago, corporate victims have accepted that low police prioritization of case acceptance and their investigative objectives (which may not reflect those of the victims) has transferred 'the economic burden of crime investigation' to them—and thus the shift of 'public law back into the sphere of private law' (Levi, 1987, p. 282). Indeed, the facts on the ground where a fraud strategy has already been proposed suggest problems of implementation within the police. As HM Inspectorate of Constabulary for Scotland (2008, pp. 8, 9) observed, well before the recent funding cuts and before the creation of a single Scottish police force, there continued to be limited numbers of fraud squad staff as 'the police service in Scotland generally regarded fraud as a low priority and therefore allowed high levels of staff abstraction from fraud squads'. This in turn 'contributed to the absence of strategic momentum in fraud, despite the priority assigned to it in the national control strategy' and the inclusion of fraud in a national control strategy appeared to mean in practice that there was 'no difference to the approach, or priority attached, to fraud in Scotland'.

Policing priorities and resources have shifted toward complex, sophisticated and enduring patterns of criminal activity. This typically looks at fraud principally as a medium of exploitation by those already engaged in criminality. This is in part because of government intentions, but also because fraud offenders are seen as a bigger social threat than previously and because this is seen as very costly crime pumping large sums into the criminal economy, creating a bad role model for 'criminal upcomers'. In turn, this widens the gulf between the policing of 'organized fraud' and the policing of one-off or low-value frauds, or those frauds committed by managers, staff, customers, or clients of institutions. Many such institutions will have to assume most of the responsibilities (and costs) of dealing with any reported frauds.

Responding to demand

Action Fraud took 12,269 formal crime reports in the 2010/11 financial year, alongside the 145,841 fraud reports recorded by the police in England and Wales. Between the recording of a fraud and the decision to investigate lie judgments about investigatability within resources available: this is a far from routine connection. In 2010, the City of London Police and the SFO were between them responsible for two-thirds of the value of live cases being investigated by Counter Fraud Strategy Forum members. Only 20,000 fraud and forgery cases led to successful convictions in 2010 (with less than half committed to prison), 'significant volumes of police recorded fraud and forgery offences were not actively investigated during 2010', and financial loss often determined the likelihood of investigation; 'it is likely that in most cases there are insufficient resources to investigate these crimes compared to other policing priorities' (NFA, 2010b, pp. 12 and 13).

Figure 2. Bucking the trend?

iew by a new officer in Greater Manchester Police's economic e section (ECS) of how fraud was addressed across the force, ding drawing on a separate divisional workload study by rnal consultants, suggested that fraud investigations at ional level were not been handled efficiently and effectively. nternal case for streamlining fraud was addressed through rce's priority-based budgeting and policing model processes h resulted in the centralization of a number of officers from ions within the ECS to operate both a major fraud and me fraud unit from early 2012. All cases are evaluated, with ria for the latter including vulnerable victims, repeat ders, the methods used to commit the fraud and cross-ion links. Both units draw on the ECS's financial investigations other specialisms. Levels of expertise, case completion, cost gs and divisional staff availability for front-line policing ities have all increased.

In a number of areas, moreover, until regional teams are established (for which there is currently no long-term financial provision), there is no fraud squad or ECU to report to, despite the occasional re-establishment of a fraud squad (as in the case of North Yorkshire police, and see figure 2). At the same time, priorities in one police organization in relation to fraud are often made without regard of the implications for the wider policing policy context. Thus a leaked report (*Guardian*, 16 November 2011) proposed that the Ministry of Defence police should close its fraud squad, despite being seen as 'impact significant', and that at least six 'local police forces' would take up any future caseload. Although this decision has been modified by the reduced detective squad having a greater focus on economic crime, the original proposal was primarily a cost-saving exercise, and not based on any substantive assessment of the fraud risks facing the Ministry of Defence (at a time of an increased risk of corporate motivation to bribe and defraud due to increased financial pressures in the defence sector), nor on whether or not the various forces had spare investigative capacity or even a fraud squad to take on the work.

Joining-up fraud

The strategy has emphasised the importance of sharing information both between police forces and between forces and the public and private sectors. However, as Doig and Levi (2009) have argued in relation to previous efforts at joined-up working against fraud, the practice does not always meet the intent.

The SFO has regularly expressed concern over the availability of resources for the joint investigation of cases with the reporting police force (Doig, 2006b). Despite there being a lead agency in SOCA and despite it being a government-initiated policing priority, the HMIC's review of the work on OCGs concluded that:

> ...despite evidence of impressive results achieved by a few individual forces and some collaborative efforts, the national response overall is blighted by the lack of a unifying strategic direction, inadequate covert capacity and under-investment in intelligence gathering, analysis and proactive capability...collaboration nationally and regionally between SOCA and individual forces occurs around cases rather than within the framework of a well-supported threat assessment, priorities and 'treatments' of organized crime (HMIC, 2009, p. 2).

On the other hand, where institutions have identified a common purpose and a synergy in terms of information and resources, then partnership and joined-up working, including with the private sector, has already taken place. To date, however, much of this has concerned funding for specific investigations or posts. Joint or joined-up institutional initiatives involving the police have been more limited, usually as a response to a perceived national *and* 'organized' fraud threat:

> *...since 2002, the payment card industry has chosen to pay for a specialist squad—the Dedicated Cheque and Plastic Crime Unit—to deal with 'organized payment card fraud' because the police forces in most of the UK refused to prioritize such offences, and* de facto *would not handle them: they are too labour-intensive for local constabulary forces to deal with, and not high-profile enough for central 'organized crime' police units to deal with. After much deliberation and initial unwillingness to pay twice for policing, the motor insurance industry agreed to follow on the same lines from 2012. It is establishing a 40-strong police intelligence and operational unit in order to ensure a greater level of action against 'crash for cash' and other 'organized' insurance frauds than can be relied upon via the constant negotiation of support for its cases among 43 English and Welsh police forces* (Levi and Maguire, 2012, p. 209; the actual staffing is now 34, rather than 40).

Conclusion

The interplay between government policy initiatives, policing priorities, and an emphasis on budget reductions, targets and performance remains an unending story, and the policing and risk-management of fraud does not lend itself easily to current crime control approaches. At the same time, the strategy has exposed the gap between intention, and the facts on the ground and the continuing primacy of other crime and security agendas. It will also, as with the elections of locally-elected and accountable Crime and Police Commissioners, have to take account of a likely emphasis on front-line policing issues.

Both the rhetoric and the recommendations of the strategy were necessary but have not yet been sufficient conditions for actual operational implementation work, and certainly not where other initiatives are taking precedence. Significant progress has been made in defining the issues and reshaping responses at a strategic level but the NFA—now part of the Home Office—will need to ensure that any hard-won reforms are ongoing in order to avoid the development of a uniform and enduring fraud strategy being downplayed or arrested before the commitment, resources and processes necessary to achieve its 2015 objectives are agreed, available and in place.

References

Brooks, G., Button, M. and Frimpong, K. (2009), Policing fraud in the private sector: a survey of FTSE 100 companies in the UK. *International Journal of Police Science and Management, 11.*

Button, M. (2011), Fraud investigation and the 'flawed architecture' of counter fraud entities in the United Kingdom. *International Journal of Law, Crime and Justice, 39,* 4.

Button, M., Gee, J. and Brooks, G. (2012), Measuring the cost of fraud: an opportunity for the new competitive advantage. *Journal of Financial Crime, 19,* 1.

Cabinet Office/Performance and Innovation Unit (2000), *Recovering the Proceeds of Crime* (Cabinet Office, London).

Cabinet Office/NFA (2011), *Eliminating Public Sector Fraud: the Counter Fraud Taskforce Interim Report* (Cabinet Office/NFA, London).

Cabinet Office (2012), *Applying Behavioural Insights to Reduce Fraud, Error and Debt* (Cabinet Office, London).

Doig, A. (2006a), Joining up a response to terrorism?...And agency shall speak to agency. *Crime, Law and Social Change, 44,* 4–5.

Doig, A. (2006b), *Fraud* (Willan, Cullompton).

Doig, A. (Ed), (2012), *Fraud: The Counter-Fraud Practitioners Handbook* (Gower, London).

Doig, A., Levi, M. and Johnson, S. (2001), Old populism or new public management? Policing fraud in the UK. *Public Policy and Administration, 16,* 1.

Doig, A. and Levi, M. (2009), Inter-agency work and the UK public sector investigation of fraud, 1996–2006: joined-up rhetoric and disjointed reality. *Policing and Society, 19,* 3.

Doig, A. and Macaulay, M. (2008), Decades, directions and the fraud review: addressing the future of public sector fraud. *Public Money & Management, 28,* 3, p. 185.

Dorn, N., Levi, M., Artingstall, D. and Howell, J. (2009), *FSA Scale and Impact of Financial Crime Project—Impacts of Financial Crimes and Amenability to Control by the FSA.* See www.fsa.gov.uk/pubs/other/scale_and_impact_paper.pdf

Flynn, N. (2002), *Public Sector Management* (Sage, London).

Fraud Review Team (2006a), *Interim Report.* See www.lslo.gov.uk/fraud_review.htm

Fraud Review Team (2006b), *Report.* See

www.lslo.gov.uk/fraud_review.htm

Gannon, R. and Doig, A. (2010), Ducking the answer: fraud strategies and police resources. *Policing and Society, 20*, 1.

HMIC (2009), *Getting Organized: A Thematic Report on the Police Service's Response to Serious and Organized Crime* (London).

HMIC (2011), *Adapting to Austerity: A Review of Police Force and Authority Preparedness for the 2011/12-14/15 CSR Period* (London).

HM Inspectorate of Constabulary for Scotland (2008), *Thematic Inspection: Serious Fraud* (Edinburgh).

Home Office (2009), *Extending our Reach: A Comprehensive Approach to Tackling Organized Crime* (The Stationery Office, London).

Home Office (2011), *CONTEST: The United Kingdom's Strategy for Countering Terrorism* (London).

Home Office (2011), *Local to Global: Reducing the Risk from Organized Crime* (The Stationery Office, London).

Levi, M. (1987), *Regulating Fraud* (Tavistock, London).

Levi, M., Burrows, J., Fleming, M. and Hopkins, M., with the assistance of Matthews, K. (2007), *The Nature, Extent and Economic Impact of Fraud in the UK* (ACPO, London).

Levi, M. and Burrows, J. (2008), Measuring the impact of fraud in the UK: a conceptual and empirical journey. *British Journal of Criminology, 48*, 3.

Levi, M. and Maguire, M. (2012), Something old, something new; something not entirely blue: uneven and shifting modes of crime control. In Newburn, T. and Peay, J. (Eds), (2012), *Policing: Politics, Culture and Control* (Hart Publishing, Oxford).

Maguire, M. and John, T. (2006), Intelligence-led policing, managerialism and community engagement: competing priorities and the role of the national intelligence model in the UK. *Policing and Society, 16*, 1, pp. 67–85.

NFA (2010a), *A Fresh Approach to Combating Fraud In the Public Sector: The Report of the Smarter Government Public Sector Fraud Taskforce* (National Fraud Authority, London).

NFA (2010b), *The Work of the Counter Fraud Strategy Forum 2010: Supporting an Improved National Enforcement Response to Fraud* (London).

NFA (2011a), *Fighting Fraud Together* (London).

NFA (2011b), *A Quantitative Segmentation of the UK Population: Helping to Determine How, Why and When Citizens Become Victims of Fraud* (London).

NFA (2012), *Annual Fraud Indicator* (London).

NFSA (2008), *The National Fraud Strategy. A New Approach to Combating Fraud* (London).

Tiffen, R. and O'Donnell, I. (2012), The continuing evolution of fraud and the local authority response. In Morales, C. and Boardman, F. (Eds), *Public Service Reform in the UK* (PMPA, London).

Treasury (2009), *Putting the Frontline First: Smarter Government*, Cm 7752 (The Stationery Office, London).

Treasury (2010), *Spending Review 2010*, Cm 7942 (The Stationery Office, London).

Tunley, M. (2011), Uncovering the iceberg: mandating the measurement of fraud in the United Kingdom. *International Journal of Law, Crime and Justice, 39*, 3.

Understanding the police response to fraud: the challenges in configuring a response to a low-priority crime on the rise

Michael Skidmore, Janice Goldstraw-White and Martin Gill

ABSTRACT

Previous research has demonstrated the comparative lack of priority fraud receives from government and law enforcement in the UK compared to other serious offences, as well as shortcomings in the overall approach to investigation. This paper examines the current state of affairs in the light of changes aimed at addressing these limitations. It incorporates findings from a national survey of police forces, as well as a local survey of police personnel in three forces supplemented by interviews. The findings suggest that the situation has become more complicated. Many police officers interviewed did not feel that the police response in their own area was effective, and that their colleagues often lacked the appropriate skill sets needed. Moreover, forces were not confident they were recruiting the right people to tackle fraud. The paper has important lessons for policing internationally.

IMPACT

The authors provide a review of current police structures, resource and their effectiveness in tackling fraud, one grounded in empirical evidence collected at the national, regional and local level. The paper contextualizes the local police response within national response systems and identifies the key gaps in existing strategies, highlighting the challenges to tackling fraud within the established police structures and resource configuration. A number of key areas of policy and practice that might be developed are discussed, which have relevance to policy-makers and practitioners working nationally and in local jurisdictions.

Previous research has identified that fraud has a significant and sometimes very damaging impact on local communities, but is not a priority for many police forces and is largely perceived by police officers to be outside of their remit (Crocker et al., 2017). This creates significant gaps in the local elements of the response, including enforcement, the support and protection of victims and crime prevention. To address this gap, this paper examines in more detail the response to fraud that is impacting in local police force areas in England and Wales.

It is only in recent years that the true scale, nature and impact of fraud in the UK has begun to become clear. The UK Crime Survey for England and Wales estimated that, for the year ending March 2018, 3.2 million fraud offences occurred (Office for National Statistics, 2018a and 2018b), though only a minority of these were reported by the victims. In total, 638,882 frauds were recorded in 2017/1918, of which only 277,561 (43%) were reported by the public to the police through Action Fraud, the central point of contact for reporting fraud and financially motivated internet crime. Action Fraud also houses the National Fraud Intelligence Bureau (NFIB), which is responsible for the assessment of the reports and allocation to police forces. The remainder were referred by membership organizations in the public and,

primarily, private sectors from reports by members; 276,993 (43%) by Cifas (a not-for-profit fraud prevention membership organization comprised primarily of financial services and corporate businesses) and 84,328 (13%) by UK Finance, the industry body representing finance, banking, markets and payments-related services in or from the UK (Office for National Statistics, 2018b).

Thus, the crime data on which the police force bases its response are incomplete. A recent Home Affairs Committee emphasised the need here in stating that 'the police response to fraud is in desperate need of a fundamental overhaul, and we welcome Government ministers' recognition that the current system is not fit for purpose' (Home Affairs Committee, 2018, para. 66). Further, that response is considered to be poor in comparison to the response in other areas of crime. For criminal investigation, the detection rate for fraud has been found to be low (Button, Lewis, Shepherd, Brooks, & Wakefield, 2012; Home Affairs Committee, 2018) owing not only to gaps in capability but also, at the national level, becoming strategically submerged into policies in which it has struggled to rise above competing, higher-priority crimes. Fraud has, to an uncertain extent, been incorporated into the serious and organized crime policy framework (see Gannon &

Doig, 2010) but these resources have been commonly allotted to other high-profile areas, such as drug supply or modern slavery. As a consequence, fraud has received relatively little of these resources (Crocker et al., 2017; Levi & Maguire, 2012). Similarly, specialist economic crime investigation teams, with a role in tackling serious fraud, began to focus resources less on fraud and more on other, higher-priority areas of business, for example money laundering and criminal asset recovery (Button, Blackbourn, & Tunley, 2014a; Gannon & Doig, 2010).

From the perspective of the victim, decisions made by police forces over whether to investigate appeared to be guided by unreasonably high thresholds and simultaneously lacked transparency (Sanderson, 2018) and, in the case of businesses, were passing the costs of investigation on to the victim (Fraud Advisory Panel, 2012). The nationalization of crime recording, which reduced police contact to remote communications by phone or email, compounded the sense of disenfranchisement for some victims (Home Affairs Committee, 2018). Besides falling short of expectations around criminal investigation, the police were also found to be failing in their duty of care to fraud victims, with research identifying risks and support needs that were going unrecognized and unaddressed by police (Button, Lewis, & Tapley, 2009). Much research has focused on countering the narrative that fraud is a 'victimless' crime, one in which the harm caused to individuals could go unacknowledged, or blame attributed to victims due to for example a perceived lack of judgement or greed on their part is corrected as appropriate (Button, Lewis, & Tapley, 2014b; Button & Cross, 2017; Cross, 2015). The extent to which such beliefs permeate police culture and practices for responding to fraud is uncertain, but any influence is likely to be detrimental to the service provided.

Investigating fraud: the context

The actual and perceived complexity of fraud investigations and police capability to manage them, an issue that seems exacerbated for online fraud, further confounds the prospects of successful prosecution and asset recovery (Gannon & Doig, 2010; Levi, 2013; Levi, Doig, Gundur, Wall, & Williams, 2015). The length of time taken to investigate was considerably higher for fraud than many other offence types; an average of 400 days, which was four times longer than for burglary (Button et al., 2012). Often serious and complex cases are specified as being beyond the reach of police generalists (Button et al., 2014a). The precise characteristics that render a fraud as 'serious' or 'complex' to investigate are unclear, but there is indication that not all frauds fall into this category (Brooks & Button, 2011).

Moreover, it is the regulatory landscape itself which fragments and complicates the context in which those responsible for tackling fraud operate; there is a proliferation of non-statutory organizations taking responsibility for substantive elements of the response (Button, Blackbourn, & Shepherd, 2016). This creates a complex network to navigate and clouds the responsibilities of the police, with the de facto effect of decriminalizing large segments of fraud (for example fraud targeting the public sector). In addition to strategic and cultural barriers, fraud also poses a number of operational challenges to the police and other legal bodies.

First, it is accepted by some forces that, because of the high numbers of cyber-enabled crimes, it is neither feasible nor viable for all reported cases to be investigated (Levi et al., 2015, 2017). Even if a 'volume' fraud is assessed to be worth investigating, the artificial boundaries between what the police classify as volume fraud and what is 'serious and complex' fraud may push the specialist resources toward the latter category (see King & Doig, 2016), rather leaving unanswered the question as to which ones then should be addressed and which ones ignored. That said, a changing police agenda has seen a move away from tackling volume crime—a shift that may have merited a focus on fraud—towards harm reduction, thus rendering fraud less of a strategic priority (Hales & Higgins, 2016; Crocker et al., 2017).

Second, fraud poses a different challenge to many other local offences in the physical separation between the crime and the offender. Police forces (and other agencies) continue to work largely within the confines of their geographical boundaries, while the changing nature of fraud means that offenders and victims can be nationally or globally dispersed, complicating the process of assigning roles and responsibilities within this patchwork of response (Skidmore et al., 2019).

Third, the nature of fraud offences has been impacted by technology and the police has been slow to adapt to this new digital landscape (HMIC, 2015). Although the term 'digital policing' is starting to gain traction within UK police forces, the rudimentary understanding of cyber crime, along with the necessary skills that are critical for collecting and utilizing digital evidence, are still not mainstream competencies (Bossler, Burruss, & Holt, 2016; HMIC, 2015). With much of fraud being cyber-enabled (Levi et al., 2015; Skidmore et al., 2018), there are very serious questions around the suitability of existing police resources. Equally, the numbers of police staff devoted to tackling economic crime (including fraud) have been and are relatively low. In the face of resource pressures, the City of London Corporation cautioned that compromises would be necessary as they lacked the resources and skills/technology to tackle every type of economic cyber crime (City of London Corporation, 2015, p. 7). Although it is difficult to measure priorities, investment in specialist economic crime teams has been used as a barometer for the level of police commitment to tackling fraud, and on that criterion, research has found police commitment to be lacking (Button et al., 2014a; Doig & Levi, 2013; Skidmore et al., 2018).

Despite the radical shift in the approach to fraud in the UK since the launch of the NFIB and Action Fraud, the view that there is a lack of competence or appetite across law enforcement is unchanged (for example Button et al., 2014a; HMICFRS, 2019). It is in this context that the research reported here—sponsored by the Dawes Trust—was conducted, focusing on understanding the local response to fraud and the factors that impact on it.

Research methods

This paper draws on evidence taken from wider, practitioner-focused research looking at the effectiveness of the police response to fraud (see Skidmore et al., 2018) and places the findings within the context of the academic and other literature on the policing of fraud. Data sources include semi-structured interviews with personnel in police forces ($N = 45$), regional–national law enforcement bodies ($N = 22$) and partner agencies ($N = 40$), a survey of the fraud strategic leads in 32 police force areas, and a survey of the workforce in three police force areas ($N = 405$).

All 43 police forces in England and Wales were sent a survey with the aim being to map out the fraud response landscape, including local strategies, structures and decision-making processes. Nearly three-quarters ($N = 32$, 74%) of those contacted completed and returned a survey; responses were received over two months (July–August) in 2017. While the local strategic lead was requested to complete the survey the extent to which each followed this instruction cannot be certain. Those completing the survey include officers ranked detective chief inspector and above ($N = 10$), detective inspectors ($N = 15$) and detective sergeants ($N = 3$). It should be noted, when considering the paper's findings, that a number of the larger urban police forces did not respond, thus limiting the national representativeness of the survey, not least since a substantive proportion of demand is concentrated in a small number of large urban police force areas (Skidmore et al., 2018).

The perspectives of police operational staff on the ground were collected from three specific police forces (Avon and Somerset, Kent and Essex); indeed, two of these areas were the focus of 39 of the 45

semi-structured interviews with police practitioners. A survey of operational staff was also completed in these areas, referred to as the 'workforce' survey. The aim of the survey was to collect cross-sectional data on perspectives of the workforce in these three areas and it was distributed to using internal police email. Four hundred and five completed surveys were received, but the response rate was uneven, with 211, 95 and 23 being received from each respective area (responses were received in November and December 2017). The survey did not reflect a representative local or national sample of the police workforce; rather, it should be seen as an opportunity to assess different perspectives in an area which has hitherto rarely been researched. Respondents from investigation ($N = 141$) or neighbourhood ($N = 104$) teams were most prominent in the sample.

Local governance of the police response

Understanding the demand

Local police forces reported being challenged in managing the demand centrally streamed to them from Action Fraud and the NFIB. Partly this was a 'big data' challenge, requiring techniques in data analysis for understanding levels of harm, risk and need. Coupled with this, the offence classification process was viewed as problematic as there are 48 separate fraud categories (Home Office, 2018). One consequence of centralizing processes was to separate the knowledge, understanding and expertise accrued by those at the centre from those working on the ground. Strategic assessments and victimization data were regularly streamed to local police forces, but there was no common understanding of how to apply these. Many practitioners, particularly non-specialists, reported difficulty in understanding the fraud offence categories, and only half of police forces ($N = 16$, 52%) reported having a designated analytical lead to systematically examine these data. At a national level, information pertaining to each crime is collected and shared, however much of the contextual information about people and places is recorded in local police and partner systems (for example prior victimization). These two sources of information are seldom integrated; as one fraud lead commented:

> … there is no integration between NFIB and force IT systems, which makes information sharing inefficient and complex.

Our research found that only some forces had begun to develop data-matching systems in order to identify priority offenders and victims.

The challenge in contextualizing offences, victims and offenders raises a barrier between fraud and many of the established decision-making frameworks for assigning resources. The police commonly utilize operationalized definitions and classifications for levering specific interventions; for example, assessment against a range of factors to determine if someone was vulnerable provided the means to direct certain victim support resources. Yet these frameworks are less able to elucidate the demand from fraud: partly because of limited information, but also conceptual ambiguity.

At the national level, fraud policing strategies are currently encompassed by the National Serious and Organized Crime Strategy (SOCS); a 2015 draft policing fraud strategy developed by the City of London Police's Economic Crime Directorate which placed the emphasis on organized crime or criminal networks but left responsibility for 'local' fraud to local force discretion was largely ignored. SOCS posits a diversified set of responses that incorporate law enforcement and crime prevention (HM Government, 2018), and this was widely cited by practitioners as a means to frame and understand both the fraud problem and the response. However, acceptance of the links to serious and organized crime did not translate to strategic or operational prominence in many jurisdictions. Police force leads described fraud as a low priority or absent from key strategic documents; nearly half ($N = 15$, 47%) described it as a low priority, and for others ($N = 5$, 15%) it was not deemed applicable to local assessments of serious and organized crime. The extent to which fraud is made a local priority will reflect both national priorities and the views of the local public but, regardless, its absence or low status in local assessments will impact on the comprehensiveness of the response. When asked to describe the challenges in conducting effective fraud investigations, 14 local strategic leads (44%) highlighted a lack of prioritization in their police force, with resources being drawn to competing serious offences such as child sexual exploitation.

There were few fraudsters that the police recognized and responded to as an organized crime group (OCG) (see Table 1). Eight (28%) police forces reported either having none or not knowing if they had fraud OCGs and 12 (41%) reported managing

one or two of these groups. The applied definitions of organized crime could vary depending on the operational focus of different agencies, and there was inconsistency between assessments at the national centre and those in local police forces, the latter more resistant to operationalizing fraudsters as OCGs despite being flagged as such by the former. Responses to organized crime were shaped by broader resourcing issues, with practitioners reporting a wide gap between available specialist economic crime resource and the potential scale of demand for complex fraud investigation.

National and regional cyber crime practitioners reported working to stringent definitions that restricted their focus to cyber-dependent, as opposed to cyber-enabled crimes. Cyber-dependent crimes are those which would not exist without the internet. Cyber-enabled crimes are those which, if the networked technologies were removed, could still take place. Being cyber-enabled allows these crimes to be carried out more easily, sometimes with fewer criminal staff than would be needed for similar crimes offline, and with less risks to the offenders (see Levi, Doig, Gundur, Wall, & Williams, 2017).

Much of fraud occurs online and, in some cases, overlaps with computer misuse crimes (for example hacking to perpetrate mandate fraud), but these cases were differentiated on the basis of either how online technology was applied (i.e. many are cyber-enabled) or the motivation behind the crime (i.e. to perpetrate fraud). Such distinctions put specialist cyber crime resources out of reach for most fraud cases. In three-quarters ($N = 24$, 75%) of police forces, few, or no fraud investigations were conducted by cyber crime teams (see Figure 1).

Similarly, fraud was excluded by the definitions in use for identifying victims who were vulnerable. A criminal justice definition of vulnerability (MoJ, 2015) has been adopted by many police forces to steer resources to victims most in need of them. However, this criterion was insensitive to fraud-related risks, with eligibility determined on the basis of physical harm rather than financial harm, and thereby rendering most fraud victims ineligible for a service. Some local police had developed separate systems to draw out a subset of victims who were vulnerable, with a particular focus on individuals who were susceptible to repeat victimization.

Previous research has demonstrated that there is serious and organized criminality (Mills, Skodbo, & Blyth, 2013) and victims who are in various way vulnerable, contained within the high volumes of reported fraud (Age UK, 2015; OFT, 2009). However, fraud falls short of the definitions in use for brokering access to relevant police resources. As with other areas of high-volume demand (for example anti-social behaviour) fraud victims are treated as an

Table 1. Organized crime groups involved in fraud as a primary or secondary form of criminality.

No. of OCGs	Primary activity	%	Secondary activity	%
1–2	12	40%	5	17%
3–5	3	10%	3	10%
6–10	2	7%	2	7%
More than 10	2	7%	1	3%
Number not specified*	3	10%	6	20%
None or don't know	8	26%	13	43%
Total	30	100%	30	100%

*Some police forces reported having OCGs linked to fraud but did not report how many.

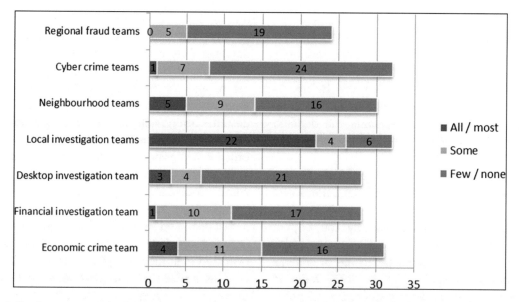

Figure 1. Police force strategic leads' perception on the proportion of fraud investigations conducted by different local police teams.

'undifferentiated mass' (Innes & Innes, 2016) which obscures in the first place the nature of the demand, but also the degree to which resources are unaligned with it.

Accounting for the response

The nationalization of responsibilities for recording and processing fraud reports introduced an unprecedented model of law enforcement—a nationalized police network for co-ordinating fraud investigations across the police service (HMICFRS, 2019). It introduced more robust and consistent processes for recording and assessing these crimes. However, it failed to produce a more consistent service, because the response continues to be primarily assigned to local police forces which operate to variable policies and protocols. There is an absence of national direction, in the form of a specific strategy for tackling fraud. In the context of this nationalized police network, there is little consensus on what 'good' practice looks like for local policing and limited clarity on who has the remit for determining and disseminating any such guidance. Therefore, policies and practices are shaped by local concerns, reflecting localized resources, structures and priorities, which creates variations in decision-making across different jurisdictions.

The introduction of Action Fraud as a national reporting hub separated the functions of crime recording from service delivery. For victims of crime who are assigned a response, the national centre 'owns' the crime, but has no accountability for service delivery or the outcome. Equally, many police force leads reported on the absence of fraud from their local performance management regimes and a failure to feed into national systems for recording outcomes, creating strategic blind-spots on effectiveness across

the system. Few had introduced new systems to account for their performance in tackling fraud. While a high percentage ($N = 23$, 72%) reported monitoring the effectiveness of their investigations, most cited procedural file checks for this, rather than strategic assessments. One respondent summarised that there was:

> … no performance regime around fraud, no accountability framework that is proactive, and no real understanding of the Action Fraud data.

Similarly, a victim's contact with the police is often limited to a phone call to the national reporting centre, leaving ambiguity over where the responsibilities lie for any follow-up support that may be required (many of whom were not assigned a local police, or any other type of investigation). It was noted that the national crime recording centre is under pressure, principally focusing on monitoring for acute risks (such as threat to life) at the time of calls and signposting to other relevant services (though many victims report online). All police forces are notified of fraud victims in their jurisdiction, but well over a quarter ($N = 9$, 28%) reported having no structures or systems in place for monitoring these or delivering additional support.

Police structures and resource for tackling fraud

Local structures for investigation

In the majority of police forces, most fraud investigations are conducted by non-specialists. Figure 1 shows that 22 police forces reported that all, or most investigations were conducted by local investigation teams and in five police forces, neighbourhood policing teams.

Most police forces had economic crime teams that incorporated specialist capabilities for investigating fraud and other forms of financial crime. These resources are allocated based on the capability requirement, with a loosely defined distinction made between 'serious and complex' and 'volume' fraud. The majority fall into the category of 'volume' fraud and are assigned to non-specialist investigators. In recognizing few frauds as 'serious and complex', they are able to restrict the flow of demand to small specialist teams that would quickly become overwhelmed.

Four out of 32 police forces reported that all, or most, investigations were conducted by their economic crime team, reflecting the small number of larger police forces (that experience high volumes of demand for investigation) that had established specialist units for undertaking both 'volume' and 'serious and complex' fraud investigations. While this approach helped in consolidating expertise, systems and protocols which foster more consistent standards in decision-making and investigation, it created a more tightly bound, less flexible, pool of resources for managing high volumes of fraud. Consequently, some forces had raised their eligibility thresholds, screening out many cases prior to investigation to maintain a more manageable workflow (see King & Doig, 2016).

Skills, capabilities and attitudes in the police

A number of police forces reported difficulty in hiring and keeping specialists with the appropriate skills to conduct fraud investigations. The most frequently cited challenges included:

- Loss of staff to the private sector, which is more able to provide better opportunities and pay.
- Lack of institutional recognition of fraud as an area of work in terms of resources and focus.
- Fraud viewed as an end-of-career move by people preparing to work in the private sector.
- A police professional development model that is not suited to a fast-moving area like fraud.

In relation to being able to recruit staff with the necessary skills to tackle fraud, 27% ($N = 8$) of fraud leads were 'very confident' that they were recruiting the right people, with 40% ($N = 12$) 'somewhat confident' and 33% ($N = 10$) 'not confident'. This problem was felt most acutely in the specialist units. One respondent commented:

In the [National Cyber Crime Unit] it's really hard to keep people in … we lose people to banks and any other sector. There's a massive technical skills shortage in cyber crime, investigation and intelligence … anyone with a pinch of knowledge and you are a desirable resource.

Two local police leads noted the tedency to recruit people without all the necessary skills:

… specialist knowledge around fraud investigations is acquired by on-the-job experience.

Similarly, one force reported that staff with a variety of other skills could be recruited and trained. However,

Due to other commitments, limited capacity and lack of specialist training these skills are not always developed or utilized.

The workforce survey carried out in three police forces (see Table 2) revealed that more respondents agreed that fraud should be a priority (39%), compared to those who disagreed (21%), but many did not provide a clear view. However, half (49%) considered that other organizations were better placed to deal with fraud, with many referring to national enforcement agencies and the finance sector. Over four in 10 (41%) did not consider the response from their own police force to be effective; many of the stated reasons related to a perceived misalignment between the resource and capability available to them (for example time and training) and what was needed to effectively investigate fraud.

Only half of the respondents in our national survey agreed that practitioners in local investigation and neighbourhood teams considered fraud investigation to be important ($N = 18$, 56%). Some attributed this to a lack of understanding of harm and vulnerability in the context of fraud. This is an important issue. In Figure 2, vulnerability is reported to be the most influential factor in determining whether to proceed with an investigation in 23 (74%) police forces. One lead commented:

Vulnerability is a key factor and even in cases which cannot be investigated then vulnerable victims will be supported.

Table 2. Attitudes in the police workforce on the role and effectiveness of their police force in tackling fraud.

Police resource	Strongly agree	Agree	Neutral	Disagree	Strongly disagree	Don't know	Total*
Fraud should be a priority in my police force	11 (2.7%)	148 (36.6%)	148 (36.6%)	71 (17.6%)	12 (3.0%)	14 (3.5%)	404
In comparison to other areas of crime, my police force is putting in place adequate resource and capability to tackle fraud	12 (3.5%)	73 (21.3%)	76 (22.2%)	80 (23.3%)	43 (12.5%)	59 (17.2%)	343
My police force is effective at responding to fraud	5 (1.2%)	72 (17.8%)	99 (24.5%)	104 (25.7%)	63 (15.6%)	61 (15.1%)	404
Other organizations are better placed to deal with fraud	44 (12.7%)	124 (35.8%)	96 (27.7%)	35 (10.1%)	8 (2.3%)	39 (11.3%)	346

*The total number of survey respondents was 405 but the rate of response varied by each question.

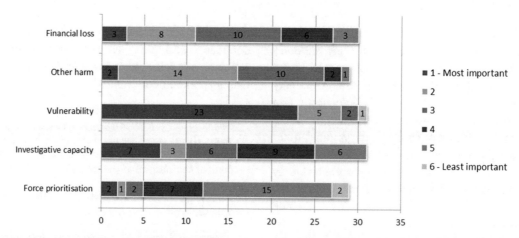

Figure 2. The perception of police force strategic leads for fraud on the importance of different factors on whether the police choose to investigate a fraud.

Many fewer considered investigative capacity ($N = 7$, 23%); financial loss ($N = 3$, 10%) and force prioritization ($N = 2$, 6%) to be the most important factors. It is, however, possible that these responses came from a point of principle, rather than pragmatism, with vulnerability representing a central value framework in police, albeit one that is inconsistently applied and understood in the context of fraud (Skidmore et al., 2018). In many jurisdictions there were no formal processes to assess which cases are assigned for investigation, but rather all cases were disseminated to local investigators to manage.

Not forgetting the influence of corporate-level strategies and frameworks in policing, the culture and attitudes of staff in the workforce are also important for determining the response (for example see Button & Cross, 2017). Our interviews and survey revealed a number of commonly held views which shaped approaches and motivations when responding to fraud. Broadly, these fell into perceptions of their own capabilities to respond to fraud, the distinct nature of the work in the context of broader responsibilities, and finally, appraisal of victims and their experiences. The police staff survey showed that 47% of participants would prefer not to be involved with fraud cases, though whether this demonstrated a true preference, or was reflective of other factors (such as lack of time and training; complexity; and

overwhelming volumes related to fraud cases) needs more work. Comments included:

> No one wants a fraud, it means paperwork, banking, accounting, details ... it's going to take too long, it's too hard, it's too complex ... they need half a day to type up, [you] submit production orders and then just need to wait a week, but they [officers] are slaves to the radio and the phone.

> It's not the [glamorous] side of policing, [appealing to] officers leading up to retirement, very methodical, who like a good spread sheet ... investigating from afar.

As previously stated, much fraud investigation is conducted by non-specialist teams. When asked for the most significant challenges in investigations, many specialists cited the lack of knowledge in their general workforce. A particular gap was digital investigation; over half ($N = 19$, 59%) did not consider their workforce to have sufficient skills and capabilities to investigate cyber crime, which is significant considering 69% of fraud investigations were found to be linked to cyber crime (Skidmore et al., 2018).

Many in the workforce perceived gaps in their own capabilities and those available within their own police force. First, many considered the skills and capabilities needed in fraud were distinct from those required for other areas of their work. Table 3 shows the majority

Table 3. Attitudes in the police workforce on the skills and capability for tackling fraud.

Police resource	Strongly agree	Agree	Neutral	Disagree	Strongly disagree	Don't know	Total*
There are enough people with the right skills in my police force to tackle fraud	8 (2.3%)	27 (7.8%)	47 (13.6%)	118 (34.2%)	82 (23.8%)	63 (18.3%)	345
Effective fraud policing requires a different set of skills to other crimes	97 (28.0%)	184 (53.0%)	27 (7.8%)	29 (8.4%)	3 (0.9%)	7 (2.0%)	347
I have the skills I need to effectively deal with a fraud case or victim	11 (2.9%)	71 (18.8%)	51 (13.5%)	125 (33.2%)	91 (24.1%)	28 (7.4%)	377
I would like more training to deal with fraud	131 (35.3%)	146 (39.4%)	42 (11.3%)	27 (7.3%)	10 (2.7%)	15 (4.0%)	371
Fraud should be dealt with by specialists	129 (37.1%)	171 (49.1%)	26 (7.5%)	20 (5.7%)	1 (0.3%)	1 (0.3%)	348
I would prefer not to be involved with fraud cases	72 (19.3%)	91 (24.3%)	55 (14.7%)	78 (20.9%)	51 (13.6%)	27 (7.2%)	374

*The total number of survey respondents was 405 but the rate of response varied by each question.

($N = 281$, 81%) agreed that policing fraud requires a different set of skills to other crimes and a similar proportion, felt that it should be dealt with by specialists ($N = 300$. 86%). Second, many reported not being equipped with these capabilities; three-quarters ($N = 277$, 75%) wanted more training to deal with fraud; and only one in five ($N = 82$, 22%) agreed they had the necessary skills to deal with a fraud case or victim.

These specific skills and capabilities reflect the features that render fraud distinct from other crimes that the local police deal with. These include:

- The intrinsic financial and technological characteristics of fraud.
- Their occurrence in cyberspace.
- The associated geographic dispersion and anonymity of the actors.
- The sophistication and considerable variance in the methods employed by fraudsters (for example money laundering and social engineering techniques) reflected in the unwieldy number of fraud offence categories.

For some economic crime investigators, the common view of fraud investigation as being intrinsically complex was out of kilter with their own experience. They believed that fraud covered a broad spectrum of complexity and that it was necessary to demystify fraud and the processes of investigation. There was no agreed criterion or defined view of what constitutes complexity, but the general workforce perceived that many cases allocated to them extended beyond their capabilities. At the point of allocation, there is only a surface level understanding of offenders and offending (for example an online shopping fraud), but practitioners reported that it was common for cases to unravel and reveal offending that is serious and/or complex. However, a paucity of specialist investigation resource could restrict opportunities to escalate the enforcement response accordingly.

Despite the existence of tools and techniques to aid fraud investigators (Betts, 2017), the evidence about what is effective in disrupting fraud offenders is limited (Levi et al., 2015). The diversity of the offence means investigators are often faced with unfamiliar contexts. Victims reporting fraud may be only partially aware (or not aware at all) on how the offence was committed and, in some cases, there is a reliance on third parties to help build an understanding. This, for example, includes the private sector, where practitioners must navigate a wide range of stakeholders typically operating to their own polices and protocols for how to engage with the police. Added to this is the need to liaise with a multitude of victims located across the country, as

well as other police forces, to assist with evidence gathering.

The gap between the skills and capability required and those made available, most likely affects not only judicial outcomes, but also the decision-making and approach to investigations. Some offences are perceived as low harm, others may entail protracted enquiries, with limited prospects of a successful outcome (i.e. criminal prosecution) and these can be influential to decision-making. Indeed, key considerations are whether it represents a proportionate use of resource and is in the public interest, in terms of likely to be successful and generating a positive outcome, which might include the likely sentence severity. These latter points were previously hard-wired into national policy (Home Office, 2004), but in practice the nature and quality of investigative resources available can be as important in determining the time and resources needed to investigate and prospects of success, as the specific nature of the fraud.

To compound matters further, the national recording and allocation processes mean that fraud information is received several months after the incident takes place (Scholes, 2018). In many instances, enquiries are directed to actors outside of the local jurisdiction (for example other police forces or web companies) and investigations involve more administrative, desk-top based enquiries that are considered to not mesh well with conventional duties. And time is always a consideration:

As a response officer, the demand on my time is so intense I can go a full set of shifts with barely enough time to make a phone call, let alone investigate fraud, which can be very lengthy.

Due to operational needs and demands, the lengthy enquiries required on a fraud do get left until there is time to sit and complete them, therefore, increasing the time the victim has to wait for an outcome.

Finally, in terms of the behaviour of fraud victims, research has highlighted a propensity to overlook the full extent of the harm caused by fraud and the experiences of victims (Button et al., 2014b; Button & Tunley, 2015; Cross, 2015). Practitioner responses in surveys and interviews highlighted a perception of an active role played by some victims in their own victimization, which made it difficult for some in the police forces to empathise with them. A considerable majority in the workforce survey agreed that the public needed to take more responsibility to protect themselves against fraud ($N = 303$, 86%). The absorption of crime recording into a national contact centre also severely restricts the opportunities for local services to engage with and assess victims, in essence reducing their local victims to data streams sent out from the national centre. Some police forces have begun to acknowledge the spectrum of fraud-related harm and develop bespoke frameworks that draw fraud into the vulnerability agenda, a central framework for directing police resources (Hales & Higgins, 2016). A particular focus has gone to the elderly demographic known to contain a segment of individuals less able to protect themselves from fraud and to be at risk of repeat victimization (Age UK, 2015). An age variable is one that can be readily used to make sense of the crime data, but the conflation of vulnerability and old age hard-wires an established 'confirmation bias', evident in the views of many practitioners. It is an explanation for fraud victimization that accentuates the role of the victim and the absence of specific social or personal resource, i.e. a deficit model (Cross, 2016). Equally, a consequence is that much shorter shrift is then given to victims, without any such excuses.

Discussion

Although the introduction of new structures for recording and processing frauds experienced by the public and the business community has brought the fraud problem more into focus, this paper has highlighted some distinct barriers to the effective policing of fraud. The year-on-year increase in the volumes of fraud reported to the police since 2011 in the UK has been, at least in part, generated by new structures for recording and processing offences (ONS, 2018b), although the now quite striking levels are still an underestimate of the scale of fraud experienced in England and Wales (Blakeborough & Correia, 2018). Still, the clearer focus generated via improved data capture naturally raises public expectations of an improved law enforcement response (Button & Tunley, 2015; Levi & Burrows, 2008) and there is growing disquiet in the business community (Fraud Advisory Panel, 2016) and more broadly across the public (Home Affairs Committee, 2018; NAO, 2017). The findings from this research reveal a similar dissatisfaction held by many working in the police.

It is ironic that the nationalized structure for recording, processing and co-ordinating the response to fraud was introduced following a national review that highlighted the failings of the local policing model (HM Government, 2006). This research exposes the fragmentation in policies, resources and commitment across the different 43 police forces (see also HMICFRS, 2019). It has untethered the roles and responsibilities in enforcement, victim support and crime reduction, that would traditionally be contained and managed within a single police force jurisdiction. And there are questions for how criminality, that extends beyond local concerns, can be integrated into decision-making that is predominantly inward-facing and focused on harm reduction within local borders (Levi et al., 2015; Wall, 2007 and 2010). Cross-border offending is not unique to fraud, but national direction and leadership is limited. It has ambiguous coverage in national strategies for serious and organized and cyber crime, and similarly, in the government's Strategic Policing Requirement for guiding the local police response to cross-border crime (Home Office, 2015). Linked to this, is the need for analytical capability for translating high volumes of recorded crime data into demand that is meaningful to local police forces. Although the police configure their response around key policy constructs such as harm, vulnerability and serious crime they are insensitive to the risks and need contained within fraud (Skidmore et al., 2018).

UK police have been slow to adapt to the substantive changes in the offending landscape (particularly with the rise of cyber crime), partly due to challenges in accounting for what the state of current police capability is against what capabilities are actually needed to respond in this new landscape (Loveday, 2017). Further, research has identified not just deficient skills and capability, but a cultural resistance across the workforce in accepting responsibilities for tackling online crime (Bossler et al., 2016; Police Executive Research Forum, 2014). In the case of fraud, structural reform at a national level has not been mirrored by reform at the local level, with most police forces managing the influx of so-called 'new' demand with resources that are relatively unchanged. It is evident that some police forces have come to see more value in their efforts to identify and support 'vulnerable' victims, than in criminal investigation (not least when suspects are difficult to trace).

Recommendations to improve the police response to fraud have included taking responsibility away from local police and centralizing the fraud response into national or regional hubs because investigations are complex; requisite capabilities are scarce; there is an OCG dimension to certain cases; and because the prospect of raising this low-priority crime up local strategic agendas is limited. This is a model some local police forces have already introduced for co-ordinating criminal investigations and, in some cases, victim support. However, the ubiquity of online crime, most likely calls for a balance to be struck between re-calibrating the skills and training available in the generalist police workforce (HMIC, 2015) and warehousing expertise within specialist teams that will have less capacity to manage large volumes of demand.

Conclusions

The nationalization of crime recording and analysis in the UK has introduced unprecedented scope to understand the scale and nature of fraud, and considerable potential to co-ordinate a national response to what is commonly a borderless crime. However, co-ordination requires a robust and common understanding of roles and responsibilities across the range of bodies and agencies involved. The implementation of the nationalized response framework in 2011, without a national policing strategy, has created a substantive rift between what is known about fraud at the national level, and what is done about it on the ground. A coherent, evidence-based approach to integrating fraud into decision-making frameworks that are central to configuring local service delivery—threat, harm, risk and vulnerability—would be one step for introducing more consistent, rationalized decision-making in the police. A byproduct of nationalization has been a detachment of the problem from responders on the ground, with local decisions made singularly on the basis of data disseminated from the national intelligence centre. There is a big data challenge in interpreting this complex stream of 'demand' to guide police investigators who have historically failed to prioritize or understand fraud.

Acknowledgement

We are grateful to the Dawes Trust for sponsoring this research.

Disclosure statement

No potential conflict of interest was reported by the author(s).

References

Age UK. (2015). *Only the tip of the iceberg: Fraud against older people evidence review*. London: Author.

Betts, M. (2017). *Investigation of fraud and economic crime*. Oxford: Oxford University Press.

Blakeborough, L., & Correia, S. (2018). *The scale and nature of fraud: A review of the evidence*. London: Home Office. Available at: https://assets.publishing.service.gov.uk/government/uploads/system/uploads/attachment_data/file/720772/scale-and-nature-of-fraud-review-of-evidence.pdf [Accessed 29 September 2018].

Bossler, A. M., Burruss, G. W., & Holt, T. J. (2016). *Assessing police perceptions of cybercrime and the law enforcement response in England and Wales*. USA: Georgia Southern University. Available at: https://www.cambridgecybercrime.uk/slides-2016-bossler.pdf [Accessed 2 August 2018].

Brooks, G., & Button, M. (2011). The police and fraud investigation and the case for a nationalized solution in the United Kingdom. *The Police Journal, 84*.

Button, M., Blackbourn, D., & Shepherd, D. (2016). *The fraud 'Justice Systems': A scoping study on the civil, regulatory and private paths to 'Justice' for fraudsters*. Portsmouth: University of Portsmouth.

Button, M., Blackbourn, D., & Tunley, M. (2014a). 'The not so thin blue line after all?' Investigative resources dedicated to fighting fraud/economic crime in the United Kingdom. *Policing: A Journal of Policy and Practice, 9*(2), 129–142.

Button, M., & Cross, C. (2017). *Cyber frauds, scams and their victims*. London: Routledge.

Button, M., Lewis, C., Shepherd, D., Brooks, G., & Wakefield, A. (2012). *Fraud and punishment: enhancing deterrence through more effective sanctions*. Portsmouth: University of Portsmouth.

Button, M., Lewis, C., & Tapley, J. (2009). *A better deal for fraud victims: Research into victims' needs and experiences*. London: NFA.

Button, M., Lewis, C., & Tapley, J. (2014b). Not a victimless crime: The impact of fraud on individual victims and their families. *Security Journal, 27*(1), 36–54.

Button, M., & Tunley, M. (2015). Explaining fraud deviancy attenuation in the United Kingdom. *Crime, Law and Social Change, 63*(1), 49–64.

City of London Corporation. (2015). *The implications of economic cybercrime for policing: research report*. London: City of London Corporation.

Crocker, R., Webb, S., Garner, S., Skidmore, M., Gill, M., & Graham, J. (2017). *The impact of organized crime in local communities*. London: The Police Foundation/Perpetuity Research.

Cross, C. (2015). No laughing matter: Blaming the victim of online fraud. *International Review of Victimology, 21*(1), 187–204. http://eprints.qut.edu.au/83702/

Cross, C. (2016). 'They're Very Lonely': understanding the fraud victimisation of seniors. *International Journal for Crime, Justice and Social Democracy, 5*(4), 60–75.

Doig, A., & Levi, M. (2013). A case of arrested development? Delivering the UK national fraud strategy within competing policing policy priorities. *Public Money and Management, 33*(2), 145–152.

Fraud Advisory Panel. (2012). *Obtaining redress and improving outcomes for the victims of fraud: Research into the experiences of smaller business fraud victims in recovering their money (case studies)*. London: Fraud Advisory Panel. Available at:.

Gannon, R., & Doig, A. (2010). Ducking the answer? Fraud strategies and police resources. *Policing & Society, 20*(1), 39–60.

Hales, G., & Higgins, A. (2016). *Prioritisation in a changing world: seven challenges for policing*. London: The Police Foundation.

HM Government. (2006). *Fraud Review: Final Report*. Available at: http://webarchive.nationalarchives.gov.uk/20070222120000 / http://www.lslo.gov.uk/pdf/FraudReview.pdf [Accessed 5 August 2018]

HM Government. (2018). *Serious and organized crime strategy*. London: The Stationery Office.

HMIC. (2015). *Real lives, real crimes: A study of digital crime and policing*. London: HMIC.

HMICFRS. (2019). *Time to choose: An inspection of the police response to fraud*. London: HMICFRS.

Home Affairs Committee. (2018) *Policing for the future: Tenth report of session 2017–19*. Available at: https://publications.parliament.uk/pa/cm201719/cmselect/cmhaff/515/515.pdf [Accessed 24 June 2019]

Home Office. (2004). *Home Office circular 47 / 2004: Priorities for the investigation of fraud cases*. Available at: http://webarchive.nationalarchives.gov.uk/20130125153037 / http://www.homeoffice.gov.uk/about-us/corporate-publications-strategy/home-office-circulars/circulars-2004/?d-7095067-p=3 [Accessed 2 September 2018]

Home Office. (2015). *The strategic policing requirement*. London: Home Office.

Home Office. (2018). *Home Office counting rules for recorded crime: Fraud*. Available at: https://www.gov.uk/government/publications/counting-rules-for-recorded-crime [Accessed 3 October 2018]

Innes, H., & Innes, M. (2013). *Personal, situational and incidental vulnerabilities to ASB harm: a follow up study*. Cardiff: Cardiff University.

King, J., & Doig, A. (2016). A dedicated place for volume fraud within the current UK economic crime agenda? The greater manchester police case study. *The Journal of Financial Crime, 23*(4), 902–915.

Levi, M. (2013). *Regulating fraud (Routledge Revivals): White-collar crime and the criminal process*. Routledge.

Levi, M., & Burrows, J. (2008). Measuring the impact of fraud in the UK: A conceptual and empirical journey. *The British Journal of Criminology, 48*(3), 293–318.

Levi, M., & Maguire, M. (2012). Something old, something new; something not entirely blue: Uneven and shifting modes of crime control. In T. Newburn, & J. Peay (Eds.), *Policing: Politics, Culture and Control*. Oxford: Hart Publishing.

Levi, M., Doig, A., Gundur, R., Wall, D., & Williams, M. (2015). *The implications of economic cybercrime for policing*. London: City of London Corporation.

Levi, M., Doig, A., Gundur, R., Wall, D., & Williams, M. (2017). Cyberfraud and the implications for effective risk-based responses: themes from UK research. *Crime Law and Social Change, 67*(1), 77–96.

Loveday, B. (2017). Still Plodding Along? The police response to the changing profile of crime in England and Wales. *International Journal of Police Science & Management, 19*(2), 101–109.

Mills, H., Skodbo, S., & Blyth, P. (2013). *Understanding organized crime: estimating the scale and the social and economic costs*. London: Home Office.

Ministry of Justice. (2015). *Code of practice for victims of crime*. Available at: https://www.gov.uk/government/publications/the-code-of-practice-for-victims-of-crime [Accessed 15 January 2018]

National Audit Office. (2017). *Online fraud*. London: National Audit Office.

Office for National Statistics. (2018a). *Crime in England and Wales: year ending March 2018*. London: ONS.

Office for National Statistics. (2018b). *Overview of fraud and computer misuse statistics for England and Wales*. London: ONS.

Office of Fair Trading. (2009). *The psychology of scams: Provoking and committing errors of judgement*. London: OFT.

Police Executive Research Forum. (2014). *The role of local law enforcement agencies in preventing and investigating cyber crime*. Washington, DC: Police Executive Research Forum.

Sanderson, D. (2018). https://www.thetimes.co.uk/article/computer-says-no-to-police-action-in-cyberfraud-cases-below-100k-znsvwcp3s.

Scholes, A. (2018). *The scale and drivers of attrition in reported fraud and cyber crime: Research Report 97*. London: Home Office.

Skidmore, M., Ramm, J., Goldstraw-White, J., Barrett, C., Barleaza, S., Muir, R., & Gill, M. (2018). *More than just a number: Improving the police response to victims of fraud*. London: The Police Foundation/Perpetuity Research.

Wall, D. (2007/10). Policing cybercrimes: Situating the Public police in networks of security within cyberspace. *Police Practice & Research: An International Journal, 8*(2), 183–205.

When opportunity knocks: mobilizing capabilities on serious organized economic crime

Kenneth Murray

ABSTRACT

This paper is primarily concerned with organized crime structures and how they adapt and modify to take advantage of fraud opportunities. It is illustrated with case studies which show a growing capability within UK organized crime to pool and deploy criminal monies in legitimate markets. The theme and purpose of the paper is to raise awareness of this in a way that encourages collaborative and strategic responses from law enforcement and relevant institutions, including academia.

IMPACT

The accumulation of criminal funds under the guise of legitimate funds is not something that should be tolerated and accepted as a necessary evil of the modern world. Markets and economies are, however, increasingly vulnerable to the corrosive and corruptive effects of serious organized crime. Using real-life case studies, this paper explains why a raised awareness of societal and professional attitudes is required to more effectively tackle the problem of serious organized economic crime and how the problem needs to be prioritized as a national strategic challenge. The paper will have value to law enforcement and policy- and law-makers worldwide.

Introduction

A recent article in *The Times* newspaper, reporting on the *Crime Survey for England and Wales* for the calendar year 2018 (Office of National Statistics, 2019), noted that the 'police are failing to investigate fraud cases even when there is compelling evidence because of a defeatist culture' (*The Times*, 2 April, 2019). The article reported claims that fraud was never close to top of law enforcement priorities, because it did not 'bang, bleed or shout'.

Whether or not this contention is justified (see Levi, 2013, originally 1987, for a historical comparison), serious organized crime groups (SOCGs) appear to have become increasingly involved in fraud and other serious economic crimes. It is an alternative use of the skill sets built up through the practice of money laundering and a profitable avenue for diversification. It is also an area law enforcement continues to find challenging for a variety of reasons. From the point of view of serious organized crime (SOC), access to corporate style financial and business expertise has become a valuable business attribute—a means by which wealth can be realized behind a legitimate veneer through establishment of evidential breaks between the individual or group commissioning a crime, its execution, and receipt of its pay-off.

This capability also improves the range and quality of criminal activities SOC can take an interest in and influence. Either directly or through criminal network connections, they have access to the relevant technology and to the necessary professional expertise that enables them both to perpetrate the crime of fraud and do it in such a way that secures its proceeds. It is an accessible skill set, as finely tuned and honed as large-scale drug trafficking logistics. As a result, when opportunity is available, the incentive for SOCGs to take advantage of fraud opportunities when they see them often proves irresistible.

This paper considers generic case studies which illustrate these points, borne from actual investigative experience in Scotland. It considers the challenges involved in preventing such schemes and in bringing them to justice. It also considers the broader implications of this activity becoming an increasingly prominent and influential aspect of our culture.

Case studies

Pension liberation fraud

The first case study illustrates how a fraud opportunity can be discovered by one set of criminal actors and exploited by another set with access to more sophisticated financial networks.

The initial fraud relates to the offer of a cash withdrawal hook to pension holders in return for consent to transfer their pension assets from a legitimate pension fund to another fund set up (unknown to the targets) by criminal associates. The receiving fund, with professional help, is pulled together with the minimum necessary administrative requirements to obtain HMRC approval status as a pension fund. Onerous tax consequences attach in the UK to pension holders cashing in pension assets before the age of 55. The technical aspects of the initial fraud relate to failure to advise pension holders of the tax consequences of such cash withdrawal. The attraction of a quick cash pay-out—achieved through the provisions of 'loans' from a supposedly separate investment company—is in many cases sufficient to persuade the pension holder to provide the necessary instruction to the existing pension fund to transfer funds to the new 'pension fund', without undertaking any diligence as to how this might adversely affect their tax position.

The selling team claim to the pension holders that they deal at arm's-length from the new pension fund. On this basis they obtain from them, in respect of each transfer, a sign-on fee, as well as a percentage of the amount transferred from the pension fund. The pension holders are assured that their money (i.e. the money left in the pension fund after their cash withdrawal) will be safely invested to provide suitable pension benefits in the future when needed. What actually happens is that these funds become a source of working liquidity for various schemes involving the deployment of criminal money pooled from this and other criminal sources. The main element of the fraud, therefore, relates to the treatment of the monies retained after the cash pay-outs are provided to the pension holders. The process involved is illustrated in Figure 1.

The process commences with the activities of the sales people who earn the immediate signing on fee from the clients, as well as a cut of pension funds transferred to the bogus pension fund. The company represented by these sales personnel (i.e. the victim-facing 'marketing company' box in Figure 1) is separate from the companies involved in setting up the bogus pension funds (i.e. the pension holder box), which are the initial recipients of the monies transferred from the original pension funds. The funds are then transferred on, after various deductions and personal expenditures, to an 'investment' company under different formal ownership (i.e. the investment company box), which uses these funds to fund the necessary cash pay-outs to pension holders (usually around 40% of the pension assets transferred). The cash withdrawal element to the pension holder is provided as a 'loan' from a separate company to which the funds have been transferred. The balance

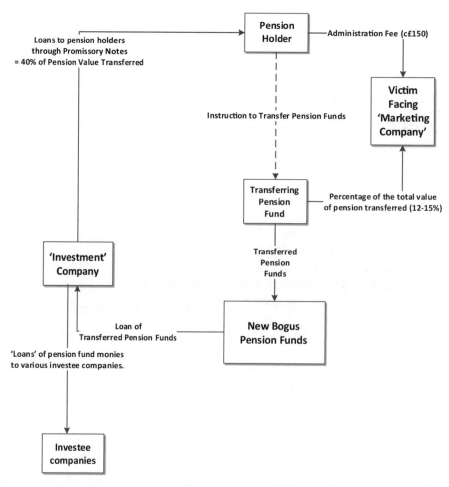

Figure 1. Pension holder fraud.

remaining is not applied in ways consistent with the objectives of pension assets: it is used to provide working capital for various false investment schemes through investee companies involved in money laundering schemes. The true owners of these companies are either criminals or associates of criminals, although these identities are hidden through the use 'clean skin' directors and shareholders.

The key individual overseeing this composite process is the controller of the investment company (i.e. the investment company box in Figure 1) who is likely to be a qualified professional, such as a lawyer or chartered accountant, operating a fully regulated practice side-by-side with high-level professional service provision to major SOC players. The enabling services provided include the design and administration of mechanisms to account for and track the investment monies and also to deal with any pension holder enquiries. Meanwhile the funds being enquired about are transferred to pools of criminal funds, otherwise funded through a number of other criminal sources, including drug trafficking. These pooled funds are often located in offshore financial centres such as Dubai.

The funds obtained from the pension fund source are treated as just another source of criminal revenue to be managed in in accordance of the objectives of these criminal clients under the veneer of a bogus investment narrative. The pooled funds are available for later repatriation to the UK under the guise of legitimate investment funds—usually into various schemes where the beneficial owners are nominees acting on behalf of criminals.

The design of this kind of overall scheme, in particular the modular nature of the criminal processes involved in its execution, presents considerable logistical challenges for prosecutors. The requirements for the offence under Scottish law may be met by the activities of the sales group in terms of their remuneration, but the illicit use of use of the transferred pension funds more readily fall into the requirements for an embezzlement charge. The issue, then, is who to prosecute and whether it is feasible to prosecute the different groups together—proving collusion is usually not straightforward and neither is the 'whole scheme' knowledge necessary for conspiracy charges. In addition to the challenges involved in presenting such a case to a non-specialist jury, the court disclosure requirements in such cases are very onerous and can present significant logistical challenges. Regulatory or criminal action against licensed professionals does happen sometimes, but does not alter the challenges above.

Carousel tax fraud

The second case study shows how a mechanism set up to achieve criminal fraud can be used to launder the profits arising from other crimes including drug and human trafficking. The scheme described here is a product of explicit collaboration between different SOCGs, exchanging access to their own separate capabilities to achieve mutually beneficial results.

The crime process is outlined in Figure 2. It relates to the money flows relevant to the carousel tax fraud known as 'MTIC' (missing trader intra community) fraud. This involves setting up a series of linked but separate companies to execute repeated sales and purchases of a staple commodity (for example mobile phones—although some of the transports organized across continents to provide the cover story will carry nothing at all). Transactions between EU member

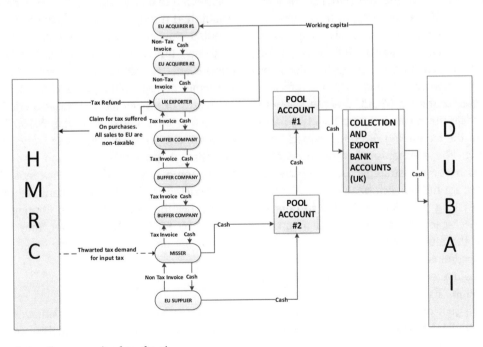

Figure 2. Laundering the proceeds of tax fraud.

countries do not attract VAT, whereas transactions between companies within the UK do. This loophole has now been plugged by HMRC, but variations on it can still emerge where there is disconnects can be exploited between collection and claim of input taxes.

The criminal scheme essentially involves a VAT reclaim being submitted by the last company in a chain of UK companies, all engaged in rapid-fire sales and purchases (i.e. all the various sales and purchases in the chain will happen on the same day, often simultaneously). This last company sells product to an 'EU acquirer' company and charges no output VAT, thus creating the conditions for a reclaim to be made on the input tax suffered—essentially an accumulation of all the input tax suffered on each link of the chain. HMRC then seeks to claim the relevant input tax from the first company in that chain, i.e. the company which has initially bought the product from an EU supplier on a no input tax basis, and then charged output VAT on sales to the next UK link in the chain. This is the 'misser'—the company that goes 'missing'. HMRC have made the pay-out at one end of the chain, but failed to collect the tax due to it at the other.

This type of fraud has generated huge amounts of criminal profits for SOC in the UK (and in some other European countries). The criminal monies obtained were collected in pool accounts of companies with UK domiciles but which were owned by associated companies, mostly in Dubai. Various schemes were initiated to provide trade cover for the relevant money transfers enabling the creation of pools of investment money in Dubai banks. As with the first case study, the criminal funds obtained could then be repatriated to the UK under the guise of investments in property or corporate assets via apparently legitimate overseas investment funds.

One such scheme involved the purchase of land with planning for industrial use, with a view to realizing a capital gain when the planning status improved to commercial status. This was to be achieved by the exploitation of corrupt relationships between local SOCG players and planning officials. The *quid pro quo* for the local SOCG was the ability to use the deal chain mechanisms set up for MTIC fraud as channels for the laundering of profits earned from drug trafficking. The mechanism set up to enable fraud had thus become a strategic asset, capable of being 'hired out' for further illicit benefit.

Where painstaking investigation is able to unravel the detailed mechanics of such schemes, it might be supposed that the requirement in money laundering cases to prove criminality would be readily achieved. The criminal nature of the mechanism is essentially exposed through its purpose—relevant here in establishing the guilt of the local SOCG handling and investing the criminal money once repatriated. Here again, though, difficulties can arise where the constituent parts of such a scheme relate to different companies, different owners and different SOCGs. Use of criminal conspiracy type charges can be challenged on the basis of the requirement that all accused have full knowledge of the entire criminal scheme.

Money laundering charge options, until relatively recently, have also been prone to fail because of the UK courts restricting application of the doctrine of 'irresistible inference', whereby proof of criminality of the funds can be inferred from the way in which they were handled (Murray, 2016). Until the 2017 Otegbola case (Otegbola v R. [2017] EWCA Crim 1147), the courts appeared to take a narrow view that the funds, or property, deemed to be criminal had to be proven to be such *before* the action was applied to it that qualified as a money laundering offence. It was not clear, therefore, whether it was possible to infer this retrospectively, where the available evidence was restricted to how the money or property was handled during the course of the action that qualified it as a money laundering offence. This was a particular issue where money was routed through Dubai and obtaining evidence from that jurisdiction proved very slow to obtain—a situation that has improved in recent years and which impetus may well be further boosted by the preparations for the FATF Mutual Evaluation Review 2019–2020. In most money laundering cases of any sophistication there are likely to be engineered breaks in the audit trail—whether this involves Dubai or even mechanisms using UK corporates as discussed below. Relying on cases where the route to the predicate offence is obvious is essentially condemning the POCA money laundering offences to be blank-firing weapons, certainly against the most serious offenders.

This is why the Otegbola case is of such significance. It appeared to finally establish that criminality could be established through the way in which the money was handled, thus encouraging the belief that, in terms of case law, the matter had at last reached a stable conclusion. However, there are still influential academic commentators who continue to question the status of money laundering as a criminal offence at all (see, for example, Alldridge, 2016). Prosecutorial commitment to such cases can vary; the relevant expertise to prosecute them can also be in short supply some 17 years after the Proceeds of Crime Act was enacted in the UK. The recent rather favourable report on the UK's AML (anti money laundering) regime by FATF (2018), however, may indicate that matters are beginning to improve.

Investment fraud

The third case study relates to situations where the pooling of criminal funds enables entry to the mainstream investment stage. In this example, a specialized 'hedge fund' is set up to provide short-term bridging loans offering investors premium returns on a fully asset-backed basis. The fund is initially funded through legitimate and reputable sources but is subject to a criminal 'cuckoo in the nest' influence at board level which turns it into a major laundering asset for criminals.

The criminal nature of a substantial portion of the investment funds held is indicated by the profiles of the borrowers it 'lends' its funds to, and also the uncommercial terms upon which the loans are provided. Finally, when market conditions move against it (as Warren Buffet might put it: 'when the tide goes out', see Buffett, 2001) the money that remains available for distribution to investors finds its way into the hands of criminal investors at the expense of legitimate investors, as shown in Figure 3.

The endgame for the genuine investors arrives when the fund is placed into administration, probably after being advised of a self-imposed redemption ban owing to 'adverse market conditions'. It will then transpire that all the available funds for redemption have been dissipated through a series of fraudulent loan deals. The available funds will have been invested in companies whose balances sheet values are propped up by grossly overvalued property assets. After transfer to these companies, the funds are then siphoned off through nominee accounts to offshore bank accounts.

Again, in terms of bringing such unravelled schemes to justice, there are difficulties to surmount, even with all confirmatory evidence assembled. In Scotland, for example, the requirement under Scots Law to obtain corroboration in respect of every material piece of evidence can become a source of technical challenge. If the only admissible corroboration available in respect of the necessary documentary evidence to establish the fraud is from the professional enabler who received the emailed instructions and executed them, the prosecutor has to consider whether they can rely on evidence from such a tainted source. This is especially the case where this is the crucial weight-bearing evidence carrying the main burden of proof for the prosecution case.

OCG themes and practice

Fraud begets money laundering

The case studies illustrate how fraud, as practised by SOCGs, is inextricably wrapped up in money laundering—even when it is not an intrinsic part of the frauds themselves. The liquidity provided by access to criminal funds, and the mechanisms established to launder them, provide scope to take advantage of revenue earning opportunities from whatever fraud opportunities present themselves. This can be in the form of investor frauds requiring some direct interface with the victim, or internet based frauds which can be executed anonymously, or a combination. The key difference between these finance-based revenue streams and the more traditional sources of large scale criminal revenue earning, such as drug trafficking, is that, in the former, the money is already in a banking system and does not have to be physically inserted risking the

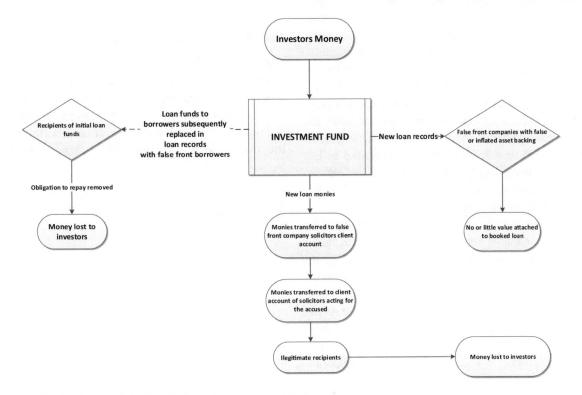

Figure 3. Distribution of criminal funds through investment vehicles.

arousal of suspicion. Both in terms of making the crime pay and keeping the funds away from exposure and possible confiscation, there are obvious laundering advantages to be had if these two disparate types of source can be intermingled, and there is access to the kind of professional skill sets that are able to do this successfully.

The higher echelons of the SOCG sector have access to a range of financial services dedicated to their needs: a pooled network of professional-level finance and business skill capability honed over the past 17 years or so in the UK by the constraints imposed by the Proceeds of Crime Act 2002 and its associated money laundering regulations. Purely as a function of the existence of such capability, participation by SOC in major economic crime is therefore likely to be an increasingly prominent trend. The question arises whether the institutional response will be sufficient to offer adequate protection against the public interest exposures this implies. Continued reliance on compliance and systems based prevention, allied to opportunistic conviction when the circumstances, or luck, allows, may not be enough. So what needs to change?

Wising up to the wise guys

The answer to this question is tied to how serious the consequences are perceived to be if such an approach is *not* adopted; whether the accumulation and deployment of increasing volumes of criminally derived money in our legitimate markets constitutes something to get worried about; and whether some or all economic crime has, or can attain, the necessary priority status to encourage the development of more strategic responses to combat it. The FATF inspection on the UK's AML regime concluded that it was as effective as could be found pretty much anywhere (FATF 2018). Critics of the UK AML effort argue that this, if true, does not say very much. The volume of criminal cash that continues to be laundered through the British economy indicates that any claim to success in this field is bound to be partial; something clearly not unconnected to London being a top global financial centre where bad money can be hidden among good.

The modes of laundering experienced in investigated criminal cases in Scotland the UK have become more sophisticated, making them more difficult to differentiate as suspicious, never mind criminal. Platt (2014) points out that this has implications for how money laundering is perceived as well as taught; the bulk of criminal money from financial crime is laundered in a way which cannot be properly described in accordance with the traditional 'placement—layering—integration' model. The proceeds of fraud crimes in particular are sourced

from within the financial system, meaning there is no need for a 'placement' phase, which has implications for how money laundering patterns associated with fraud can be recognized and understood.

Platt suggests an alternative money laundering descriptive model of 'enable–distance–disguise', which conveys two features of particular importance in understanding the nature of modern money laundering. The first is that money laundering comprises a mechanism which has to accommodate necessary connections between the three reference points of crime, perpetrator and crime proceeds, and yet introduce breaks in the lines that connect each of them. The second is that to achieve this objective the observable transactional patterns that attach to such laundering more often present as circular rather than linear. The money is hurtled round a carousel of different nominal owners in a manner echoed by the MTIC fraud process as previously described and illustrated in Figure 4.

From this perspective, the importance of understanding context in respect of money laundering schemes, rather than merely source, is emphasised in terms of detecting the criminal nature of the activity. This is of crucial importance in terms of maximizing the effectiveness of the two principal cornerstones of the current AML regime: the identifying and reporting of suspicious transactions; and obtaining prosecutions and convictions. But it also suggests we need an approach to tackling this problem, especially as it relates to the activities of SOC, in a manner that is explicitly strategic rather than reactive and tactical.

Nobody said it would be easy

The reported effectiveness of the UK AML regime as reported by FATF represents a return on the huge amount of capital that has been invested in it by financial institutions and government in constructing the reporting regime. The compliance departments of the major banks are now able to track predictive

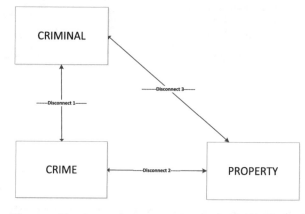

Figure 4. The three reference points of money laundering.

criminal transaction patterns not visible to the human eye, or even comprehension. Collectively they represent a cutting age technical capability on the side of crime prevention that is increasingly relied upon by law enforcement. From the perspective of law enforcement, the standard and quality of suspicious activity reports has continuously improved, with purely defensive reporting now less of an issue than previously. Accordingly, despite the relative lack of resources devoted to them in some enforcement bodies, the intelligence conveyed by these SARs collectively provides a precious resource of intelligence for law enforcement, often overlooked by critics of their effectiveness.

When it comes to turning of this intelligence into money laundering prosecutions, however, the UK achievement record is less impressive. The pace of progress has been slow, with the courts, academia, and other priorities in law enforcement all contributing, either knowingly or unknowingly, to a collective impression of underperformance. The ambivalence in influential legal quarters about the effectiveness, even worth, of the relevant legislation (Alldridge, 2016), and the connected lack of enthusiasm on the part of some practitioners in terms of delivering on it (*The Times*, 2019; ONS, 2019), bear some responsibility for this, but a continuous and persistent stream of criticism from academia that the AML regime serves limited worthwhile social function relative to its cost (Van Duyne, Harvey, & Gelemerova, 2019 ch.9) does so too. In such an environment, the attractiveness of money laundering as an area of investigation for law enforcement, especially on very restricted fiscal budgets, is not obvious.

In terms of most of the technical functions and applications necessary to perpetrate serious economic crime, there is no distinction to be drawn between those involved in money laundering as opposed all the other serious economic crimes perpetrated by SOC such as fraud. This is therefore not just a problem with money laundering: it extends to all other serious economic crime offences too, including fraud. A criminal trial in Scotland involving a multiple mortgage fraudster finally concluded in 2017 having lasted over two years and reached the dubious accolade of becoming the longest criminal trial in Scottish legal history. The convictions obtained were at a cost in terms of money effort and resource that the 'victory' to prosecutors felt distinctively Pyrrhic. It then served as something of a cautionary tale whenever other serious economic crime cases were considered for prosecution. The heavy burden of disclosure that usually attaches to such cases also does not help in promoting their appeal to prosecutors.

A threat that hides in plain sight

The threat presented is not going to go away, however. There are good grounds for considering that public exposure to serious economic crime will keep on increasing. The exposure of virtually everyone to the internet—which provides such a multi-faceted, versatile and often highly lucrative platform for criminal activity—has done much to raise awareness of vulnerability to acquisitive crime. What it has also done is increase the scope for SOC to pool skill resources in such a way as to transform the rogue characteristics of criminal profits into powerful earning streams.

It is access to these revenue streams that enables influence to be exerted across a whole range of legitimate markets. They enable corrupt access to the professional services necessary for participation in high-level economic crime—indeed, it is access to such services that provides an obvious means of differentiating major SOC players from less major players. The correlation between access to high powered money management and seniority in SOC hierarchy becomes substantively a study of the exercise of economic power.

The founding influences for this development are Russian. Economic crime is the dominant business of Russian SOC, with the principal revenue streams being various forms of fraud, sophisticated or otherwise. Galeotti's (2018) history of Russian organized crime *The Vory* chronicles how Russian SOC morphed into big business in the wake of the collapse of communism and thus provided an influential model for international SOC to follow. According to Galeotti, the principal implication for power relationships within Russian SOC is that there are essentially two underworlds at play: an upper level where appearances are almost indistinguishable in appearance from legitimate players; and a lower where people look and more obviously act like criminals. These are characteristics which are becoming increasingly apparent in the UK too. There is a fertile research area, yet to be fully cultivated, which relates to how the two emerging levels of SOC relate to each other in the UK. Experience of relevant intelligence disseminations confirms that access to financial and professional services is a key differentiating characteristic.

Corporate finance criminal-style

The 'Managing Criminal Revenues Business Process' below in Figure 5 is illustrative but it provides a broad visual template for the business process of managing criminal revenues as practised by the dominant 'first-tier' SOC players. The essential game plan is to develop a business profile that appears legitimate and is resilient to challenge or investigation. The corresponding law enforcement

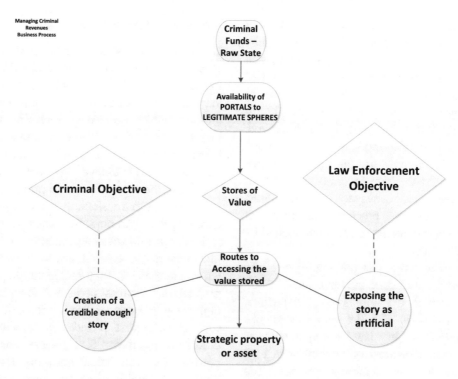

Figure 5. Managing criminal revenues.

objective is to expose the criminal support mechanisms that sustain this façade, and to disable the unfair competitive advantage that arises from the deployment of criminal revenues in legitimate markets.

The mechanisms deployed involve structures which are designed to both hide the ultimate funding source and separate the strategic asset from the trading company that earns the profits from its use. For example the structure illustrated in Figure 6 involves the use of parallel companies with associated, but distinct, ownerships to respectively acquire and run the business involved with the strategic asset. The typical scenario is where the legitimate company originally holding the asset acquired has run into cash difficulties or requires further funding to stabilize an overleveraged balance sheet. The scheme arrangement shown allows funds to be funnelled to the acquiring company from the side company, which in turn is funded by third party loans of undisclosed provenance.

There are certain signs to look out for which indicate SOC influence. An exceptionally generous dividend policy for example; or recapitalizations using opaque sources. Other indicators relate to how tangible influence is exerted on the markets concerned. Public sector contracts can end up being awarded to SOC sponsored businesses because the only bidders on the tendering short list come from that cohort. Such influence is also indicated by the acquisition of companies owning strategic public assets in an area of public concern—such as, for example, waste recycling assets—by companies and players new to the industry with access to considerable, if unfathomable, sources of funding. If and when such assets cease to function, or do not function in the way they were designed to

function, and environmental costs start to accrue in a visible way that government appears powerless to do anything about, there may at that stage be some form of public enquiry process to understand how this could all have happened. Public welfare in the meantime continues to suffer until a solution emerges to fix the problem.

As already indicated, the main reason why such things can happen is that SOC sponsored companies operating in legitimate commercial and public markets are able to exploit a powerful competitive advantage—the ability to tap into illegitimate revenue streams as a source of working capital. That such capability exists within SOC carries consequences for society as a whole. These consequences are underappreciated, however—in part because they tend to be hidden, or at least are not visible until it is perceived too late to do anything about them that wouldn't be prohibitively disruptive.

Fighting back effectively needs collective will

Effective counter-strategies against this trend have to start with a raising of public awareness that this is actually happening. This is an effort that requires sustained institutional effort and commitment, involving suitable resource deployed to obtain the necessary intelligence, and then the will to use it to practical advantage. The collective energies and skills of UK law enforcement may possess these, but it is not always clear that they are co-ordinated in such a fashion that the true significance of SOC activity in strategically important commercial and public markets is properly appreciated.

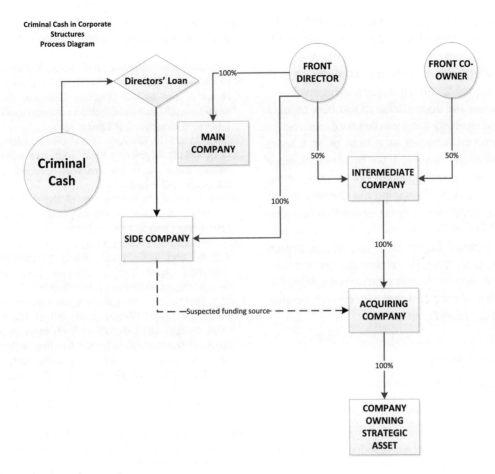

Figure 6. Concealment and separation: structures.

The formulation of suitable responses requires collective effort involving all facets of the domestic regulator culture affected: prosecutors, tax authorities, trading bodies, market regulators. The professions who educate and regulate the necessary enablers are also key players. Overall strategic aims are a useful starting point for establishing intent, but the practical read-through is to devise meaningful strategies for breaking up business models which involve SOC sponsored companies in public and commercial markets; in crude terms to muck up SOC engines by challenging and then exposing the falsehood of the narratives that underpin pretence to legitimacy. If we therefore need to tackle fraud in a strategic way, rather than a tactical, reactive way, what does this involve?

Understanding what is going on requires an understanding of the distinctive capabilities of SOCG criminal processes and the strategic assets used for their deployment. Law enforcement needs to work with stakeholder partners on a sector by sector basis to develop understanding and appreciation of what the strategic risks actually are. Some of the required disciplines, such as the ability to plot and understand criminal business systems, have hitherto not been associated with the standard law enforcement skill set. Modern policing, however, is obliged to transform itself to deal with rapidly changing criminal landscapes requiring the development of new skills

to deal with the challenges of cybercrime, sex crime and social media based hate crime. There seems no reason why the business analysis skills necessary to develop adequate profiles of criminal business processes, and the money laundering processes that form part of them, should not be a 'must have' feature of modern law enforcement.

Until the tackling of economic crime is accepted as an issue of national priority, the chances of sufficient will and resolve being applied to prevent these kinds of consequences will remain open to question. This is a challenge that has to involve the forging of collaborative game plans across agencies where actions can be agreed on the basis of a strategic understanding of the business models and a full appreciation of their harm potential. The first priority is to raise awareness—to shine a light on the strategic significance of SOC involvement in economic crime. The second is to formulate effective and co-ordinated counter-measures.

Conclusions

The accumulation of criminal funds under the guise of legitimate funds is not something to be tolerated and accepted as a necessary evil of the modern world. The competitiveness of public markets, not to mention their fairness, can only be defended properly against the corrosive and corruptive effects of SOC if the problem is acknowledged and appreciated, preferably before its worst effects come to be felt. A serious reboot of societal and professional attitudes to SOC and serious economic crime is required. This involves a raised awareness and appreciation of just how capable SOC is of undercutting the foundation of our society and its institutions, whether at a local or at a more national level. It also requires a willingness to engage on the basis that the main game is not primarily about locking people up, but in stopping the effectiveness of SOC business models that rely on interaction between criminal and legitimate spheres. For that to happen requires institutional buy-in to a strategic approach where all the major law enforcement players and their partners face up to a common responsibility to recognize this challenge and deal with it in a collective, effective and coherent manner.

Disclosure statement

No potential conflict of interest was reported by the author(s).

References

Alldridge, P. (2016). *What went wrong with money laundering law?* Palgrave Macmillan.

Buffett, W. (2001). Berkshire hathaway inc., annual report 2001, chairman's letter. In *After all, you only find out who is naked when the tide goes out*. Retrieved from http://www.berkshirehathaway.com/letters/2000pdf.pdf

Financial Action Task Force (FATF). (2018). *Mutual evaluation report of the United Kingdom*. Retrieved from https://www.fatf-gafi.org/media/fatf/documents/reports/mer4/MER-United-Kingdom-2018.pdf

Galeotti, M. (2018). *The vory*. Yale University Press.

Levi, M. (2013). *Regulating fraud (routledge revivals): White-collar crime and the criminal process*. Routledge. (Originally published 1987).

Murray, K. (2016). In the shadow of the dark twin: Proving criminality in money laundering cases. *Journal of Money Laundering Control, 19*(4), 447–458.

Office of National Statistics (ONS). (2019). *The crime survey of England and wales*, (year ending 31 December 2018). Published April 2019. Retrieved from http://www.crimesurvey.co.uk/en/SurveyResults.html

Platt, S. (2014). *Criminal capital*. Palgrave Macmillan.

The Times. (2019). *Defeatist police fail to investigate fraud cases*. 2 April 2019, Retrieved from https://www.google.co.uk/url?sa=t&rct=j&q=&esrc=s&source=web&cd=1&cad=rja&uact=8&ved=2ahUKEwikr-qzg77iAhWDL1AKHYDHBDAQFjAAegQIBBAB&url=https%3A%2F%2Fwww.thetimes.co.uk%2Farticle%2Fdefeatist-police-fail-to-investigate-fraud-cases-520d9k6b7&usg=AOvVaw0ZBRSqt-M_pi-z1CwfwMmh

Van Duyne, P., Harvey, J., & Gelemerova, L. (2019). *The critical handbook of money laundering: Policy, analysis and myths*. Palgrave Macmillan.

For fraud, look under 'serious and organized crime'

Simon Avery

ABSTRACT

The UK government's response to fraud cannot be disentangled from its broader 'serious and organized crime' (SOC) strategy. In order to explore whether fraud should—in public policy, criminal justice and law enforcement terms—be seen primarily as an SOC issue, there is a need to consider questions about whether or not 'SOC' is a sensible object of policy-making in the first place. Several arguments in favour of an SOC policy are identified in the paper. However, the notion of an overarching SOC policy is problematic for three reasons. First, SOC is a fundamental misrepresentation of reality, which does not correspond to a real social problem. Second, SOC policy can limit the development of more problem-specific crime strategies, Third, the 'SOC' label can negatively transform how social problems are perceived over the long term. If fraud is to be better understood and dealt with, it may therefore be necessary to extract it from its current inclusion within wider SOC strategy.

IMPACT

This paper argues that fraud has been subsumed by 'serious and organized crime' policy. It explores both the benefits and problems of this state of affairs and questions the validity of 'serious and organized crime' as an object of policy-making. It is hoped the paper will encourage policy-makers and practitioners to think carefully about how fraud is conceptualized as a problem.

Introduction

The UK government's response to fraud cannot be disentangled from broader 'serious and organized crime' (SOC) strategy. Fraud is now labelled as a form of SOC; it is included with the likes of drug dealing, modern slavery and human trafficking as part of a broader threat to national security (HM Government, 2018). The National Crime Agency (NCA) has classified fraud as a significant threat in its SOC assessments (NCA, 2018), arguing, for instance, that 'a significant proportion' of fraud is committed by 'organized crime groups' (*ibid.*, p. 41). Any attempt to analyse, evaluate or improve the UK response to fraud must begin by understanding and scrutinizing the SOC strategy within which it now sits. Yet such scrutiny needs to move beyond the usual quibbling over how much SOC costs the UK, or whether local police are doing enough against SOC, or whether the government's strategy is being implemented effectively. Such questions reinforce the notion that SOC is a naturally-occurring phenomenon, rather than a fallible public policy construct. The more important questions to ask are: should fraud be subsumed within SOC strategy and, more fundamentally, is SOC a sensible object of strategy-making at all? Answering these questions is an essential first step if new approaches to the prevention and investigation of fraud are to be developed. In following this line of questioning, this paper begins by describing the emergence of SOC as a public policy concern and explains the current UK strategy, before exploring the advantages and pitfalls of adopting SOC as an object of policy.

The UK government's SOC policy

SOC has been a major policy concern in the UK for some time. If official pronouncements are to be believed, it is an ever-increasing threat, requiring an ever-stronger response. In 2013, the UK government labelled SOC as 'a threat to our national security [that] costs the UK more than £24 billion a year' (Home Office, 2013, p. 5). The NCA recently said; 'the threat from SOC is increasing in both volume and complexity' (2018, p. 8), while the official SOC strategy 2018 claimed that 'serious and organized crime is the most deadly national security threat faced by the UK' (p. 3). It is a policy area with a substantial budget and thousands of public servants dispersed across the police, NCA, Serious Fraud Office, Home Office and others, all working to further SOC strategy.

SOC policy has developed and shifted over a number of decades in the UK. Hobbs and Woodiwiss (2009) have provided a history of these developments in both British and American contexts. Their work suggests that UK law enforcement agencies were initially preoccupied with 'super-criminal organizations' (*ibid.*, p. 121), such as the Russian mafia; threats requiring both intelligence support from UK spy agencies (Levi, 1998) and more traditional police crackdowns. This gave way to a looser and more general conceptualization of SOC by the mid 1990s; one that blended criminal activities and criminal organizations. For instance, a Home Affairs Committee investigation into SOC in 1994–1995 argued that the 'Italian mafia' and 'former criminal gangs in Britain such as the Krays … are examples of organized crime, but to confine concern to such relatively tightly organized groups would be to miss most of today's criminal activity' (Home Affairs Committee, 1995, p. x). The committee went on to establish a number of 'special features' of organized crime; arguing that it is a 'group activity', 'undertaken for profit', 'long term' and entails 'internal discipline amongst the group' (*ibid.*, p. x). Yet the committee also suggested there was 'little purpose in worrying about a precise definition' (*ibid.*, p. x). Their concerns were mostly centred around the illegal drug trade, although 'fraud, benefits fraud, credit card crime and other financial crime' were mentioned in passing (*ibid.*, p. xvi). The policy suggestions developed from this investigation emphasised the need to expand the 'fight' beyond just law enforcement and to use intelligence more effectively (*ibid.*, pp. xx-xxii).

By the mid 2000s, SOC policy had started to become fused with wider national security concerns. In 2004, the UK government produced a new strategy—*One Step Ahead: A 21ˢᵗ Century Strategy to Defeat Organized Crime*—in which organized criminals were said to 'share many characteristics with terrorists' (p. 1). This, it was argued, meant that 'a successful approach to organized crime is therefore inseparable from our wider effort against threats to national security' (*ibid.*, p. 1). Over time, the affinity with national security and counter-terrorism grew ever stronger. In 2008, SOC was included in the UK's National Security Strategy alongside terrorism and nuclear attack (Cabinet Office, 2008). In 2013, the government adopted a counter-terrorist strategy known as 'CONTEST' for use against SOC (Home Office, 2013; Sergi, 2015). The strategy was based on four strands:

- *Pursue* (prosecute and disrupt people engaged in SOC).
- *Prevent* (prevent people from engaging in SOC).
- *Protect* (increase protection against SOC).
- *Prepare* (reduce the impact of this criminality when it takes place) (Home Office, 2013, p. 9).

Local police were subsequently instructed to start producing 'serious organized crime local profiles' (Home Office, 2014); a new kind of assessment based on pre-existing counter-terrorism local profiles (*ibid.*).

The most up-to-date manifestation of SOC policy can be found in the UK government's 2018 strategy. Here, SOC is defined as:

> *Individuals planning, co-ordinating and committing serious offences, whether individually, in groups and/or as part of transnational networks. The main categories of serious offences covered by the term are: child sexual exploitation and abuse; illegal drugs; illegal firearms; fraud; money laundering and other economic crime; bribery and corruption; organized immigration crime; modern slavery and human trafficking; and cyber crime* (HM Government, 2018, p. 11).

The strategy for dealing with this variegated range of individuals and activities is comprised of four objectives: 'relentless disruption and targeted action against the highest harm serious and organized criminals and networks'; 'building the highest levels of defence and resilience in vulnerable people, communities, businesses and systems'; 'stopping the problem at source', 'identifying and supporting those at risk of engaging in criminality'; and 'establishing a single, whole-system approach' (HM Government, 2018, pp. 6–7). This new strategy places less explicit emphasis on CONTEST, although the first three objectives have strong parallels with 'Pursue', 'Protect' and 'Prevent'. The strategy seeks to enrol a huge array of different agencies and actors into its programme of governance, including local police, Regional Organized Crime Units (ROCUs), the Foreign Office, intelligence agencies and the private sector.

Today, the SOC problem is no longer considered to be one of large, hierarchical mafias from outside the UK; the primary focus is now on types of criminal activity, such as drug dealing, child exploitation and cyber crime, although the notion of the 'organized crime group' is still prevalent. This is not a narrow-minded, police-dominated strategy, but one that seeks to prevent crime and protect victims, rather than just arrest 'Mr Bigs'. In 2013, there seemed a real risk that SOC policy would be completely subsumed by that of counter-terrorism, although the 2018 strategy has pulled back somewhat from this. Nevertheless, SOC has now become well-established as an issue of national security (Sergi, 2015).

Absorbing fraud

The UK approach to fraud has also undergone several changes in recent decades. The cost of fraud and its use by a range of perpetrators—from corporate entities to terrorist groups—has been well-documented for some time. The increasing risks and costs of fraud have been deemed to require a national policy response at law enforcement and government levels (see Doig, Johnson, & Levi, 2001;

Home Office, 2004). Concerns have continued over the costs of fraud, the continuing decline in police resources, perceptions that fraud was used to fund other crimes, such as terrorism and organized crime, and that new opportunities for fraud are increasingly being opened up by new technology; for example the growth in identity and internet fraud (see National Criminal Intelligence Service, 2003; Fraud Review, 2006). In October 2005, the attorney-general proposed a national policy review whose final report recognized a number of these concerns, recommending a primarily, but not exclusively, criminal justice approach and making a range of thematic and institutional proposals. The recommendations were to be shaped by a national strategy and led by the then National Fraud Strategic Authority (NFSA) which, in 2008, produced a national fraud strategy. This was followed by an annual measurement of the cost of fraud, regular updates on progress, lessons from pilot projects and a complementary strategy for local government.

In 2011, the National Fraud Authority (NFA) published an over-arching national 'strategic plan'—*Fighting Fraud Together*—to revise the existing strategy. This was based on a review of current issues and post-Fraud Review responses, and an analysis of factors inhibiting the implementation of the previous strategy. In particular, it suggested that the NCA's Economic Crime Command (EEC) would provide a stronger institutional focus, including addressing constraints on police resources by developing 'innovative, partnership solutions working across police forces, the NCA and its EEC, other law enforcement organizations and the public, private and voluntary sectors' (NFA, 2011, p. 20). Within two years, the government unilaterally announced the closure of the NFA and the distribution of many, but not all, of its roles and responsibilities. In doing so, the government claimed that the NFA had been successful in raising awareness of fraud and improving the co-ordination of those who fought it, but argued there should be a single national focus on cutting economic crime. That focus was to be the NCA's EEC and its primary focus on SOC fraud.

On the one hand, this fragmented a uniform or national approach to fraud. One of the consequences of the 2006 fraud review was to designate a lead police force for fraud—the City of London Police took on national training and advice roles—but the absence of resources and means to direct law enforcement approaches to fraud meant that fraud continued to be a low local policing priority. In 2015, the National Police Co-ordinator for Economic Crime housed by the City of London Police issued a draft strategy on the policing of fraud, supplemented by a draft strategy on prevention. In 2019 the Police

Inspectorate (Her Majesty's Inspectorate of Constabulary and Fire & Rescue Services [HMICFRS]) reported that, with the closure of the NFA and distribution of roles and responsibilities, 'the notion of a single national fraud strategy such as Fighting Fraud Together was largely forgotten … we did not find any evidence of general awareness of the document, or that it had ever been formally adopted by police forces' (HMICFRS, 2019, pp. 30–31).

On the other hand, fraud had now been recognized as a priority in the 2013 SOC strategy, which stated that: 'the aim of this strategy is to substantially reduce the level of organized crime in this country and the level of serious crime that requires a national response (notably fraud and child sexual exploitation)' (HM Government, 2013, p. 25). However, in 2018, the Police Foundation, a police-focused think-tank, reported on the impact of competing policy agendas:

> The last national strategy for tackling fraud was published in 2011 by an agency that no longer exists … and we found few practitioners at any level made reference to it. Instead, strategic direction is derived to some extent from the Modern Crime Prevention Strategy … but more prominently from broader strategies to tackle serious and organized crime … where other problems with a higher profile and stronger intelligence base (for example, drug offences) gain greater priority and attract more resources … More recently there has been a greater national strategic focus on cybercrime. There is now a national agency, the National Cyber Security Centre, which helps to co-ordinate efforts to improve cyber security (Skidmore et al., 2018, p. 67).

This gradual absorption of fraud into SOC strategy presents several issues. As suggested by Skidmore et al. (2018), there was concern that fraud may not get enough attention and resources if it has to compete with the likes of drug trafficking and child exploitation within the SOC policy space. There is also the question of whether fraud has been properly included within the SOC strategic approach. Yet the more fundamental question is whether or not 'SOC' is a sensible object for strategic decision-making at all. It is the very idea that there should *be* an SOC strategy which requires scrutiny, and this takes precedent over arguments about whether fraud is best situated within it. This question is an essential starting-point for thinking about fraud and how it might be addressed more effectively.

The value of an SOC policy

What then, are the advantages of adopting SOC as an object of policy? What are the advantages of situating fraud within it? One major advantage it can be argued, is that SOC is a broad, inclusive and 'elastic' concept (Edwards & Gill, 2002, p. 204) capable of appreciating inter-relationships between different kinds of offending. This is suggested in the NCA's strategic assessment 2018:

> SOC threats are increasingly interlinked. There are significant overlaps between Modern Slavery & Human Trafficking (MSHT) and Organized Immigration Crime (OIC)...Upstream, offenders often move seamlessly between MSHT and OIC. There is also a strong connection between drugs supply and firearms, with firearms being used for protecting and enabling the wider criminal interests of OCGs (NCA, 2018, p. 8).

Undoubtedly, there are overlaps between many activities designated as SOC. Urban street gangs, for example, often have ties to the illegal drug trade; high-level fraud in certain countries can be linked to money laundering in the UK; online child exploitation can depend upon other forms of cybercrime. It can be argued that SOC is broad enough to include these inter-relationships; for instance it does not sever connections between different criminal phenomena; it does not cut-off the problem of violent street gangs from that of illegal drugs. It attempts to encapsulate a wider picture of serious and organized criminality, allowing broad-ranging strategy to be developed. Much the same point can be made about individual SOC offenders. Research has shown how they move between different areas of 'business' throughout their careers, smuggling drugs when conditions are right, engaging in mortgage fraud as a side-line, stealing goods from lorries if the opportunity arises—all the while running a legitimate business (Hobbs, 1998, 2013). If SOC policy were to be fragmented, then such offenders may slip through the gaps as they move from one criminal activity to another. Fraud, from this perspective, does not stand alone; it is part of a portfolio of illegal money-making ventures committed by career criminals.

Some may go further than this, arguing that fraud, drug dealing, human trafficking and other such activities all share an essential underlying characteristic and are actually just different manifestations of the same thing. It might be said, for example, that they all involve prolonged, complex interactions between offenders, or that they are all carried out by 'organized crime groups', or that they are all forms of illicit enterprise. The UK government's SOC strategy draws on this kind of argument but stops short of identifying some fundamental core feature of these activities, beyond the notion they all involve: 'individuals planning, co-ordinating and committing serious offences, whether individually, in groups and/or as part of transnational networks' (HM Government, 2018, p. 11).

From this perspective, fraud might be said to share some deep-seated common features with drug dealing, human trafficking, money laundering etc.

Such activities are imagined to be just sub-species of a broader SOC phylum; any differences between them are deemed superficial. The implication is that SOC is a valuable object of policy because it isolates some deeper, common 'core' to the problems of fraud, drug dealing, human trafficking etc. Without it, policy and strategy would treat these as separate problems, ignoring their congruities.

Allied to this, it can be argued that an over-arching SOC policy leads to a more 'joined-up' response. Given the supposed connections between different kinds of criminality, there is a need for diverse agencies to work together to combat such problems. Local authorities, police, the Serious Fraud Office, NCA, the Border Agency, banks, HM Revenue & Customs and others each have the potential to control forms of SOC. Those dealing with fraud can call upon these other organizations for help; they can create joint taskforces using the common language of SOC. Having an SOC policy helps to co-ordinate the efforts of these different agencies, allocating them specific roles and creating a policy framework for them to work together more effectively. This is deemed to be important given the fluid and flexible nature of many so-called 'SOC' offenders who, as described above, may have fingers in many different pies throughout their 'careers'. SOC policy is, in this sense, a helmsman helping others row in the right direction. Without it, there would be no co-ordinated response, or so the argument goes.

A similar argument is that the criminal activities labelled as SOC all demand the same response and should therefore fall under one overarching control strategy. So even if fraud *is* significantly different from drug dealing, modern slavery, and other SOC activities, it could be argued that they are all best dealt with through a strategy such as 'CONTEST', involving elements of Pursue, Prevent, Protect and Prepare. From this perspective, the strategy comes first and various crime problems are subsequently allocated to it if they are an appropriate 'fit'. Much the same argument was used to align SOC strategy with that of counter-terrorism; the CONTEST model was deemed to be working effectively in the latter domain and so it was transposed over to SOC (or SOC was transposed into CONTEST, depending on your perspective). This is made clear in the official SOC strategy 2013: 'our new strategy is built on the successful framework we use to counter terrorism' (p. 5); 'We want to see much more sharing of capabilities between the separate police networks which deal with organized crime and terrorism' (p. 10); 'Organized crime Prevent work should also be co-ordinated with work on preventing terrorism. It may be possible in some areas for the same local team to take responsibility for both issues. In many regions these programmes will be operating in the same geographical area: there is considerable overlap between the priority places for both these agendas' (p. 46). These kinds of argument put policy and strategy first and then seek to apply them to different social problems. SOC, in this sense, is a valuable object of policy-making because it demarcates those illegal activities and groups amenable to governance through CONTEST or similar strategies. It is a circular argument, but an argument, nonetheless.

SOC can also be said to have political traction beyond the sum of its parts. In other words, SOC can attract more political attention than fraud, drug trafficking or human trafficking could as a separate object of policy-making. By joining forces, these public policy concerns can exert a greater influence on politicians, the public and the media, possibly leading to more resources and more publicity (Edwards & Levi, 2008, p. 364; Levi, 1998). If a particular criminal activity becomes labelled as SOC, it somehow takes on a new status; its claims to be taken seriously are bolstered. This means that emerging crime problems ignored by politicians, media and the public can become more visible if portrayed as SOC. An SOC policy can, in this way, have an empowering effect on less well-known crime problems.

A further argument is that SOC should be preserved as an object of policy in the interests of continuity. Officials in the police and NCA are generally familiar with the term 'SOC'; it is a concept that has survived the last few decades and elbowed its way into media and public discourse. It can be claimed that a body of official knowledge on SOC has built up over the years, for example through 'Organized Crime Group Mapping'—a computerized system for counting and ranking so-called 'organized crime groups' (HMIC, 2015)—and through national strategic assessments. There is now a whole machinery of policing built around SOC—institutions, procedures, relationships, data flows, command and control mechanisms—and these are constantly being inspected and refined. If SOC were to be abandoned as an object of policy, or substantially changed, this continuity and progress would be lost. It would take years to embed a replacement concept in police and public discourse and the SOC machinery would be rudderless. This sort of argument might well acknowledge that SOC is not a perfect concept about which to make policy, but that the perils of abandoning it outweigh the problems of keeping it.

The problems of SOC as an object of policy

A number of objections can be raised against these arguments. The first is that SOC is so broad and inclusive that it ends up lumping together a range of very different kinds of crime problem. Activities such as fraud, drug dealing and online child exploitation, for example, are all very different from each other; they take place in distinct socio-economic contexts, involve different skills and expertise, and have different impacts. It seems strange to suggest, therefore, that they can all be subsumed under one SOC strategy. This is akin to having a single strategy to deal with speeding, burglary and corporate manslaughter. While some of these offences may have links to others, there is no guarantee those links are meaningful and it is ridiculous to suggest that all of those activities labelled as SOC comprise some kind of unified underground web.

Similarly, the idea that SOC isolates some 'core' common features of drug dealing, fraud, cybercrime, human trafficking and the like, is highly dubious. The SOC concept did not emerge from a careful, scientific study of these phenomena; it was cobbled together by police and policy-makers during the 1980s and early 1990s (Hobbs & Woodiwiss, 2009). Proponents of this argument suggest SOC activities are all illegal; all motivated by profit; and all require a degree of organization—and should therefore be grouped as one. While problems such as fraud, drug dealing and human trafficking may be superficially similar to each other in their illegality, profit-motive and degree of organization, each has different causal connections. Drug dealing is often driven by drug addiction and street-gang rivalry in deprived communities; high-level fraud is often connected to poor oversight in financial institutions and high-risk attitudes to money-making, while human trafficking can be generated by demand for cheap labour in massage parlours, nail salons and car-washes. These are the sorts of social, economic and cultural factors that actually drive crime problems (Edwards & Levi, 2008) and they are different for different 'SOC' activities. It makes far more sense, therefore, to build strategy and policy around specific crime problems and their underlying social, economic and cultural causes rather than to group very different things together based on arbitrary similarities (*ibid.*).

A second objection follows from this point. The UK SOC policy effectively imposes one homogenous strategy onto an eclectic jumble of criminal activities. Given the sheer diversity of those activities, the strategy may have variable effects; it may work against some kinds of offending, but not others. There can be no guarantee, for instance, that the best way to reduce fraud is also the best way to reduce human trafficking. There is even the risk that an over-bearing SOC strategy has detrimental or unintended effects in some areas. For example, 'relentless disruption and targeted action against the highest harm serious and organized criminals and networks' (HM Government, 2018) might have a lasting impact on human trafficking but lead to an increase in gang violence when applied to drugs. By contrast, a strategy of long-term demand reduction, gang mediation and social support for addicts might be more effective against the illegal drug trade. Yet attempts to develop this kind of alternative strategy could be stifled by the constraints SOC strategy places on the police and others. Indeed, an all-encompassing SOC strategy can limit the development of more targeted crime interventions. So while some may argue that SOC strategy creates a joined-up response, it can be countered that a joined-up response is not really needed in the first place because those things labelled as SOC are so different from each other. Instead, more problem-specific strategies are required.

The third objection is the potential transformative effect the SOC label can have when applied to a public policy concern. It was mentioned earlier how unacknowledged crime and social problems can gain greater status if they become labelled as SOC. The political value of SOC is undeniable, especially for those seeking resources and government attention, but the label can have other effects too. The UK government conceptualizes SOC as a threat to national security; it seeks to govern SOC through counter-terrorist inspired strategies (HM Government, 2013; Sergi, 2015). These strategies often have implicit connotations (Sheptycki, 2003), such as secrecy, the need for intrusive surveillance, the protection of an oblivious and vulnerable public, and for policy-making behind closed doors by vetted officials with high-level access. When a crime or social problem is labelled as SOC it is enrolled into this wider 'governmentality'; it is subsumed by these national security and counter-terrorist narratives (Sergi, 2015, 2016). As a result, such problems can become perceived differently over time. The issue of unemployed youths dealing cannabis on a street corner (technically a form of SOC) has the potential to become viewed as part of a vast, interlinked national security threat, rather than, say, a problem of unemployment or broken families or failing schools. Similarly, a group of immigrants paddling a dinghy across the English Channel is seen as part of the same shadowy threat to the UK, rather than a risky and desperate attempt to seek a better life. The SOC label can change how these issues are viewed; it can restructure them in our minds (Sheptycki, 2003). This is an especially serious risk given the vagueness and flexibility of the SOC concept; just about any form of illegal activity could fit some of its looser definitions (Levi, 2002). Levi has made the argument that '"organized crime" can mean anything from major Italian syndicates in sharp suits or peasant garb, to three very menacing burglars with a window-cleaning business who differentiate by having one as look-out,

another as burglar, and a third as money-launderer' (Levi, 2002, p. 883).

SOC strategy has also proven to be highly invasive when it comes to local policing. SOC does not merely exist in the national arena; it increasingly attempts to penetrate local policing strategy. For example, police forces must now produce 'serious and organized crime local profiles' of their area in line with official guidance (Home Office, 2014). These profiles have to adopt the government's CONTEST strategy and render local crime problems into the language of threat and national security and make recommendations for intervention on those terms (ibid.). Through such assessments, the SOC label can recode local crime problems, transforming how they are seen and governed.

Admittedly, this remains more of a long-term risk than an immediate certainty; rival policy groups may contest how these social issues are conceptualized: a drug-treatment NGO might inhibit attempts to treat cannabis-dealing teenagers as a national security threat; some media outlets might help change official attitudes to illegal immigrants crossing the English Channel. The danger though, is that the SOC label becomes normalized over the long term; that it becomes normal and seemingly natural to view teenagers dealing cannabis and immigrants paddling dinghies as national security threats requiring counter-terrorist inspired interventions. Once something is enveloped within the national security apparatus, it can be difficult to free it again (Hobbs & Woodiwiss, 2009); it can recede from public view and become the preserve of vetted officials behind closed doors. As long as SOC is problematized in such terms, it has the potential to insidiously transform those social problems it touches.

Conclusions: a way forward for fraud and SOC

The question of whether or not SOC is a sensible object for strategy cannot be decided by simply weighing up pros and cons. The arguments against SOC fundamentally undermine those in favour. Claims that SOC is useful in its ability to attract political attention, co-ordinate disparate agencies or capture inter-relationships—even if true—are trumped by its fundamental misrepresentation of reality, its failure to correspond to a real social problem, its capacity to limit the development of more targeted and innovative strategies and the potential it has to transform social problems over the long term.

In a broader sense, this boils down to questions about how crime problems should be isolated and defined as objects of strategy in the first place. For those who have to implement and 'sell' government strategies to others, it may be political expediency, continuity, flexibility and symbolic value that make a policy area 'workable'. Yet for those who believe crime strategy should—first and foremost—be *problem-oriented*, SOC is a flawed concept. Problem-oriented strategy demands the careful isolation of specific, real social problems; it requires that the problem be understood in a holistic way without it being conflated or confused with other problems. Ultimately, SOC fails on both these counts.

For those of the latter disposition, the way forward may be to disaggregate SOC into a series of more specific problems. A sound basis for doing this is to think of social problems as harmful systems and processes. By understanding how the 'system' works, by mapping out the system's component parts, its drivers and its enablers, it becomes possible to identify what is, and what is not, really part of the problem. In essence, this means, according to Edwards and Levi (2008, p. 368), asking: 'how are serious crimes organized?' The boundaries of the systems themselves could then be used to delineate sensible objects for policy-making and strategy. For example, if 'heroin dealing' were to be freed from the SOC label, it could be re-located within a more coherent system which includes causal factors and drivers like heroin demand in deprived inner-city estates, the sub-cultural status of drug dealers and inter-gang rivalry. By taking this kind of harmful system as an object of policy-making, it then becomes easier to understand and address the causes, drivers and enablers of the problem. Conceptualizing problems in systemic terms means that individuals are grouped together in a meaningful way—because they are inter-related, not because they have superficial similarities (Edwards & Levi, 2008). It subsequently becomes possible to develop specific, targeted strategies to reduce or mitigate the effects of the system as a whole. Contrast this with the notion of one single SOC strategy for drugs, fraud, cybercrime, child exploitation, modern slavery and everything else now labelled as SOC.

This implies a need to rescue fraud from broader SOC strategy. Doing so would provide greater autonomy for those charged with tackling fraud. It would allow specific fraud problems to be mapped-out and situated within broader social or economic systems. By identifying the underlying causes and vulnerabilities that drive these problems, targeted intervention strategies can be developed, free from the constraints of a homogenous SOC strategy. Such an approach replaces generalistic top-down strategy with a bottom-up problem-orientation. Some may perceive the removal of fraud from the official list of SOC activities as a demotion of sorts, perhaps implying a decline in importance and resources. Yet any loss of status would be out-weighed by the potential created for developing unique, bespoke interventions based on an understanding of specific fraud problems.

This process of extracting, breaking-up and re-fashioning SOC into more coherent policy problems seems to the best way forward, although whether or not such an enterprise can succeed is another question entirely. SOC is now so well-established, so embedded in UK policy and policing circles that such grand ambitions may fall on deaf ears. Perhaps the best that can be hoped for is a gradual extrication of specific problems from underneath the SOC label; perhaps through evidence and argument, policy-making can be taken forward in a positive direction.

Regardless of the likelihood of achieving any such change, this is the context out of which new ideas about fraud must emerge. Fraud is not considered by government to be a stand-alone crime problem; it has been enrolled into and enveloped by SOC strategy. Those interested in developing fresh ideas about fraud—about how it can be understood, assessed and reduced—need to appreciate this strategic framework; they need to understand the pitfalls of allowing fraud (and other crime problems) to be dominated by an over-arching SOC strategy.

Disclosure statement

No potential conflict of interest was reported by the author(s).

References

Cabinet Office. (2008). *The national security strategy of the UK: Security in an interdependent world*. Retrieved from https://assets.publishing.service.gov.uk/government/uploads/system/uploads/attachment_data/file/228539/7291.pdf

Doig, A., Johnson, S., & Levi, M. (2001). New public management, old populism and the policing of fraud. *Public Policy and Administration, 16*, 91–113.

Edwards, A., & Gill, P. (2002). Crime as enterprise? The case of 'transnational organized crime. *Crime, Law & Social Change, 37*, 203–223.

Edwards, A., & Levi, M. (2008). Researching the organization of serious crimes. *Criminology and Criminal Justice, 8*, 363–388.

Fraud Review Team. (2006). *Final report*. Retrieved from http://www.lslo.gov.uk/fraud_review.htm

HM Government. (2013). *Serious and organized crime strategy*. Retrieved from https://www.gov.uk/government/publications/serious-organized-crime-strategy

HM Government. (2018). *Serious and organized crime strategy 2018*. Retrieved from https://assets.publishing.service.gov.uk/government/uploads/system/uploads/attachment_data/file/752850/SOC-2018-web.pdf

HMIC. (2015). *Regional organized crime units: A review of capability and effectiveness*. Retrieved from https://www.justiceinspectorates.gov.uk/hmic/wp-content/uploads/regional-organized-crime-units.pdf

HMICFRS. (2019). *Fraud: Time to choose. An inspection of the police response to fraud*. London: HMICRS.

Hobbs, D. (1998). Going down the glocal: The local context of organized crime. *The Howard Journal, 34*, 407–422.

Hobbs, D. (2013). *Lush life*. Oxford: Oxford University Press.

Hobbs, D., & Woodiwiss, M. (2009). Organized evil and the atlantic alliance: Moral panics and the rhetoric of organized crime policing in America and Britain. *British Journal of Criminology*, *49*, 106–128.

Home Affairs Committee. (1995). *Organized crime*. London: House of Commons, Session 1994-5.

Home Office. (2004). *Fraud law reform. Consultation on proposals for legislation*. London: Home Office.

Home Office. (2013). *Serious and organized crime strategy*. Retrieved from https://assets.publishing.service.gov.uk/government/uploads/system/uploads/attachment_data/file/248645/Serious_and_Organized_Crime_Strategy.pdf

Home Office. (2014). *Serious and organized crime local profiles: A guide*. Retrieved from https://www.gov.uk/government/uploads/system/uploads/attachment_data/file/371602/Serious_and_Organized_Crime_local_profiles.pdf

Levi, M. (1998). Perspectives on organized crime: An overview. *The Howard Journal*, *37*, 335–345.

Levi, M. (2002). The organization of serious crimes. In M. Maguire, R. Morgan, & R. Reiner (Eds.), *The Oxford handbook of criminology*. Oxford: Oxford University Press.

National Criminal Intelligence Service. (2003). *United Kingdom threat assessment of serious and organized crime 2003*. London: National Criminal Intelligence Service.

National Fraud Authority. (2011). *Fighting fraud together: The strategic plan to reduce fraud*. Retrieved from https://assets.publishing.service.gov.uk/government/uploads/system/uploads/attachment_data/file/118501/fighting-fraud-together.pdf

NCA. (2018). *National strategic assessment of serious and organized crime*. Retrieved from http://www.nationalcrimeagency.gov.uk/publications/905-national-strategic-assessment-for-soc-2018/file

Sergi, A. (2015). Divergent mind-sets, convergent policies: Policing models against organized crime in Italy and in England within international frameworks. *European Journal of Criminology*, *12*, 658–680.

Sergi, A. (2016). Serious, therefore organized? A critique of the emerging 'Cyber-Organized Crime' rhetoric in the United Kingdom. *International Journal of Cyber Criminology (IJCC)*, *10*, 170–187.

Sheptycki, J. (2003). Against transnational organized crime. In M. Beare (Ed.), *Critical reflections on transnational organized crime, money laundering and corruption*. Toronto: University of Toronto Press.

Skidmore, M., Ramm, J., Goldstraw-White, J., Barrett, C., Barleaza, S., Muir, R., & Gill, M. (2018). *More than just a number: Improving the police response to victims of fraud*. London: The Police Foundation/Perpetuity Research.

UK Government. (2004). *One Step Ahead: A 21st Century Strategy to Defeat Organised Crime*. Retrieved from: https://assets.publishing.service.gov.uk/government/uploads/system/uploads/attachment_data/file/251075/6167.pdf

Implementing a divergent response? The UK approach to bribery in international and domestic contexts

Nicholas Lord, Alan Doig, Michael Levi, Karin van Wingerde and Katie Benson

ABSTRACT

This paper analyses UK domestic bribery. The authors argue that in both domestic and international contexts, cases are not numerically significant but that changes in how the UK government approaches bribery in the international context means that, where once domestic bribery was addressed more rigorously than bribery in the international context, this imbalance may be being steadily reversed. The paper concludes by setting out the implications that this identifiable divergence may have for the effective policing of bribery in the domestic context. The paper makes an empirical and theoretical contribution to the literature on corruption in the UK.

IMPACT

This paper analyses the UK response to bribery and corruption and provides evidence of a divergent approach, in terms of strategy, policy and enforcement action, to addressing bribery in the domestic and international contexts. This has adverse implications for the prevention, detection, and investigation of bribery. In order to reduce the divergence and reinforce the domestic focus, governments need to ensure better and more detailed data for monitoring of the extent of bribery, the presence of a single lead for the domestic context to ensure consistency and co-ordination, and the availability of training for relevant staff to make certain relevant stakeholders are alert to emerging corruption issues. The empirically informed insights and arguments in this paper are relevant to policy-makers and practitioners working in the area of anti-corruption, as well as non-governmental organizations seeking to scrutinize anti-corruption strategies, policies and practice in the UK.

Introduction and context

Historically in the UK, there has been a divergence in the attitudes and responses of governments towards domestic and international bribery by UK persons (including corporations). Domestic bribery, particularly of political and public sector personnel, was increasingly presented as being less acceptable within a growing expectation of high public standards and the public interest (Doig, 1984). The Acts passed in 1889, 1906 and 1916 provided the legal framework for behaviours, relations and acts being labelled as 'corrupt' in the context of the domestic (local and central) duties of public officials with public inquiries (such as those relating to the Poulson and other corruption scandals in the early 1970s) demanding not only effective anti-bribery legislation but also related legislation (for example, conflict of financial interests in local government). The UK Bribery Act (UKBA) 2010 consolidated and updated the existing legislation.

Apart from the limited domestic jurisdictional reach of the longstanding pre-UKBA legislation (though the Anti-terrorism, Crime and Security Act 2001 gave them extra-territorial jurisdiction), much of the lack of interest in bribery overseas arose from perceptions among government departments on what was or was not acceptable abroad in terms of the primacy of UK economic/political interests (see Doig, 2011), particularly involving countries where corruption was prevalent or a pragmatic necessity in a highly-competitive export environment (see Gutterman, 2017).

Neither the 2001 extension of the jurisdiction of existing legislation, nor being a signatory to the OECD Convention on Combating Bribery of Foreign Public Officials in International Business Transactions, were enough to address the concerns of OECD's Working Group on the Convention about the adequacy of the UK's response to bribery in the international context. Indeed, the inadequacy of the legislative framework, including the inadequacy of corporate criminal liability alongside this in terms of, for example, the restrictive nature of identification principle (Lord, 2014), for both the domestic and the international context had long been a concern of a range of bodies, from 1976 Royal Commission on Standards of Conduct in Public Life to the UK's ratification of UNCAC in 2006. This was publicly accepted by UK governments and led (*a*) to the UKBA and a number of policy and strategy documents; and (*b*) in order to implement the intent of the UKBA for the international context, a clearly-defined set of institutional changes and resourcing arrangements within a very public statement of commitment through a 'landmark' [*sic*] international anti-corruption summit in London in 2016.

The research context and methodology

The absence of similar changes and arrangements for effective implementation of the UKBA for the domestic context is reflected in the 2018 City of London Police's statement that, while it has lead responsibility for fraud within the UK, there is no lead responsibility for bribery within the UK and, even if there was, there would be 'a need for infrastructure, investment and resourcing' to ensure an effective law enforcement response (House of Lords Bribery Act Committee, 2018, p. 15). This suggests a change to the historical divergence in terms of priorities for the domestic and international contexts, and a major research gap in terms of the contemporary nature and control of domestic bribery. This paper contributes to the current discourse on bribery in the UK by asking if there is a divergence in enforcement of domestic and international bribery by the UK through four research questions:

- Does the contemporary response to domestic and international bribery diverge?
- What do we know about the nature, extent and scope of domestic bribery in the UK?
- If the contemporary responses to domestic and international bribery diverge, are there identifiable reasons for this?
- What are the implications for future approaches to bribery in the domestic context?

The research was undertaken between October 2016 and September 2018 with funding from the British Academy/Leverhulme Small Research Grants 2016 round. The research involved both intensive and extensive research approaches and the implementation of mixed methods over three phases to triangulate and corroborate the findings:

- A systematic search of the literature to identify relevant academic and 'grey' scholarship on bribery and corruption, as well as a desk review of official reports and publications (see Saunders, Lewis, & Thornhill, 2009).
- A Freedom of Information (FOI) request to all police forces in the UK plus specialist anti-corruption enforcement authorities such as the Serious Fraud Office (SFO), the Ministry of Defence Police and the City of London Police ($N = 45$; all replied) to establish the number, type and outcome of cases

recorded for investigation in relation to the bribery of public and/or private sector personnel under the 1889, 1906, 1916 and 2010 Acts.
- Semi-structured interviews with six informed experts in the areas of anti-bribery and corruption, including senior prosecutors, and senior bribery trainers and investigators, to gain insight into the nature of domestic bribery and issues relating to the regulation and control of these behaviours.

Is there a divergence? Legal framework, government attention, institutional change, and the research issue

Legal context

Bribery is a transactional crime—it consists of an illicit exchange involving the transfer of a benefit to the recipient(s), directly or indirectly, immediately and over a longer term, which may comprise both monetary payments and other types of inducements, to facilitate the circumventing of legally prescribed rules and procedures, and usually consists of the abuse or misuse of otherwise 'normal' relationships (Doig, 2006, p. 116), to the advantage of the provider directly or on behalf of another party. Note that the terms 'corruption' and 'bribery' are often used interchangeably. Corruption is essentially about the 'corruption' of public office or its use for private, personal or partisan interests. This may take a number of criminalized forms, such as embezzlement or bribery, or ethical issues, such as conflict of interest or nepotism; this paper focuses on bribery, as defined by the UKBA. In legal terms, common law offences of bribery and embracery (bribery of a juror) in England and Wales, and bribery and accepting a bribe in Scotland, have existed for centuries, with focus placed on the corruption of those in 'public office' (whose definition invariably relied on case law interpretation).

This was reinforced in statute: the Public Bodies Corrupt Practices Act 1889 sought to criminalize local government officials acting 'corruptly' in connection to their public body. The Prevention of Corruption Act 1906 brought into scope the private sector (agents acting corruptly in relation to a principal's business) and central government officials. The Prevention of Corruption Act 1916 introduced a presumption of corruption component, shifting the burden of proof to public sector defendants to prove that their behaviours were not corrupt in offences involving public sector contracts under the 1889 and 1906 Acts where it had already been proved that a bribe had been given or received. In 2002, the Anti-Terrorism, Crime and Security Act 2001 came into force and introduced an overseas element to ensure that bribery and corruption, as legislated for in the

Prevention of Corruption Acts, committed by UK persons in other jurisdictions was also punishable in the UK.

This latter amendment was an attempt to satisfy the requirements of the OECD's 1997 Anti-Bribery Convention. However, the OECD's monitoring process considered the changes in the 2001 Act to be insufficient and recommended 'that the UK proceed at the earliest opportunity to enact a comprehensive anti-corruption statute' (OECD, 2003, p. 17). The outcome was the UKBA, which consolidated all bribery offences, accounting for domestic and foreign bribery by natural and legal persons, and including four specific offences relating to giving or offering a bribe, receiving or soliciting a bribe, bribing a foreign public official, and a failure of commercial organizations to prevent bribery. The UKBA refers to bribery as the offering, promising or giving (active bribery), or the requesting, agreeing to receive or accepting (passive bribery) of a financial or other advantage with the intention to induce improper performance in relation to a relevant function or activity (such as a public function or in the course of employment).

Government attention

In line with this developing legal framework, corruption and bribery were identified as a high-priority public policy concern by the UK government (see HM Government, 2014). They also remain high on the agenda of other sovereign states and inter-governmental bodies such as the UNODC, the Working Group on the OECD Convention and the European Union (see European Commission, 2014). The 2016 Anti-Corruption Summit convened by the UK government spelt out the rhetoric of the UK's commitment in terms of the international context, and the UK government also stated that corruption is a threat to the UK's 'national security and prosperity, both at home and overseas' (HM Government, 2017, p. 7). The then Home Secretary Amber Rudd asserted that 'although the UK enjoys higher levels of integrity than many other countries, we are not immune from the effects of corruption. Stories of corruption can undermine confidence in the institutions and the business reputation more widely' (HM Government, 2017, p. 7, 5).

The UK government has taken an active role in developing a policy framework to address bribery. The 2014 Anti-Corruption Plan, which has both domestic and international perspectives, outlined the government's intention to build a better picture of the threat from corruption and the ways in which the UK is vulnerable by increasing protection against the organized criminals who corrupt public sector officials; strengthening integrity in key sectors and institutions; and strengthening the UK's law enforcement response to more effectively pursue those who engage in corruption or launder their corrupt funds in the UK. Most recently, the UK Anti-Corruption Strategy 2017–2022 was published focusing on six priorities: reducing the insider threat in high-risk domestic sectors such as borders and ports; reducing corruption in public procurement and grants; promoting integrity across the public and private sectors; strengthening the integrity of the UK as an international financial centre; improving the business environment globally; and working with other countries to combat corruption.

Institutional change

In addition to the policy framework and a very public commitment to addressing corruption underlined by the Anti-Corruption Summit in 2016, where several commitments were made by the UK government as part of a drive to 'galvanize a global response to tackle corruption', the government also introduced institutional reforms. Most of these, however, were focused on or prioritized international bribery.

On the enactment of the UKBA, the SFO was designated with lead responsibility for international cases, to whom Foreign and Commonwealth Office (FCO) staff were advised to report allegations (FCO, 2011; see also OECD, 2017, p. 104). In the same year, an All-Party Parliamentary Group on Anti-Corruption was established to bring together interested members of the House of Commons and House of Lords to raise awareness of the impact of international corruption and to enhance and strengthen UK anti-corruption policies and mechanisms. In 2014, the government established a post of Anti-Corruption Champion. In 2015, an Inter-Ministerial Group on Anti-Corruption was created and the City of London Police Overseas Anti-corruption Unit, along with the Metropolitan Police's International Proceeds of Corruption Unit, were transferred to the National Crime Agency's (NCA's) Economic Crime Command to become the International Corruption Unit (ICU), funded largely by the Department for International Development (DFID) and with some 50 staff focusing on bribery, money laundering and financial sanctions evasion (see Harvey, *this issue*). An integrated approach to restitution of illicit funds held in the UK was drafted and agreed by a number of agencies (see Campbell & Lord, 2018).

In July 2017, the International Anti-Corruption Coordination Centre (IACCC), hosted within the NCA, was launched to bring together specialist law enforcement officers from multiple agencies around the world to tackle allegations of high-level corruption where co-ordination and cooperation was crucial. In December 2017, the UK government announced the creation of the National Economic Crime Centre

(NECC)—also hosted within the NCA—in order to plan, task and co-ordinate operational responses across agencies bringing together the UK's capabilities to tackle economic crime more effectively, with particular focus on bribery and corruption. It also established a memorandum of understanding in 2017, entitled 'Tackling Foreign Bribery', signed between various law enforcement bodies, including the SFO, the City of London Police, the Crown Prosecution Service (CPS), the Scottish government's Crown Office and Procurator Fiscal Service, the Financial Conduct Authority, the Ministry of Defence Police, the NCA and HM Revenue and Customs. Further legislative reform—such as 'unexplained wealth orders' (UWO) under the Criminal Finances Act 2017—has underlined the continuing emphasis on the international context (even though such orders were addressed domestically through applications to the UK High Court).

Developing the research issue: reviewing the domestic context

The UK continues to be rated an 'active enforcer' (Transparency International, 2018) of the OECD Anti-Bribery Convention in the international context based on the number of investigations commenced and sanctions brought in relation to its share of world exports (only six other countries are considered 'active'). Yet, in contrast to the developments outlined above, it was being argued that bribery *within* the UK has not been given the same level of attention and support as it has in the international context, despite both domestic and external criticisms of this: an early UNCAC review noted that 'there is no typology of corruption available, or any analysis and evaluation of the situation in the UK … nor is there any specialised agency which is responsible for a centralized co-ordination of nation-wide anti-corruption work' (UNODC, 2011, p. 7; see also Transparency International, 2011).

A few years later, in 2018, evidence to a House of Lords inquiry into the UKBA from a senior officer from the City of London Police noted that 'domestically, the picture has not been articulated particularly well. The spotlight has not been on what happens within the United Kingdom and the response to it. One might say that that allows the growth of corrupt activity, as we are not really focusing on those aspects' (House of Lords Bribery Act Committee, 2018, q108). In the same year, GRECO noted that, in relation to what it terms 'persons who are entrusted with top executive functions', it 'did not come across a co-ordinated system for analysing major corruption risk factors … in an unconditional strategic manner at central governmental level' (GRECO, 2018, p. 13).

The paper argues that, while the legislative framework and the publication of policy documents

suggest a common approach by governments, that approach diverges in terms of institutional changes and resourcing arrangements. Thus the question underpinning our research was why there appears to be a lack of implementation focus on bribery in the domestic context?

What do we know about the nature, extent and scope of domestic bribery in the UK?

The scale of domestic bribery

In the second phase of the research, the FOI data showed the actual number of recorded cases of domestic bribery in the UK. Table 1 presents the absolute number of bribery offences recorded by UK police forces from 1989 onward and differentiated by the legislation used. The recording periods of the different forces varied quite significantly—some forces' records went back to 1989, while others only recorded one year, making direct comparison of the pre- and post-Bribery Act periods impossible. Forty two out of the 47 forces and authorities surveyed provided detail as to whether the offences were recorded under the Bribery Act 2010 or earlier legislation. However, in five responses, the specific legislation was not noted, though the year of recording was provided (except for one force) and in these cases we inferred that those recorded in 2011 onwards would have been recorded under the UKBA.

For research data, this means that one case included in the 202 pre-UKBA legislation cases may have been a UKBA offence, and that 58 of the cases included in the 125 post-UKBA figure may have been offences relating to earlier legislation: this may be due to the time delay between offence and detection, and the inability to make UKBA charges retrospective. However, the figure of 58 includes 41 cases recorded by Police Scotland, all of which were recorded between 2013 and 2016. According to Police Scotland, 'crimes in Scotland are recorded in accordance with the Scottish Government Justice Department crime classification codes and are not thereafter subcategorised' (FOI response). It is therefore possible that some of these 41 cases were pre-UKBA offences, though we cannot estimate how many.

Based on responses to the FOI requests, 327 bribery offences were recorded between 1989 and 2017, including 125 since the UKBA came into force in 2011. If we break down the data further, authorities with national jurisdiction, such as the Ministry of

Table 1. Recorded bribery data (1989–2017).

Legal framework (dates)	Number of recorded cases
Prevention of Corruption Acts (1989–2011)	202
UKBA (2011–2017)	125
Total	327

Defence Police (63 cases between 1999 and 2016) and the SFO (43 cases between 2012 and 2016), recorded the highest number of cases. In terms of police forces, Thames Valley Police, (44), Police Scotland (41), West Mercia Police (22), the Police Service of Northern Ireland (15), Warwickshire Police (12) and Greater Manchester Police (12) recorded the highest numbers. For the time period 2011–2017 (which may not entirely be cases investigated under the UKBA), a total of 125 cases was recorded, with the greatest numbers recorded by Police Scotland (41), Thames Valley Police (15) and Greater Manchester Police (11).

Given the problematic variation in time periods for which responses were received, and to provide a better reflection of recorded cases over time, we calculated the rate of recording per year for each force. From this analysis, it can be seen that the Ministry of Defence Police and SFO recorded a high number of total cases, with 3.5 and 8.6 cases per year. In terms of constabulary police forces, Police Scotland (10.2), Thames Valley Police (4.8) and West Mercia Police (2.2) have the highest rate of recording per year. For the period 2011–2017, the analysis indicates that the forces with the highest rate of recording of UKBA offences were Police Scotland (7.5), Thames Valley Police (2.7) and Greater Manchester Police (2). The current research thus suggests that while a significant minority of UK police forces have had no recorded domestic cases under the UKBA, some 25 police forces plus the Ministry of Defence Police and the SFO have had a total of 125 cases over a 6-year period (or ≈21 a year).

The research data were triangulated against the annual average of cases with two further sets of data. The first was provided by the Home Office on cases brought under the 1889 and 1906 Acts (the 1916 Act increased the maximum penalty under these Acts for certain offences) between 1965 and 1978—see Table 2.

These data suggest that the annual average number of cases brought under the 1889 Act was less than three, while the number brought under the 1906 Act was over 30; conspiracy to commit corruption cases were less than four per year. The other set of data was provided by the Office for National Statistics (ONS) in 2018 when it published for the first time data on corruption related offences recorded by the police. These 'experimental statistics' include all four UKBA offences, plus the offence of misconduct in public office—see Table 3.

Table 3. ONS corruption data (ONS, 2018).

Offences/dates	July 2016–June 2017	July 2017–June 2018	Total
Offences relating to offering, promising or giving bribes (s.1 and s.6 UKBA)	13	9	22
Offences relating to requesting, agreeing to receive and accepting bribes (s.2 UKBA)	4	6	10
Commercial organization—failure to prevent associate bribing another with intent to obtain or retain business or advantage (s.7 UKBA)	0	1	1
Misconduct in a public office	62	106	168

As the ONS indicates, other than for unlawful deaths, police recorded crime data are not designated as national statistics. Furthermore, data collected prior to April 2018 are not comparable with data after April 2018, as improvements in data collection procedures mean that for the period April to June 2018, data were only available from 38 of the 43 police forces in England and Wales. In terms of bribery specifically, the absolute numbers of recorded offences here are low relative to the FOI data but it is very difficult to make comparisons between the two years of corruption data published by the ONS (currently classed as Experimental) and the FOI data, because they relate to different numbers of police forces and varying time periods of available recorded data across forces. Most offences in the ONS data relate to the broader construct of 'misconduct in public office' which can range from the exploitation of an official position to facilitate a personal or sexual relationship, or acting while under a conflict of interest in a prejudicial manner (see Law Commission, 2016), raising questions over how many may involve bribery.

Nevertheless, when comparing the current data with the data in Tables 2 and 3, the number of recorded cases shows no significant increase or decrease since 1965. If a small number of significant variations often occasioned by a single case with multiple offences and offenders are taken into account, then the number per force is about two to three recorded cases a year. There are other means at the disposal of police forces, including decisions taken by local police forces to investigate under the Fraud Act 2006 (for example fraud by abuse of position) cases where bribery allegedly occurred, and by the CPS to prosecute accordingly; the use of money laundering provisions in the Proceeds of Crime Act (POCA); the use of the 1889 Act for offences committed prior to the coming into force of the UKBA; and—for the moment—the common law offence of misconduct in public office. Within the limits of the research and the current state of recorded bribery data—which continues to be a function of what is chosen to report, record, and investigate, and by whom—the paper has demonstrated that there continue to be few bribery

Table 2. Bribery offences from 1965 to 1978 (Doig, 1984).

| Charges | Crown Court | | |
	Cases	Annual average	Convicted
1889 Act; s1(1)	43	>2.9	32
1889 Act; s1(2)	24	>1.6	23
1906 Act s1	483	>32.0	350
Conspiracy to commit corruption	52	>3.4	45

cases and that there is little evidence from which it may reasonably be concluded whether or not the UKBA has had an impact on levels of domestic cases investigated or prosecuted.

The nature and scope of domestic bribery

The FOI data provided qualitative insights into the nature of the cases, as descriptions were provided by forces as to whether the bribery was public or private, domestic or international, and the outcome of the case. However, the information was very inconsistent, with some forces providing elaborate accounts of the bribery offences, some providing brief and unspecific accounts, for example 'corruption (public sector)'; some providing no description at all other than stating the offence (for example a section 1 UKBA violation, or 'giving bribe'); and, finally, some providing nothing beyond the number of cases and year recorded. Most cases were recorded under section 1 of the UKBA (offering, promising or giving a bribe), section 1 of POCA (primarily in SFO cases, but in other forces also) and section 1 of the Public Bodies Corrupt Practices Act 1889. From the data collated, many of those involved had a modest socio-economic status. The range of actors implicated in the FOI responses and (where available) an indication of the purpose of the bribe shows low-level appointments (such as driving test inspectors, hotel workers and planning officers) and routine offences (insider information, award contracts etc.); there was no data in the FOI responses about the financial value of the bribes. However, in other research analysing domestic and international bribery in England and Wales, domestic bribes tend to be 'cheaper' than foreign ones (Andresen & Button, 2018, p. 9). More specifically, 95% of convictions involving bribes under £100,000 were domestic (and 5% were overseas), whereas only 40% of convictions involving bribes over £100,000 were domestic, with 60% overseas (Andresen & Button, 2018). This was later reinforced in interviews with senior CPS staff who alluded to domestic bribery involving relatively small amounts in terms of payments made and a wide geography of cases. Overall, domestic cases coming to the CPS were generally lower-level, 'petty' bribery cases and involve small businesses rather than larger, more complex schemes. That said, small and medium size enterprises can be more readily prosecuted and so may appear more in official data. The data received do not indicate anything about the lapse of time from offence commission to reporting/recording to investigation or to prosecution; nor about the benefits sought from the bribes, which might be larger from overseas cases, being mainly about very large contracts. The scale of the rewards sought might account for their higher average bribe size.

Only a few forces provided enough information for insights into the 'bribers', i.e. those who gave, offered or promised a bribe. More detail is given on the 'bribee', i.e. those who were offered or accepted a bribe. These included most notably bribes offered by private sector actors to those with decision-making responsibilities for awarding public contracts. Many of the Ministry of Defence Police cases involved the offering or accepting of bribes, including hospitality and gifts, for rewarding contracts to subcontractors, while there were several cases of commercial bribery, again to influence to provision of business to suppliers and subcontractors. There were also several instances of driving test examiners being bribed.

Finally, the data provided numerical information as to the outcome of the cases investigated by respondent forces—see Table 4.

The figure of 100 for 'no details on outcomes provided' is distorted by two FOI responses: Thames Valley Police (44) and Police Scotland (41). In both responses, no details were provided as to the outcomes of the offences recorded. Police Scotland does not have responsibility for charging cases, meaning outcome data was not available through the FOI request. This responsibility falls to the Crown Office and Procurator Fiscal Service (COPFS). The COPFS website contains data on all recorded offences: however, corruption is included as 'Other crimes of dishonesty', a category that includes forgery (other), 'reset' (receiving stolen goods) and embezzlement. Consequently, it is not possible to disaggregate this down to a specific focus on bribery. No further action is the most common outcome. Details provided indicated this was often due to insufficient evidence or evidential difficulties, no suspects identified or victims/allegers withdrawing support. The outcomes 'referred elsewhere' and 'internal discipline' all related to the Ministry of Defence FOI response.

Are there reasons for the divergence in terms of the domestic context?

In summary, the paper demonstrates that bribery in the domestic context is not, numerically or in terms of the status of those investigated or decisions and actions

Table 4. Outcomes of recorded bribery cases.

No further action	97
Charge	93
Ongoing investigation /pending decision	15
Caution	9
Referred elsewhere	4
Internal discipline	4
Adult restorative disposal	2
Community resolution	1
Offence changed	1
Formal action (unspecified)	1
No details on outcomes provided	100
Total	327

involved, significant. The UK approach, whether strategic or institutional, has focused on the international context, in part because of the drivers for reform and in part because of the UK's very public commitment to taking a proactive role in addressing international bribery. There may not be significant numbers of cases in the domestic context and, unlike the transnational corporations arraigned by the SFO, few involve corporations with a high visibility or reputational significance to attract the attention of the SFO and national/international media. The third phase of the research therefore sought to explore reasons as to why there may be a divergence in responses in the domestic and international contexts.

The first explanation we found was that the levels and types of cases—or at least the levels of known cases—in the domestic context, as well as the outcomes of cases, do not create a climate of concern in themselves. The lack of centralization of information means lack of sufficient records/comparable data which indeed inhibits awareness, which may lead to the self-fulfilling prophecy that if there are not many cases or serious cases of domestic bribery (based on the data) then a different response is not necessary on the basis of the existing evidence (see also Walburg, 2015). Sometimes, low data may be a reason for concern, reflecting incompetence/corruption of the criminal justice process, but there are no clear grounds for suspicion that this is the explanation here.

Second, interviews with senior CPS staff suggested that most bribery cases that came to their attention involved 'abuse by managers', for example diverting funds, sometimes via separate companies, and bribing to maintain concealment, alongside many cases that involved using bribery to maintain subcontracts in business, as the FOI data indicated also. This level of case also does not attract official concern, even though interview data may indicate that domestic bribery reflects, as one investigator argued, a 'continuing undercurrent of corruption' (see also the Chartered Institute of Building, 2013; Fazekas, 2015) and where interviewees pointed out that official statistics on bribery and corruption do not give accurate figures. Thus the research highlights that, collectively, the known cases do not show a level of seriousness that demands official or media attention (and despite reporting on cases that, individually, included multi-million pound public sector contracts, football, the Royal Household, a £4.9 million bribe for supermarket supplies, domestic companies charged with failing to have adequate procedures, the involvement of the SFO and so on; see, for example, http://www.elexica.com/en/resources/microsite/uk-bribery-act/corruption-enforcement-tracker). This confirms the research on media treatment of fraud, which likewise is tilted towards glamorous and 'famous name' cases (Levi, 2006).

Third, the divergence may be related to the current law enforcement approach which makes very little provision for bribery as a domestic law enforcement issue. In the case of fraud, which has been subject to review and institutional change, a lead police force—the City of London police—is responsible for training provision through its Economic Crime Academy. There is a centralized reporting process through Action Fraud and then the dissemination of investigative packages through the National Fraud Intelligence Bureau (although there continue to be concerns over fraud investigation capacity within police forces; see, for example, Skidmore et al *this issue*). In the case of bribery, as the City of London Police have noted, 'as a national lead force for fraud and other economic crime, we have a degree of co-ordination to enable us to do that, but we do not do it for bribery and corruption … there is no domestic sharing of intelligence on bribery' (House of Lords Bribery Act Committee, 2018, p. 4, 13). This latter issue was not helped by the recent refusal of the Home Office to fund an extension of the Action Fraud database and reporting mechanisms to include bribery. The overall perception of the priority given to the domestic bribery is a consequence of 'the focus on grand international corruption, rather than the everyday corruption that you might see in society' (House of Lords Bribery Act Committee, 2018, p. 26).

Further, prosecutorial discretion and data recording can also shape the corruption picture in the UK. For instance, many corruption cases have:

> … *been prosecuted with 'fraud by abuse of position' … This enables them to think that there is no corruption going on in the UK because no one has been prosecuted for it. They've been prosecuted for something else* (interview with NGO actor).

The logic of this argument implies that low absolute numbers of bribery/corruption prosecutions accounts for there being no (apparent) corruption. However, it is more likely to be a reflection on decision-making within the public authorities about when and on what charges to prosecute corruption. This might also reflect the consent needed from the Director of Public Prosecutions (DPP) for a bribery prosecution or the Attorney General (AG) for a corruption offence; such consent, from either the DPP or the AG, is not needed for prosecuting the offence of 'fraud by abuse of position', and thus the option of fraud prosecution offers a less bureaucratically complicated approach.

Fourth, there continues to be pressure from internal and external organizations that influence the enforcement priorities in terms of domestic and international bribery. For instance, the presence of intense scrutiny by inter-governmental bodies, such as the OECD's Working Group on Bribery, into how the

UK is implementing the OECD Anti-Bribery Convention, is a major external factor (the UK government is required to communicate in person four times a year what is being done to meet the requirements of the convention). Consequently, it would be unsurprising that policy and enforcement focus has been placed on the response to international bribery which, in an ambience of resource austerity, may detract from pursuing domestic bribery:

> … the attention to domestic corruption is swamped by the SFO and NCA's major focus on international corruption where they have specific mandates and where the latter's ICU [International Corruption Unit] is DFID-funded for that role (interview with law enforcement actor).

Fifth, while specific mandates and capacity have been created for national policing authorities, such as the SFO and the NCA, these are concerned with international bribery, rather than supporting local efforts against domestic bribery. This has been exacerbated by continuing funding cuts to fraud squads within local police forces who normally deal with bribery cases (see Doig, 2018). In addition, there have been wider changes in terms of domestic monitoring of the risk of bribery and appropriate institutional responses, including the abolition of both the NFA and the Audit Commission which took a leading role in monitoring levels of fraud and bribery, as well as running a national annual data-mining and matching initiative, and developing comprehensive performance assessment reviews to ensure relevant policies and procedures were in place.

Finally, the nature and profile of domestic bribery may in itself attract less attention because, according to one police interviewee, it is less overt and often less tangible in comparison to the nature—and traceability—of bribery in the international context. Domestic bribery is often an extension of embedded social relation(ships) and ways of operating rather than merely specific one-off bribery transactions. The context often relates to critical 'touch points'—how and where connections are made, grooming through social and sporting occasions, shared peer groups and similar interests—as the basis for favours for friends within a shared social setting. Here there may be no bribe for specific actions but, developing from existing relationships and connectivity, a reciprocity within potentially corrupt relationships that is justifiable in terms of friendship or helping each other. Thus the bribes are less explicit tangible, material inducements than more subtle benefits (for example hospitality, employment of relatives, discounts, and so on) where there may have no direct tangible exchange, or specific payments for specified outcomes.

Taking the strands noted above together, there is a divergence in how government approaches bribery in the domestic and international contexts. This has meant that, where once domestic bribery was addressed more rigorously than bribery in the international context, this may be being steadily reversed, in terms of signalled priorities, resources and institutional responses. The paper concludes that this has come about because of a lack of governmental concern and prioritization. The consequence has also meant that, unlike the international context, the domestic context lacks institutional focus, central collation of data, resources, and appropriate training when compared to the approach to transnational bribery.

What are the implications for future approaches to bribery in the domestic context?

The lack of ownership or co-ordination of the UK approach to domestic bribery is the consequence of an absence of a collective push to build up a national profile of domestic bribery and the infrastructure that would implement the existing policy statements. This has important implications for the effective policing of bribery in the domestic context. The areas we believe need to be addressed and possible consequences if no initiative is taken to redress the divergence follow.

Data on corruption

First, our research raised several notable data issues, including the absence of a centralized register of bribery or corruption offences in the UK. This creates difficulties for determining the scale, extent and nature of domestic bribery. In previous years, the Public Sector Corruption Index (PSCI) provided a centralized register of all corruption offences. The index was set up as one of the recommendations of the 1976 Royal Commission and required all police forces to report allegations of corruption to the Metropolitan and City Police Company Fraud Branch (as it then was) which would maintain a register and would undertake a collating, evaluation and co-ordinating role. This Index was initially held by the Metropolitan Police before being moved to the Serious and Organised Crime Agency (SOCA, now NCA) before being allowed to lapse.

Related to this issue, as highlighted in the systematic use of FOI requests to obtain data from across UK policing agencies, is the current inconsistency of data collection and retention methods. There are no centralized expectations on how data should be stored, what data should be recorded, and for how long the data should be retained. We found that how far back data records go is dependent on individual force policies, ranging from over 20 years to 12 months. The data that are available also vary in detail, with some forces supplying rich, contextual insight into individual cases, but others only superficial numbers, although this may reflect internal decisions over which, or how much, information to share. This is further complicated as different software and systems are being used across the different forces which, in turn, creates compatibility issues. For instance, Police Scotland gave details of 41 recorded 'corruption' offences since 2013 but, while these data include the Acts for which data was requested, we cannot be certain that they did not also include non-bribery offences. In other cases, some forces withheld some information due to sensitivities relating to potentially identifiable cases.

Prosecutorial discretion

Second, as mentioned earlier, the interviews with senior CPS actors indicated that many substantive bribery cases may be prosecuted as 'fraud by abuse of position' under the Fraud Act 2006, also reflecting police force decisions to record as fraud rather than bribery. Decisions over whether to pursue as bribery or fraud depends on several factors where the police look to expedite provable offences associated with the same criminality by considering which is 'easiest' to prove, where evidence is most readily available, and whether there is a corporate aspect to the case and which penalties can be invoked. We are not arguing that these judgments are unreasonable, but their unintended effect is to make collective assessment of harm and risk difficult.

Institutional configuration and engagement

Third is the current institutional configuration and engagement. Although the Home Office and Cabinet Office have presented a policy perspective in reducing domestic bribery, this has not been resourced or allocated in terms of institutional ownership (as opposed to guidance) and thus remains rhetorical, particularly as these bodies have a small staff with a policy or strategic rather than an operational focus. The abolition of the Audit Commission has underlined the significance of roles of, and co-ordination between, other audit or oversight bodies or regulators, where issues of awareness, prevention and reporting, especially those proposed in policy and strategy documents, may remain unmonitored or unreviewed for effective implementation.

Apart from the central role played by the City of London Police Economic Crime Academy in training police officers, and some limited guidance by the College of Policing, there is currently no central unit or resourcing for the support of local police forces for what are (by the standards of most other cases)

complex, resource- and time-intensive investigations. The result may be cases not pursued because they require co-ordination, often where there may be cross-police boundaries. Within local policing, and apart from the roles of police professional standards units for police corruption and Special Operations Units (*de facto* regional organized crime units linked to the NCA and focused on economic crime committed by organized crime groups), strategies for the investigation of fraud, including bribery, continue to have limited effect in persuading police forces to commit appropriate resources (Doig, 2018).

Political and enforcement complacency

Finally, the absence of a major scandal or a major corporation or municipal body may have led to a 'complacency' around domestic bribery (interview with NGO actor). For instance, while the UK's role is recognized in the international side of bribery, such as in terms of the financial and professional services sectors intentionally or otherwise servicing corrupt foreigners with money laundering opportunities, or in terms of UK companies exporting bribes, bribery occurring within the UK is not part of the UK psyche (interview with NGO actor). Whether a drip-feed of domestic bribery cases can amount to enough to change the complacency and close the divergence is not clear.

Conclusions

Through our four research questions, we identified that there is a divergence in the approach to domestic and international bribery by the UK. We found that there are data, and assumptions, about the number, type and significance of cases in the domestic context that have not resulted in anything approaching the levels of responses that bribery in the international context has achieved. The response to transnational bribery has been driven not only by government commitment but also by implementing that commitment through specific institutional and resourcing changes. This has led to a divergent approach to addressing bribery in the domestic and international contexts which will have adverse implications for the prevention, detection, and investigation of bribery generally.

Operationally, levels and types of domestic bribery may be under-reported because of investigative and prosecutorial choices. More widely, we found that the interplay between national strategies and initiatives, organizational priorities, international commitments and institutional and other responses in relation to bribery remain a continuing dynamic that has favoured the international context over the domestic context. Our research may point to both a limited number of cases and low levels of complexity or status of those involved to explain the absence of an equivalent response in the domestic context. While there is no evidence of significant levels of bribery in the domestic context, however, the failure to respond in policy, institutional and resource terms could lead to slow reaction to any emerging rise in scale or significance in the domestic context in the future.

The need for valid data on corruption

A key issue is the reliance on enforcement data to provide insights into the nature and levels of bribery, as such data are an artefact of enforcement activities and reporting mechanisms. Alongside this, there is an absence of valid empirical data on the extent and scope of bribery offences. Social scientific methodologies utilizing self-report or victimization studies may contribute to informing this debate, but the particular nature or bribery presents obstacles: the inherently clandestine nature, the lack of identifiable victims and consequences, the invisibility of those involved in the corrupt transaction given they consent to (or otherwise incentivized to remain silent) and benefit from the arrangements, are all factors that undermine such approaches. For these reasons, we suggest more can be gained analytically by developing fuller theoretical accounts of the nature of bribery in the UK so as to inform 'intelligence-led' interventions and to pursue deliberative methods that utilize the expertise and informed judgement of key stakeholders in this area, with a view to forecasting potential future scenarios of bribery that indicate sectors, areas, issues that may emerge as priority concerns for academia, policy and practice. These offer potential future research areas.

Current and future scenarios of corruption

In the wider domestic context, unlawful payments—often addressed in a number of contexts, by a range of agencies under various pieces of legislation—are one of the sources that undermine the integrity of UK systems and democratic processes. Whether in business, such as the awarding of contracts in the construction sector, or public services, such as NHS staff accepting excessive hospitality to promote certain products and services, or the financing of political and election campaigns by commercial and other interests, a lack of perceived fairness can reduce legitimacy, and this permeates into society more widely. Furthermore, as we see the emergence of new sectors, such as the explosion of FinTech companies and public and private services provided via the 'internet of things', there is potential for bribery in such industries that may put at risk individual and workplace data security. In addition, the potential for using new technologies for bribery,

such as utilizing anonymised cryptocurrencies as material inducements is also emerging, though very little is known about the nature of such activities.

For such reasons, in order to reduce the divergence and reinforce the domestic focus, there is a need for better and more detailed data, the presence of a single lead for the domestic context and the availability of training for relevant staff which would go a long way to anticipating such issues. In the meantime, however, the we have drawn attention to the absence of a national response and guidance to bribery in the domestic context that, given the quite substantial response for the international context, is a significant policy and strategy gap. In conclusion, governments should ensure that they have access to the appropriate levels of data to monitor the domestic context so that they may be alert to such issues in the future and address the identified divergence to enhance the implementation of the UKBA in the domestic as well as in the international contexts.

Disclosure statement

No potential conflict of interest was reported by the authors.

References

Andresen, M. S., & Button, M. (2018). The profile and detection of bribery in Norway and England & Wales: A comparative study. *European Journal of Criminology*, Online First. doi:10.1177/1477370818764827

Campbell, L., & Lord, N. (2018). *Corruption in commercial enterprise: Law, theory and practice*. London: Routledge.

The Chartered Institute of Building. (2013). *Report exploring corruption in the UK construction industry*. London: The Chartered Institute of Building.

Doig, A. (1984). *Corruption and misconduct in contemporary British politics*. London: Penguin.

Doig, A. (2006). *Fraud*. London: Routledge.

Doig, A. (2011). *State crime*. London: Routledge.

Doig, A. (2018). Implementing national policing agendas and strategies for fraud at local level. *Journal of Financial Crime*, 25(4), 984–996.

European Commission. (2014). *Report from the commission to the council and the European parliament EU anti-corruption report*. Brussels: Ec.

Fazekas, M. (2015). *The cost of one-party councils: Lack of electoral accountability and public procurement corruption: Report for the electoral reform society*. London: Electoral Reform Society.

FCO. (2011). *The Role of the FCO in UK government: Supplementary written evidence from the foreign and commonwealth office-further to the response of the secretary of state to the committee's seventh report of session 2010–12: (CM 8125)*. London: FCO.

GRECO. (2018). *Fifth evaluation round: Preventing corruption and promoting integrity in central governments (top executive functions) and law enforcement agencies—Evaluation Report United Kingdom, GRECO*.

Gutterman, E. (2017). Poverty, corruption, trade, or terrorism? Strategic framing in the politics of UK anti-bribery compliance. *The British Journal of Politics and International Relations, 19*(1), 152–171.

HM Government. (2014). *UK anti-corruption plan*. London: Home Office and Department for Business, Innovation and Skills.

HM Government. (2017). *United Kingdom anti-corruption strategy 2017-2022*. Crown Copyright.

House of Lords Bribery Act Committee. (2018). *Bribery act 2010: Uncorrected oral evidence*. London: House of Lords.

Law Commission. (2016). *Misconduct in public office. Issues paper 1: The current law*. London: Law Commission. The offence is currently subject to review by the Law Commission.

Levi, M. (2006). The media construction of financial white-collar crimes. *British Journal of Criminology, 46*(6), 1037–1057.

Lord, N. (2014). *Regulating corporate Bribery in International Business: Anti-Corruption in the UK and Germany*. Farnham: Ashgate Publishing.

OECD. (2003). *United Kingdom review of implementation of the convention and 1997 recommendation phase i bis report*. Paris: OECD.

OECD. (2017). *The detection of foreign bribery*. Paris: OECD.

ONS. (2018). *Statistical bulletin: Crime in England and wales: Year ending. June 2018*, Retrieved from: https://www.ons.gov.uk/peoplepopulationandcommunity/crimeandjustice/bulletins/crimeinenglandandwales/yearendingjune2018#main-points.

Saunders, M., Lewis, P., & Thornhill, A. (2009). *Research methods for business students* (Fifth edition). Harlow: Pearson Education Limited.

Transparency International. (2011). *Corruption in the UK: Overview and policy recommendations*. TI UK.

Transparency International. (2018). *Exporting corruption—Progress report 2018: Assessing enforcement of the oecd anti-bribery convention*. Berlin: TI.

UNODC. (2011). *Pilot review programme: United Kingdom. review of the implementation of articles 5, 15, 16, 17, 25, 46 paragraphs 9 and 13, 52 and 53 of the United Nations convention against corruption*. Vienna: UNODC.

Walburg, C. (2015). The measurement of corporate crime, an exercise in futility? In J. van Erp, W. Huisman, & G. Vande Walle with the assistance of Becker, J. (Eds.), *The routledge handbook of white-collar and corporate crime in Europe* (pp. 25–38). London: Routledge.

Tracking the international proceeds of corruption and the challenges of national boundaries and national agencies: the UK example

Jackie Harvey 🄾

ABSTRACT

Corruption is a major inhibitor to economic growth, discouraging to domestic and foreign investment and destabilizing of governments. Unsurprisingly, international attention has intensified in recent years with global initiatives to counter corruption and address the proceeds of corruption. These have placed requirements upon national governments to increase transparency, reducing opportunities for use of the legitimate legal and financial infrastructure to disguise and move the proceeds of corruption. This paper reviews the boundaries at national and agency level that can create challenges for those agencies tasked with investigating and returning the proceeds of corruption to the countries from which they came. The paper considers the mechanisms that the agencies in a returning country—the UK —have at their disposal and whether national policy changes can affect their focus and operation. Specifically it reviews the role and future of the International Corruption Unit of the National Crime Agency.

IMPACT

Following from the highly publicised anti-corruption summit hosted by the Cameron government in 2016, the UK has positioned itself at the forefront of anti-corruption initiatives. Recognizing that corruption is as much an issue for the UK as for victim countries, the UK initiated a unique response model in its International Corruption Unit. However, the proceeds of corruption continue to find their way into the London property market, hence recent initiatives to open up ownership registries. The need to 'respond', shortens timeframes, driving resource allocation towards 'quick wins'. Tracking and recovering the proceeds of corruption that may have moved across multiple jurisdictions is a slow business. The failure to evidence 'hard results' creates an uncertain future for the International Corruption Unit. Yet, its unique contribution is one that should be widely supported by policy makers.

International context

Arguing that corruption, bribery, theft and tax evasion cost some US$1.26 trillion for developing countries per year, the 17 UN Sustainable Development Goals (SDG) announced in 2015 include SDG 16 relating to peace, justice and strong institutions. SDG 16 includes an intention that, by 2030, countries will strengthen the recovery and return of stolen assets (16.4) and substantially reduce corruption and bribery in all their forms (16.5). Such rhetoric at international level is not new. Studies have indicated (see, for example, Transparency International, 2017a, 2017c) the global nature of the problem beyond those states falling victim to corruption and thus corruption should equally be viewed as a problem for the countries where the proceeds of corruption are ultimately invested. Further, effective mechanisms for tracing and recovering stolen assets can raise the potential costs faced by corrupt domestic actors and increase transnational pressures on corrupt states (Hatchard, 2014).

The need for a global response has also been supported by international conventions. Thus the 1997 OECD (Organisation for Economic Development) Convention, which establishes legally-binding standards to criminalize bribery of foreign public officials in international business transactions, talks of 'the identification, freezing, seizure, confiscation and recovery of the proceeds of bribery of foreign public officials'. The United Nations Convention against Corruption (UNCAC) article 57 includes provision for the return of confiscated assets such as embezzled public funds; 57(c) allows the return of such property to its prior legitimate owners or for compensating the victims of the crime. More recently the Financial Action Task Force (FATF—an inter-governmental body setting standards and promoting effective implementation of legal, regulatory and operational measures for combating money laundering, terrorist financing and other related threats to the integrity of the international financial system) has emphasised the role of asset recovery—the return or repatriation of the illicit proceeds, where those proceeds are located in foreign countries.

The rhetoric reflects the view that where funds are moved out of the victim country, then seizure and recovery of such funds is viewed as a 'powerful tool' to inhibit further corrupt activity. However, studies have suggested 'modest' success when it comes to either freezing or, indeed, returning stolen assets (Chêne, 2017). There may be a number of possible explanations for this, including:

- The various channels through which corrupt transactions occur, including the concealing of proceeds, and also of the identity of the real owner of the proceeds.
- Concerns expressed that, on return of such funds to victim countries, they might be further 'misappropriated'. In these circumstances, delicate negotiations have to take place to ring-fence deployment of such funds, usually in support of aid objectives.
- The costs at international level associated with identifying, tracking and recovering the proceeds of corruption—the high-profile international Stolen Asset Recovery initiative (StAR) discloses their funding during 2018 as just short of $1.5 million coming from a multi donor trust fund and from the World Bank global engagement budget (StAR, 2019).

Of particular relevance is the issue of the complexities of the movement of the proceeds of corruption. Efforts to track and recover the proceeds of corruption inevitably involve multiple jurisdictions (and laws) as corrupt funds do not respect borders and the multiplicity of flows and fungibility of money enable proceeds of corruption to become indistinguishable from other (legal) payment flows. In consequence, from any country in the world, illegal proceeds may be exported, 'cleaned' and returned for lifestyle investment or consumption. Further, they can also be exported and held in enabling country accounts or moved via conduit countries (Garcia-Bernardo, Fichtner, Takes, & Heemskerk, 2017) (or directly) into investments held in 'desirable' countries. This then focuses attention on such countries and, given that national legal frameworks have historically been bound by the principle of territoriality (Rider, 1999), what such countries can then do, to deliver at national level, the international rhetoric.

UK context

The UK became a signatory to the OECD Anti-Bribery Convention in 1997, determining at that time, that its existing legal framework would be sufficient to meet the requirements of the convention (OECD, 2001). The UK also ratified the European Council Criminal Law Convention on Corruption that entered into force in 2002 together with the UNCAC in February 2006. In order to address identified deficiencies in its existing legal framework, the UK introduced the Bribery Act (UKBA) in 2010. Prior to this, the UK had three prevention of corruption acts:

- The Public Bodies Corrupt Practices Act 1889 covering public bodies—it was an offence to offer or receive, before or after a specific decision or action (or absence of either), an advantage in favour of the giver.
- The Prevention of Corruption Act 1906 criminalized any benefit to any employee or agent that was done without the knowledge of the employer (the principal).
- The Prevention of Corruption Act 1916 transferred the presumption of guilt to the defendant charged under either Act (corruption presumed) when it is proved that a bribe has been paid or received in relation to a public sector contract.

All three were repealed by the 2010 Act unless the offences were committed prior to its enactment.

In May 2016, the Cameron government hosted a global anti-corruption summit that saw a number of initiatives including the UK committing to the creation of a specialist law enforcement International Anti-Corruption Co-ordination Centre (IACCC), whose membership comprises the UK, Australia, Canada, New Zealand, Singapore and the USA. The IACCC responds to requests from victim states and co-ordinates the investigation 'police to police' across different countries in order to minimize duplication of activity. It is currently (until 2021) hosted by the NCA with funding from the Foreign & Commonwealth Office (FCO) prosperity fund, although member countries provide their own staff. The most recent commitment to anti-corruption domestically and internationally is set out in the Anti-Corruption Strategy 2017–2022. This strategy has, as one of six priorities, 'Greater transparency over who owns and controls companies and other legal entities' (p. 8).

In terms of illicit flows, investigative journalists have exposed their ultimate disposition into the London property market (Transparency International, 2017a, b, c; 2013). This is hardly surprising, as the UK authorities have long recognized the country as one of the more attractive destinations for laundering the proceeds of corruption, particularly with respect to grand corruption (NCA 2016, 2018). The Guardian (2019), provides further details:

In 2017, 160 properties worth over £4bn were purchased by 'high-corruption-risk' individuals. As many as 86,000 properties in England and Wales have been identified as owned by companies incorporated in 'secrecy jurisdictions'—commonly known as tax havens. Between 2004 and 2015, £180m of UK property was subject to criminal investigation as suspected proceeds of corruption; many suspect that is the tip of the iceberg.

Mindful of the importance of international transparency with respect to the real owner of assets, the UK government has committed to launch a public beneficial ownership register for properties owned by overseas companies and legal entities in early 2021 (see https://researchbriefings.parliament.uk/ResearchBriefing/Summary/CBP-8259). Until that point, it will be possible to request access to the UK Land Registry Overseas Companies Ownership Data (OCOD), however, this only records legal ownership. Opening up ownership registers to scrutiny together with the creation of the People with Significant Control Register (PSC) within Companies House is a key part of the UK's delivery of its Anti-Corruption Strategy. It also ensures that it has attended to its own house before drawing attention to deficiencies in other countries.

As a member of the OECD, the UK submits itself for review under the terms of the OECD Anti-Bribery Convention. The most recent review of the UK under the convention was a phase 4 evaluation in 2017, together with the recent follow up report which was produced in March 2019 (OECD, 2019a). This report noted 'Overall, the UK has demonstrated active enforcement of its foreign bribery laws'. However, it also mentioned a 'plethora of agencies' working within the anti-bribery space, although noting that the SFO is the 'lead agency' (OECD, 2019b). This same point was made by Transparency International (2011) who listed the range of different agencies, in addition to the Serious Fraud Office (SFO), including multiple police forces and central government agencies, all of which included anti-corruption within their mandate. The focus of this paper is on one specific agency among the plethora—the International Corruption Unit (ICU)—which is the main co-ordinator of the UK's external corruption recovery effort.

Focus and methodology

There are two reasons for studying the ICU. One concerns its national level responsibility for delivering the UK's response to the international rhetoric relating to the proceeds of corruption and how far this also reflects FATF's proposals in support of confiscation (FATF Recommendations 4 and 38) and a framework for ongoing work on asset recovery in terms of, at national level, implementing:

> 6(b): ... mechanisms to co-ordinate asset tracing and financial investigations with a view to ensuring that such efforts are not impeded by regionalised or fragmented systems, or competing local priorities;

> 6(c): ... specialised units or dedicated personnel with training in specialised financial investigation techniques. Such personnel should be adequately resourced and trained (FATF, 2012).

The second reason is its unique model of funding, and hence accountability to more than one 'paymaster', within the UK domestic context. The duality of paymasters can give rise to two sets of organizational objectives possibly responding to different agendas and potentially requiring different emphasis and alignment of resources. Such organizational boundaries may give rise to unintended consequences. In light of this, the paper seeks to understand the history and operations of that unit, the scope of the ICU's remit and any challenges it has faced in operationalizing the international dimension of the UK's counter-corruption agenda.

The methodology was qualitative. Following an initial review of the academic literature and of official government documents that provided background and lines of enquiry, semi-structured interviews were carried out in January 2019 with two key respondents. Given the small sample size, no claims are made regarding generalizability from the output of this work; rather, its contribution lies in providing a more detailed understanding of one important agency from the perspective of two 'knowledgeable insiders'. The respondent interviews were carried out separately and lasted 1 hour 20 minutes (ICU) and 45 minutes (from the Department for International Development: DFID). The interviewers (two) both took notes only. After the interviews, the notes were transcribed and agreed between the two interviewers. An interim draft of the paper was shared with the respondents to check for factual accuracy. What is presented here is the collective output from those interviews in relation to the history and operations of the unit. In addition, this paper offers comment on the main discussion points that emerged from both interviews, together with reflection on their implications for the future operation of this important agency.

The development of the ICU

DFID and engaging with corruption

The first review of the UK's record in counter-corruption as part of its accession to the OECD Anti-Bribery Convention (OECD, 2001) was highly critical of the UK's effort in this arena (U4, 2011). Subsequently, the Africa All-Party Parliamentary Group (Africa APPG) report on the UK and Corruption in Africa (2006) noted two issues. (The Africa APPG is an externally-supported cross-party group of UK MPs and peers which studies and reports on African led-development agendas through positive relationships between the UK and African countries.) First, in terms of the UK policing UK companies abroad, 'the fragmentation of the investigatory and prosecuting authorities' was making enforcement difficult. Indeed, no British individual or organization has yet been prosecuted for bribery of a foreign public official, indicating that enforcement is an area of particular weakness (where) the primary obstacles faced by the police in mounting investigations into cases of bribery overseas are lack of funding and expertise' (Africa APPG, 2006). Second, inquiries by the UK Financial Services Authority into the Abacha case—where the former President of Nigeria between 1993 and 1998, family and associates stole up to $5 billion—found that 'in excess of US$1.3 billion linked to Abacha went through 42 bank accounts in the UK between 1996 and 2000 ... more than 20% of the estimated total stolen by Abacha and his entourage' (Africa APPG, 2006). At the same time, however, issues were identified about powers to freeze such assets, where responsibility lay among the 'several agencies involved in preventing, investigating, acting on and enforcing money laundering issues', and the absence of 'earmarked resources to work on repatriating the proceeds of foreign corruption' (Africa APPG, 2006).

The U4 report (2011) noted, as reinforced by one of our respondents, that early on, DFID recognized that if it wished to improve this situation it would have to contribute to the funding of anti-corruption effort. Certainly, DFID had been concerned about corruption in aid-recipient countries but as one of our respondents shared with us, in 2001 Clare Short (then secretary of state for international development) also saw corruption as a two-way exercise for DFID. As a donor agency, they were focused on corruption in the developing countries that were recipients of UK aid. However, they were aware of the transfer of assets out of those countries to the UK as a 'haven'. The approach was to retain the focus of DFID work on the developing countries but at the same time, they saw the need to tackle two key areas. First, other Whitehall departments seen to be 'allowing' companies to pay bribes to officials and politically-exposed persons (PEPs) in order to secure lucrative contracts. Such action being viewed as a necessary business expense (BBC, 2006). (PEPs are individuals whose prominent position in public life may make them vulnerable to corruption. The definition extends to immediate family members and known close associates. The full definition of a PEP in the UK context is set out in the UK's Money Laundering, Terrorist Financing and Transfer of Funds [Information on the Payer] Regulations 2017.) The second area of focus was the financial system itself, which was seen as responsible for 'accepting' the proceeds of corruption.

One of our respondents referred to the OECD review discussed in the previous section as having 'pilloried' the government and that it was DFID who used this sharp criticism as a lever to lobby the Home Office to change the bribery legislation, eventually leading to the UKBA. At the same time, the UK Treasury was persuaded of the reputational damage to the UK financial system when they were contacted by Swiss prosecutors investigating Abacha and informed that the funds had passed undetected via London. Another respondent separately noted that when full details of the Abacha case emerged providing evidence that proceeds of corruption had clearly ended up in London, law enforcement was deemed 'woeful'. They further noted that DFID (and Clare Short) felt that the UK could not tell other countries how to improve if the UK was 'laundering all the cash'.

Post 9/11, a paragraph was included in the Anti-terrorism, Crime and Security Act 2001 to extend the provisions to foreign public officials and this was viewed as having provided assurance to DFID that it could pursue foreign bribery and proceeds of corruption flows. Further, the passage of this act gave it confidence to ask overseas missions—DFID has country officers in its countries of operation—to share knowledge and intelligence. The problem they faced at the time was, however, that information would be passed by the police to the police force where the headquarters of the UK company was located. Results were, therefore, dependent on that force's resourcing and level of interest. There was no other way to deal with international cases of bribery unless they were within the remit of the SFO.

Rather than depend on the vagaries of the local police force, DFID concluded there was a need for centralization. DFID's choices were limited—they could try to get a line in the police strategy to raise the profile of anti-corruption or they could provide dedicated capacity and fund a central national base. Having received legal clearance that DFID could use aid funds in such anti-corruption efforts, in 2006, DFID agreed to fund dedicated units within both the Metropolitan Police (the Proceeds of Corruption Unit—POCU), and the City of London Police (the Overseas Anti-Corruption Unit—OACU). From 2010, the Serious Organised Crime Agency (SOCA) and from 2013 the National Crime Agency (NCA), hosted a DFID funded anti-bribery unit (Mason, 2013). This unit (the International Corruption Intelligence Unit—ICIC) was able to gather and share intelligence from its in-country international liaison officers providing additional information to both POCU and OACU to support intelligence generated from the UK Financial Intelligence Unit's Suspicious Activity Reports (SARs) that had been reported by designated financial services institutions as possible money-laundering offences. POCU (demand side) was located in Scotland Yard and had 20 officers dedicated to investigating money-laundering offences (James Ibori, former governor of Nigeria's Delta State, who was jailed for 13 years in the UK in 2012 was referred to by our correspondents as the 'poster case' for POCU) looking at the illicit flows side within the UK jurisdiction. On the anti-bribery (supply side) it created OACU with some 20 officers tasked with prosecutions under the (old) bribery legislation and was well renowned for successful case management achieving 14 or 15 convictions. As DFID does not directly fund prosecutions (Mason, 2013, p. 201), from 2012 it funded a small unit (two lawyers) in the Crown Prosecution Service (CPS) to ensure asset recovery in developing countries was serviced. By 2013, the operational arrangement has been as shown in Figure 1.

Consolidating the focus

Our respondents both mentioned two major international events as being influential in changing the UK's approach towards corruption:

- The 2011 Arab Spring saw capital move from Egypt to the UK and criticism of POCU by the Egyptian authorities for its inability to respond positively to their enquiries.
- The 2014 crisis in Ukraine which saw the proceeds of corruption flow into the UK.

Our respondents were aware that anti-corruption did not really fall within the remit of SOCA and this was seen to contribute to the rationale for the refocused NCA, with the broader remit beyond organized crime. This wider remit included investigating the 'Ukrainian money' and the formation of the Kleptocracy Investigation Unit (KIU). At the same time, it was noted by our respondents that the lack of intelligence and information sharing was becoming a problem despite the earlier attempts to address this. With ICIC in SOCA, which also housed a significant intelligence resource developed out of the NCIS, both the London police forces were having to ask SOCA for intelligence relevant to their work on anti-corruption. Our respondents talked of 'in-fighting and back-biting' between SOCA (where intelligence had priority) and the Metropolitan Police (with a focus on prosecution) over co-ordination and co-operation, as well as formal issues of information-sharing.

DFID felt it necessary to ensure intelligence-based work by the two police-located units (albeit with an ODA—Official Development Assistance—focus) to move away from the 'lottery of what was coming up through the system'. They were also aware that the

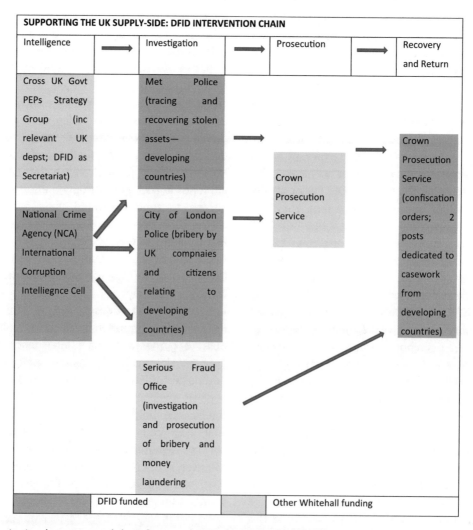

Figure 1. Organizational structure and the influence of DFID. Source: Mason (2013).

tidy demarcation between POCU and OACU did not hold in practice as the division between illicit flow and bribery was artificial. In consequence, they were aware of the need to consider merging the two entities. As with many things, in the event, the changes did not emerge from policy but from practical need. The immediate push came from the sale of Scotland Yard in 2014 which, simply, meant that POCU needed to find a new physical location. NCA was willing to host POCU; DFID indicated it would be willing to fund provided an identified key individual seen as important to the success of its anti-corruption agenda would also move from the police to the NCA.

A unified ICU—'the multi-agency team will be operated by the National Crime Agency and be the central point for investigating international corruption in the UK' (DFID, 2015)—was proposed within the NCA from May/June 2015 and identified as one of the commitments within the 2014 UK Anti-Corruption Plan (HM Government, 2014). This unit was to bring together the work of the different anti-corruption units from the Metropolitan and City of London police together with ICIC and the KIU, with input from the continuing CPS-based legal team. The establishment of the ICU meant that, with most of POCU having come over to ICU on secondment, they and the rest of the POCU joined the NCA along with the ICIC and the KIU which were already part of the NCA. OACU staff, however, did not join the ICU instead, they dealt with legacy cases and all new cases were picked up by the ICU. This was because of terms and conditions of service implications. This largely related to retirement; the NCA is classed for employment purposes as a government department and not a police force where the latter allowed retirement on full pension from age 50 onward.

ICU: case sources

As noted in the OECD review (2019), the ICU's focus:

> … is to investigate money laundering in the UK resulting from grand corruption overseas; Trace and recover the proceeds of international grand corruption; Support foreign law enforcement agencies with international anti-corruption investigations; Investigate bribery involving UK-based entities which have an international element and other cross-border bribery with a UK nexus.

The review draws attention to the funding model of the agency that defines the geographical focus of its operations to ODA developing countries. It also notes that the ICU had a staff of 45 persons, of whom 30 were frontline investigators, as well as officials from the SFO and the Financial Conduct Authority (FCA—the regulator for financial services firms and financial

markets in the UK) to facilitate the flow of information between these different agencies. Staff are supported in financial investigator training and bribery investigations training through a bespoke course run by the City of London Police Economic Crime Academy.

The ICU currently numbers 50 full-time and seconded staff split roughly equally between bribery and money laundering, and financial sanctions evasion, with defined responsibilities for:

- Money laundering in the UK resulting from corruption of high-ranking officials overseas.
- Bribery involving UK–based companies or nationals which has an international element.
- Cross-border bribery where there is a link to the UK.
- Tracing and recovering the proceeds of international corruption.
- Supporting HM Treasury with the enforcement of financial sanctions.
- Supporting foreign law enforcement agencies with international anti-corruption investigations.
- Engaging with government and business to reduce the UK's exposure to the proceeds of corruption.
- Working with businesses to support increased compliance with the UKBA.

As already mentioned, there were multiple agencies operating in the counter-corruption space. Separate to the creation of OACU and POCU and already in existence was the SFO. Our respondents noted that the SFO will only take on cases that are 'complex or significant in some way'. Further, in line with the Roskill model (combining prosecutors and accountants/financial investigators within a single team), they had the ability to mobilize large teams in pursuit of 'reactive investigations against high profile organizations'. The NCA's ICU, on the other hand, was described as being closer to the police approach involving covert techniques and crime in action often with 'companies or individuals no-one has ever heard of'. The FCO will report cases to SFO; if SFO determine it does not fall within their remit the cases are passed to the ICU. In undertaking their investigations, the ICU relies on the international liaison officer network (and a flexible foreign travel budget funded by DFID) made up of NCA officers attached to embassies overseas.

In addition to the specific FCO referrals from the SFO, ICU cases are sourced both reactively and proactively with a number having been developed from SARs. Both respondents noted that POCU brought with it one big case that is still ongoing. In addition, there are some law enforcement referrals from regulators including the FCA, as well as referrals from NCA intelligence. The NCA has a range of covert intelligence collection techniques that it can deploy in pursuit of its crime reduction mandate; these are available for use by ICU but, importantly given its remit, this work is not funded by DFID.

ICU: overseas case acceptance

Current decisions about which cases to take are determined by whether they are dealing with an ODA country, and perhaps more importantly, in relation to location of evidence and whether it can be secured. One of the problems for the UK in terms of its approach to anti-corruption and asset recovery, and indeed responses to mutual legal assistance requests from other jurisdictions (MLAs), is the requirement to meet its own evidential standards. Transparency International (2013) discussed this issue 'from a UK perspective, ideally, the origin state should demonstrate—across the party-political spectrum—a sustained commitment to domestic conviction of the accused and ensure that the convicted are not acquitted at a later date'. A concern for law enforcement authorities in the UK is their uncertainty over how much reliance can be placed on convictions in third countries, whether they comply with UK human rights standards, or whether a prosecution within another country will be overturned.

There is a further dimension of uncertainty where evidence presented to support action is in respect to a PEP, but that it arose as a result of regime change. Transparency International go on to report some of the requirements placed upon the victim country to avoid 'fishing expeditions'. They have to have identified assets held by the corrupt party and be able to set out their requests clearly in English employing UK common law legal terminology. Their request should provide evidence of suspicion to a UK law enforcement standard that would secure a conviction and all within a timeframe that would facilitate asset tracing. In the view of Transparency International (2013) 'These expectations for the origin state law enforcement are, in the majority of cases, likely to be unrealistic'.

Our respondents noted that in the early days of the ICU 'there were no requests for MLA coming in as there was no infrastructure in place to respond to them'. They observed that MLAs only really work in countries where the judiciary and police functions are independent. Further, that submission of MLAs is something of an 'art form' and 'tricky' in a number of countries as they are essentially 'a 20th century response to a globalized world'. Echoing some of the comments by Transparency International, there are compliance requirements that have to be met before the requests find their way to the relevant part of the government for action. Within the UK, the relevant part is the Home Office, in other countries it is the attorney general. Our respondent noted that the

navigation from the landing point to the ICU can take some time, echoing the observations above, there is great concern over legality of request and possible human rights issues. They are wary of 'fishing expeditions' with requests under UNCAC to 'give us what you have' rather than prior sharing 'police to police' of available intelligence gathered from registries, companies house and the like in a way that would enable the requesting police force to frame a request so that it will be accepted.

ICU: resourcing

There is no doubt that high-level support and interest was critical in the establishment and continuing support for internationally focused anti-corruption activity in the UK. The ICU is, however, vulnerable to the inevitable short-term time horizon of politicians and the consequent need 'to do something' bringing out additional initiatives, changing focus and moving resource to other priorities. One of the challenges that the unit faces is that it is dependent on two different ministries for funding and thus has to demonstrate value for money against potentially different targets. Our ICU respondent shared that their ability to take on work is constrained by capacity. The ICU currently has a caseload of 23 cases running and with current resourcing levels, they can handle in the region of 23–25. They are hopeful that they will be able to obtain three to four charging decisions (based on there being sufficient evidence to provide a realistic prospect of conviction) from the CPS's Serious Fraud Division in 2020. It was noted that some cases had been dropped as 'they were not going anywhere' and that these, together with non-pursued leads and opportunities would continue to be held on the NCA case database.

The ICU is physically located within the NCA and is jointly funded by the NCA (20%) and by DFID (80%). but could face problems in arguing for maintenance of budget. This is because of the major operational investment required for investigations (including travel to potentially multiple countries) and to secure co-operation with different police forces. Against this is set the potentially small number of arrests/assets recovered to date. There are challenges in the length of time it takes to investigate cases, this figure was not disclosed to us, although we were informed that the OECD average is seven years 'cradle-to-grave from allegation to completion of prosecution'. It was also noted that the international architecture is geared (legitimately) to minimizing tax for large companies and data protections, all systems that can be mirrored by illicit finance making the detection of bribery cases much harder. Payments are moved with multiple points of change and in these circumstances, the payments are unlikely to picked up in SARs.

The ICU report on a quarterly basis to DFID against a 'log-frame' that captures activity in which it has been engaged. This focuses on the nature of their casework and performance against milestones, for example in how many countries have they open cases. It is interesting that the ICU consider themselves independent of DFID despite relying on them for funding. We were informed that the ICU has funding from DFID through to 2020.

ICU: the future

A final area of discussion is the changing environment within which the ICU works and how far this may affect its approach and resourcing. Within the NCA, the new National Economic Crime Centre (NECC) is intended to co-ordinate and task the UK's response to economic crime, and with its partners (who include the SFO, the FCA and the CPS) jointly identify and prioritize the most appropriate type of investigations, whether criminal, civil or regulatory to ensure maximum impact in addressing the illicit finance that funds and enables all forms of serious and organized crime. While this includes 'abusing UK financial services' there may be some concern that the international dimension of corruption might lose attention.

At the same time, other changes internally to the wider NCA may not recognize the role of the ICU and the purpose of DFID funding. Our respondents noted that NCA has just reorganized its structure to be on a threat-based horizontal model, with investigators and intelligence resource being 'poolable' to be more responsive, with the ICU now being 'an oddity in that it is a very specialist function' and 'one of the silos'. Such restructuring may well meet organizational objectives for the NCA, but it may have future unintended consequences in terms of the impact on the ICU and its role as part of the UK's response to the international anti-corruption rhetoric.

Conclusions

There is no argument that corruption is a major global phenomenon, negatively impacting on the development of a wide number of countries, disproportionality impacting the poor. Attempts to measure the effectiveness of initiatives to reduce corruption have been hampered by its hidden nature. International efforts, particularly by the FATF, to increase transparency of the financial system are proving positive; as too is recognition that corruption is as much a problem for countries where the funds are invested as for the victim states. The focus on identifying and recovering the proceeds of corruption that may have moved across multiple jurisdictions requires high levels of co-operation between and across agencies—not only internationally but also within national boundaries determined by legal standards and frameworks.

Prior to the setting up of the ICU in 2015 it was, according to one of our respondents, 'inconceivable that such an operation could exist' due to the existence of established agency boundaries and specialisms. The relationship between the ICU and DFID was innovative as a solution to tackling overseas corruption. Wide political support was crucial in the setting up of the ICU in 2015 and the commitment from DFID for an extension to its funding to the end of 2020 is positive. However, given the time taken to investigate highly complex cases, the unit is in danger of running into the challenges imposed by short political and organizational time frames and the need to be able to demonstrate not only action but also value for money. The IACCC may prove helpful as an organization that can 'join the dots' and generate future referrals for the ICU (one having already been secured) but there remains a risk that the ICU's consolidation and competences may be diluted or derailed as competing priorities take precedence for resourcing and other priorities.

ORCID

Jackie Harvey ⓘ http://orcid.org/0000-0003-0048-0924

References

Africa APPG. (2006). *The other side of the coin: The UK and corruption in Africa*. Africa All Party Parliamentary Group.

BBC. (2006). *Former minister admits Saudi bribes on Newsnight*. Press Office, 16th June. Retrieved from http://www.bbc.co.uk/pressoffice/pressreleases/stories/2006/06_june/16/saudi.shtml (Accessed 20 December 19).

Chêne, M. (2017). *International support to anti-money laundering and asset recovery: Success stories expert answer U4 anti-corruption resource centre, 9 March*. Retrieved from https://knowledgehub.transparency.org/assets/uploads/helpdesk/Money-laundering-and-asset-recovery-success-stories.pdf (Accessed 03 May 19).

DFID. (2015). *New crime unit to investigate corruption affecting developing countries*. Press release 9th August. Retrieved from https://www.gov.uk/government/news/new-crime-unit-to-investigate-corruption-affecting-developing-countries (Accessed 03 May 19).

FATF. (2012). *Best practices on confiscation (Recommendations 4 And 38) and a Framework for Ongoing Work on Asset Recovery* (OECD/FATF).

Garcia-Bernardo, J., Fichtner, J., Takes, F., & Heemskerk, E. (2017). Uncovering offshore financial centers: Conduits and sinks in the global corporate ownership network nature scientific reports 7.

Hatchard, J. (2014). *Combating corruption: Legal approaches to supporting good governance and integrity in Africa*. Edward Elgar.

HM Government (2017) *United Kingdom anti-corruption strategy 2017-2022* Retrieved from https://assets.publis

hing.service.gov.uk/government/uploads/system/uploads/attachment_data/file/667221/6_3323_Anti-Corruption_Strategy_WEB.pdf (Accessed 03 May 19)

HM Government. (2014). *UK anti-corruption plan, HM government*, December, Retrieved from https://assets.publishing.service.gov.uk/government/uploads/system/uploads/attachment_data/file/388894/UKantiCorruptionPlan.pdf (Accessed 03 May 19).

Mason, P. (2013). Being Janus: A donor agency's approach to asset recovery. In G. Fenner-Zinkernagel, C. Monteith, & P. Gomes Pereira (Eds.), *Emerging trends in asset recovery*. Basel Institute on Governance's International Centre for Asset Recovery. P. 201. (Accessed 03 May 19).

OECD. (2001). *United Kingdom review of implementation of the convention and 1997 recommendation* (Retrieved from http://www.oecd.org/unitedkingdom/2498215.pdf). (Accessed 03 May 19).

OECD. (2019a). Retrieved from http://www.oecd.org/corruption/anti-bribery/UK-Phase-4-Report-ENG.pdf (Accessed 03 May 19).

OECD. (2019b). *Implementing the OECD anti-bribery convention phase 4 two-year follow-up report: United Kingdom.*

Rider, B. (1999), The Crusade against money laundering—Time to think. *European Journal Law Reform*, 4, 501—527

Stolen Asset Recovery Initiative (STAR). (2019). *Annual report 2018*. International Bank for Reconstruction and Development /The World Bank.

The Guardian. (2019). *UK property register 'needed urgently' to stop money laundering* Owen Bowcott Legal affairs correspondent 2th May, Retrieved from https://www.theguardian.com/business/2019/may/20/uk-foreign-property-register-needed-urgently-money-laundering (Accessed 20 December 19).

Transparency International. (2011). *Corruption in the UK: Overview and policy recommendations*. Transparency International.

Transparency International. (2013, December). *Closing down the safe havens ending impunity for corrupt individuals by seizing and recovering their assets in the UK*. Transparency International.

Transparency international. (2017a, March). *Doors wide open| corruption and real estate in four key markets*. Transparency International.

Transparency International. (2017b). *Faulty Towers: understanding the impact of overseas corruption on the London Property market.*

Transparency International. (2017c, November). *Hiding in plain sight, how UK companies are used to launder the proceeds of corruption*. Transparency International.

U4. (2011). *Making development assistance work at home: DFIDs approach to clamping down on international bribery and money laundering in the UK*. Practice Insight, No 5 (Chr. Michelson Institute). p.5.

Estate agents' perspectives of anti-money laundering compliance—four key issues in the UK property market

Ilaria Zavoli ⓘ and Colin King ⓘ

ABSTRACT

In recent years, money laundering in the property market has come under scrutiny across the world, attracting significant attention from governments, regulators, policy-makers, NGOs, academics and others. However, there remain gaps in knowledge, which is particularly important given practical difficulties in the implementation of anti-money laundering (AML) obligations. This article offers new insights into such implementation in the context of the UK AML regime and the real estate sector. The authors analyse four important issues relating to the UK AML obligations: customer due diligence (CDD); reporting suspicion; training requirements; and letting (rental) agents.

IMPACT

Money laundering in the property market is a significant problem across the globe, yet there is limited understanding of how anti-money laundering (AML) rules are implemented in practice. This article draws on semi-structured interviews with estate agents and compliance officials in the UK to explore this often-overlooked perspective. Interviewees take AML rules seriously, however they are often faced with significant difficulties in practice. This article shows that—in the eyes of interviewees—governments and law enforcement do not understand how the sector operates. Failure to deal with this lack of understanding means that the problem of money laundering via property sales and rentals will continue.

Money laundering in the property market has attracted significant attention in recent years in a number of countries. In the UK, it has been widely suggested that corrupt capital is being used to buy property, often using offshore companies with non-transparent ownership (Transparency International UK, 2017). Indeed, in 2016, the then prime minister stated that the UK should 'clean up our property market and show that there is no home for the corrupt in Britain' (Cameron, 2016). In Canada, an expert panel was established in British Columbia in 2018 following concerns about money laundering in the real estate sector (Maloney, Somerville, & Unger, 2019). Subsequently, it was announced that there would be a public inquiry into money laundering in the British Columbian economy (Office of the Premier, 2019). Similar concerns about money laundering in the property market are evident in other jurisdictions, for example Australia (Austrac, 2015), Hong Kong (Estate Agents Authority, 2018), Singapore (Council for Estate Agents, 2017), and the USA (FinCEN, 2019). Money laundering in the property market is also attracting attention at EU level (Remeur, 2019). Clearly, this issue is now on the table for governments across the globe. The aim of this article is to offer new insights into the implementation of anti-money laundering (AML) efforts in the property market in the UK by drawing upon inside views from those on the ground: (real) estate agents and compliance officials. The research for this article included 17 semi-structured interviews with estate agents and compliance officials (responsible for AML, either in-house or on a consultancy basis). The interviews were conducted in person and via Skype/phone over a period of five months between November 2017 and March 2018.

The total amount of money laundered in a particular year, or in a particular sector, is unknown. Despite various efforts claiming to measure the extent of money laundering (UNODC, 2011), it is impossible to (accurately) do so (Levi, Reuter, & Halliday, 2018; Alldridge, 2016, pp. 15–16). Indeed, the lack of reliable figures is now explicitly recognized at a policy level. For example, a House of Commons briefing paper acknowledges: 'by its very nature it is difficult to quantify what the scale of the problem is. The proceeds are hidden and often only come to light in the event of prosecutions' (Edmonds, 2018, p. 4). In addition, the Financial Action Task Force (FATF) acknowledges difficulties with various 'estimates' on money laundering:

> … estimates should be treated with caution. They are intended to give an estimate of the magnitude of money laundering. Due to the illegal nature of the transactions, precise statistics are not available and it is therefore impossible to produce a definitive estimate of

the amount of money that is globally laundered every year. The FATF therefore does not publish any figures in this regard (FATF, 2019).

Of course, it would be desirable to have significant knowledge in this area, not least given various proclamations as to the scale of the problem or the threat posed by money laundering. In relation to the property market, concerns have been expressed that money laundering is a threat to the economy, society, and political stability (Transparency International UK, 2015, p. 6; see also van Duyne, Harvey, & Gelemerova, 2018, p. 225 for a critical perspective).

So, what approaches have been adopted to explore this area? Some studies have attempted to examine money laundering in the property market by means of 'red flags' or proxies (Unger, 2013, p. 663). Others have built on this approach by using data mining (Ritzen, 2011). Other studies have focused on suspicious activities within the sector (FinCEN, 2006). Unsurprisingly, there are significant barriers to accurately reflecting the scale of money laundering in the property market. As Petrus van Duyne colourfully puts it: 'our knowledge in this area can be likened to that of an archaeologist who has to describe the economy of a Stone Age settlement on the basis of a few pottery fragments, a spear point and half a jawbone' (van Duyne, 1994, p. 62). Given such methodological difficulties, our approach in this article is quite different. Rather than attempting the impossible (i.e. quantifying the extent of money laundering), or addressing the complexities of AML rules and obligations across the property sector in response to this perceived threat, we take a qualitative approach to explore one specific aspect: how the real estate sector in the UK is responding to its role and obligations. The focus is on four key issues that arose in our interviews: customer due diligence (CDD); reporting suspicion; training requirements; and letting (rental) agents.

Customer due diligence

Interestingly, there were varying perspectives on the role of estate agents in doing AML, with one interviewee contending that 'it is an absolutely pointless exercise' (interview 12), and another suggesting that 'we should have an obligation as a first responder if you like, we can be a very good source of information' (interview 6). However, there was more agreement with regards to the costs of compliance and the burdens that this brings for estate agencies (for example interviews 1; 9; 14). Unsurprisingly, the CDD requirements in the Money Laundering, Terrorist Financing and Transfer of Funds (Information on the Payer) Regulations 2017

(hereafter 'ML Regs') sparked significant discussion. In particular, there were criticisms that such checks involved a doubling-up or even a tripling-up of work. In other words, banks and/or solicitors will often have done the same checks already (for example interviews 4; 11; 12; 13). Thus, estate agents repeating the same CDD checks was described as 'overkill' (interview 4). Many noted that estate agents do not handle money, so should not be under any AML obligations (for example interviews 4; 10; 11; 12; 13). Others, however, noted that different actors in a transaction (i.e. banks, solicitors, estate agents) offer different eyes on a transaction and will be better placed to spot particular discrepancies and to ask for an explanation (for example interview 5).

A recurring theme was that CDD checks are being done simply 'to tick a box' (interview 9) or that systems and processes are in place 'to cover their own backsides' (interview 3). Others spoke about doing the minimum that is required to be compliant (for example interview 14). Interviewee 1 said that CDD 'must go right the way through from cradle to grave' and suggested using a traffic-light system, i.e. if everything is right, then it is green; if there is something wrong, but not a criminal offence (for example a form has not been fully filled in correctly), then it is amber; and, if something is a 'fail' under the ML Regs, then it is a red.

Interviewees identified certain areas where CDD checks can be problematic, for example where a foreign buyer is involved and there is no face-to-face contact (for example interview 1). Another difficulty is where documentation might be fake—again, this arises particularly where there are foreign clients and the documentation is in a language other than English (for example interviews 6; 8). A further difficulty relates to the source of funds (for example interview 3). There can also be issues where there is to be a quick exchange of contracts; in such instances, it might not be possible to do AML checks properly (for example interview 11). The use of internet searches and social media was noted as a means of finding further information on people if necessary (for example interviews 3; 12).

An issue raised by many participants was reliance on checks done by others. It was recognized by some that this is permitted under the current law, but that the estate agent remains liable if the required checks have not been properly carried out (for example interview 10). Some stated that they do not rely upon CDD checks by others on that basis (for example interview 8). It was noted that if an estate agent asks too many questions, then a person trying to launder money through that agency can simply withdraw from the purchase with no consequence (for example interview 9).

Reporting suspicion

It is axiomatic that deciding to file a suspicious activity report (SAR) is a significant one. It was recognized that estate agents often 'want to be on the safe side' (interview 10), to cover themselves against future action (for example interview 1). While these were recurring issues, a small number did stress that they only submit a SAR to the UK Financial Intelligence Unit where there is genuine concern (for example interview 8). There was some concern about the 'tipping-off' offence (for example interview 5), i.e. the offence of making a disclosure likely to prejudice a money laundering investigation being undertaken by law enforcement authorities. Interestingly, some noted the difficulties in maintaining confidentiality as to whether or not a report is being made. For example, while the only people who ought to know are the individual agent who reports their suspicion to the money laundering reporting officer (MLRO) and the MLRO, the reality is otherwise. As interviewee 3 stated: this type of business 'mainly works in open plan offices as a team and therefore the whole team is going to know about the situation, particularly in the market now where we're fairly low volume of transactions so everybody is going to know, and therefore the risk of something getting out is far greater than it perhaps would be indicated by the regulations'. Interviewee 3 went on to say that the ML Regs 'weren't written by someone who operates in the front-line of estate agents'.

The SAR system itself came in for criticism. It was noted that the system was designed for the banking sector and does not transfer well to other sectors (for example interview 1). There were also criticisms as to the registration process and the process of actually filing a report. For example, an estate agent will have a 'gateway' with HMRC, but if they want to file a SAR they have to do that through the NCA portal, which is not linked to the HMRC gateway. As interviewee 14 stated: 'it's more complicated than it need be ... If I want to tip off the state, that I think something's dodgy going on, why not make it easy for me to do so?' Moreover, there were concerns that the support from the state could be improved (for example interview 6). A final point to note here is whether estate agents should receive any updates on SARs submitted. At the moment, there is no individualized feedback on specific SARs. Thus, it was suggested by participants that they do not know whether their reports are useful or not. Interviewee 11 said that 'it would be helpful to have feedback, to have pointers as to what to look for, because we are very much in the dark. We can't even talk to anyone else about it because of tipping off concerns'. Others, however, stated that they had no interest in any follow-up information (for example interview 15).

Training requirements

While estate agents are required by the ML Regs to undergo regular AML training, the regulations leave room for interpretation on how, and how often, estate agents should do this. Our research revealed inconsistencies and variations between agencies. Generally, participants were aware of the need to obtain proper training on AML and of its importance in providing them with adequate understanding and tools to prevent and detect suspicious activities. For instance, interviewee 7: 'we go to as many anti-money laundering courses as we can here, read as much as we can ... to make sure we know what we can'; and interviewee 12: 'we try and be as thorough as we can be'. However, estate agents can find it difficult to fulfil this obligation in practice due to additional factors (for example lack of financial resources and precise guidelines). In particular, a difference exists between large and small agencies (for example interviews 13; 14) as to the financial resources available to them for effective training. Some agencies struggle to find enough funds to cover training costs: 'it is ... your smaller, independent [agency] that has not got access to those resources' (interview 13).

A further issue relates to differences in the quality of the training provided, given that some agencies do it in-house (for example interviews 1; 7; 12; 14; 15), whereas others prefer to outsource it (for example interviews 3; 13). Furthermore, the collection of informative material through websites (such as that of HMRC and of the National Association of Estate Agents) was highlighted as useful support. For instance, some interviewees recognized webinars as a valuable option for training purposes (for example interview 15).

A final point worth noting in relation to training relates, again, to variations across different agencies. There is no prescribed approach under the ML Regs. Thus, it is unsurprising that different choices have been made. Some said that the training should be done three or four times a year (for example interview 1); others thought that this should be done every 12 months (for example interview 13).

Letting (rental) agents

In 2018, the 5th EU AML Directive brought letting agents within the AML regime where a monthly rent is over 10,000 euro (EU Directive, 2018, Art. 1). This directive is due to be implemented in the UK in 2020 (HM Treasury, 2019, p. 4). While letting agents were not initially part of the research focus, it quickly became apparent that this sector is one of concern for (sales) estate agents. Indeed, participants identified various means by which money could be laundered through lettings. For instance, this can be done by disguising the identity of the tenant and renting a property to a person who is both the owner and the tenant (for example interview 3). Another method is to have an upfront payment for the rent of a property followed by a withdrawal from the transaction with a reimbursement of the sum paid (for example interviews 3; 6). Another approach is to invest criminal money into many cheap properties and then sub-let them (for example interviews 6; 9; 15), allowing money launderers to integrate their capital into numerous properties and being less likely to come to the attention of AML authorities (for example interview 9).

Participants expressed significant concern as to the lack of regulation of letting agents' activities. For some, this issue came as a surprise (for example interviews 1; 10) and it was widely considered a gap in the AML legislative framework (for example interview 15). Indeed, some interviewees argued that there is no difference between sales and lettings for AML purposes because 'there is just as much money laundering that goes on through lettings' (interview 3), and 'it is easier to do money laundering through lettings than it is through sales' (interview 3). Moreover, leaving letting agents out of AML provisions might prompt inconsistencies in the sector because 'there is going to be less checks and balances on letting than there is on the sale environment' (interview 3). Others suggested that the lack of regulation might be due to the nature of the letting business: 'letting is a much faster business and you would be spending days doing AML on all your tenants' (interview 12).

A further point to mention here is the sense of different legislative treatment concerning letting agents compared to (sales) estate agents. Some participants thought that the legislation does not cover letting agents because 'Letting agents are not estate agents' (interview 15). Indeed, a person banned from estate agency can, nonetheless, operate as a letting agent (for example interview 3). A further, significant distinction between letting agents and sales agents is that the former receive money in their accounts from the tenant, whereas the latter generally do not handle money (for example interviews 10; 12; 13).

Conclusions

This article has outlined some key issues in the implementation of AML legislation in the UK real estate sector. The aim of this article is not to critique the AML regime or its application in practice, rather it is simply intended to present the (often) overlooked perspective of those involved in the buying and selling of domestic property in the UK. It was clear from the interviews that participants would like to see a more tailored approach to AML obligations—one that takes account

of sector-specific circumstances and the lived reality of AML in the real estate sector. Instead, however, the current regime demonstrates a gap between policy-makers' and others' perceptions and the reality of how the sector operates; failure to consider this gap is likely to lead to continued lingering discontent in the sector.

Acknowledgement

This research was supported by a British Academy 'Tackling International Challenges' research grant: IC160112.

Disclosure statement

No potential conflict of interest was reported by the author(s).

ORCID

Ilaria Zavoli ⓘ http://orcid.org/0000-0002-0162-1103
Colin King ⓘ http://orcid.org/0000-0001-8537-5853

REFERENCES

Alldridge, P. (2016). *What went wrong with money laundering law?* Palgrave.

Austrac. (2015). *Strategic analysis brief: Money laundering through real estate.* Austrac.

Cameron, D. (2016, May 12). *Anti-corruption summit 2016: PM's closing remarks.* <https://www.gov.uk/government/speeches/anti-corruption-summit-2016-pms-closing-remarks> (last accessed 14 August 2019).

Council for Estate Agencies. (2017, October 16). *Practice circular 03-17: Checklists for estate agents and salespersons on prevention of money laundering and countering the financing of terrorism.*

Edmonds, T. (2018). *Money laundering law. Briefing paper number 2592.* House of Commons Library.

Estate Agents Authority. (2018, February 21). *Press release— EAA issues guidelines on compliance of anti-money laundering and counter-terrorist financing requirements for the estate agency sector.*

EU Directive. (2018). *2018/843 of the EU parliament and the council of 30 May 2018 amending directive (EU) 2015/849 on the prevention of the use of the financial system for the purposes of money laundering or terrorist financing and amending Directives 2009/138/EC and 2013/36/EU.*

FATF. (2019). *How much money is laundered per year?* Available at: <http://www.fatf-gafi.org/faq/moneylaundering/> (last accessed 14 August 2019).

Financial Crimes Enforcement Network (FinCEN). (2019, May 15). *News release—FinCEN reissues real estate geographic targeting orders for 12 metropolitan areas.*

Financial Crimes Enforcement Network (FinCEN). (2006). *Money laundering in the commercial real estate industry: An assessment based upon suspicious activity report filing analysis.* Office of Regulatory Analysis.

HM Treasury. (2019, April). *Transposition of the fifth money laundering directive: Consultation.*

Levi, M., Reuter, P., & Halliday, T. (2018). Can the AML system be evaluated without better data? *69 Crime, Law and Social Change, 307–328.*

Maloney, M., Somerville, T., & Unger, B. (2019, March 31). *Combating money laundering in BC real estate.*

Money Laundering, Terrorist Financing and Transfer of Funds (Information on the Payer) Regulations. (2017). S.I. 2017/692.

Office of the Premier. (2019, May 15). *News release—Government to hold public inquiry into money laundering.*

Remeur, C. (2019). *Understanding money laundering through real estate transactions*. European Parliamentary Research Service, PE 633.154 - February 2019.

Ritzen, L. (2011). Mapping "infected" real estate property. *Journal of Money Laundering Control, 14*(3), 239–253.

Transparency International UK. (2015). *Corruption on your doorstep: How corrupt capital is used to buy property in the UK*. TI-UK.

Transparency International UK. (2017). *Faulty towers: Understanding the impact of overseas corruption on the London Property Market*. TI-UK.

Unger, B. (2013). Can money laundering decrease? *Public Finance Review, 41*(5), 658–676.

UNODC. (2011, October). *Estimating illicit financial flows resulting from drug trafficking and other transnational organized crimes. Research report.*

van Duyne, P. (1994). Money-laundering: Estimates in Fog. *Journal of Financial Crime, 2*(1), 58–74.

van Duyne, P., Harvey, J., & Gelemerova, L. (2018). *The critical handbook of money laundering: Policy, analysis and myths.* Palgrave.

Forensic accounting services in English local government and the counter-fraud agenda

Mohd Hadafi Sahdan, Christopher J. Cowton and Julie E. Drake

ABSTRACT

Fraud is a growing challenge for English local government, yet the resources and support local authorities (LAs) have available to prevent, detect and investigate it are limited. Forensic accounting services (FAS) provided by external specialist private sector firms, particularly those undertaking mandatory external audit, might be one solution. Research reported in this paper suggests, however, that existing English LA users are not all convinced. Nevertheless, better awareness and understanding of what FAS have to offer, perhaps through case studies of successful implementation, would be a valuable contribution to helping local government enhance its counter-fraud capabilities and make informed decisions about how best to meet the increasingly complex fraud challenge.

IMPACT

Forensic accounting services (FAS) provided by specialist private sector firms might help local government meet the growing challenge of fraud, especially digital fraud perpetrated by organized criminal groups, at a time when in-house capacity and expertise are severely constrained. However, a questionnaire survey suggests that usage by English local authorities is currently limited, and it also found mixed levels of satisfaction amongst those that had used FAS. Nevertheless, better awareness of what FAS have to offer, perhaps through case studies of successful implementation, would help local authorities make more informed decisions about when and how to use FAS.

Introduction

English local authorities (LAs), like public sector organizations in many countries, are experiencing an increasing tension between the pressure for good quality administration and cost cutting (Hood & Dixon, 2016). At the same time, they face a growing threat from fraud, which is on the rise in the UK (Levi, Doig, Gundur, Wall, & Williams, 2017), fuelled in particular by the twin sources of digital technology and organized crime (Levi, 2017), alongside increased contracting out of services. Addressing fraud in LAs has been subject to two iterations of a strategy to address fraud in local government, in 2011 and 2016. The second of these—*Fighting Fraud & Corruption Locally: The Local Government Counter Fraud and Corruption Strategy, 2016–2019* (henceforth *Fighting Fraud*) (CIPFA, 2016)—is adamant about the need for a 'tougher response' (p. 6). It speaks of the need to 'transform' counter-fraud and corruption performance, requiring innovation to 'keep ahead of fraudsters' (CIPFA, 2016, p. 4). However, the abolition of the Audit Commission in 2015 (Tonkiss & Skelcher, 2015) and other changes have probably weakened the ability of LAs to tackle fraud. The 'flawed architecture' of counter-fraud entities in the UK (Button, 2011) and the lack of 'coherence, co-ordination, common approaches and a commitment of resources' (Doig, 2018, p. 147) mean that the rhetoric and recommendations of the various strategies that have been proposed over the years fall short of providing the conditions for actual operational implementation to take place on the ground (Doig, 2018).

Whatever the precise cost of fraud to LAs (see Levi & Burrows, 2008) and the problematic strategic support context (Button, 2011), spending money on the development of capacity and expertise to combat the threat of fraud might ordinarily be a sound business decision; 'invest to save', as *Fighting Fraud* (CIPFA, 2016, p. 5) terms it. However, in periods of austerity for public services it is difficult to increase, or even maintain, expenditure on any area of activity, especially when it is not a core one mandated by central government (CIPFA, 2016). New spending commitments, such as taking on more counter-fraud staff, are difficult to justify in a cash-constrained context. Nevertheless, in such an environment there might still exist opportunities for LAs to buy-in specialist forensic accounting services (FAS) from external specialist private sector firms, including those providing mandatory external audit services, which offer an increasingly recognized set of specialized skills (Hegazy, Sangster, & Kotb, 2017). This could be on an *ad hoc* basis when budgets allow (for example when the end of the financial year is in sight), not only to produce future savings but also, perhaps, to increase the likelihood of recovering monies fraudulently obtained. However, the option of using FAS does not receive any attention in *Fighting Fraud* or any other literature that addresses the fraud challenge faced by LAs. Drawing on the findings of a questionnaire survey, this paper examines the scope for LAs to use externally-sourced FAS as one element of their response to the counter-fraud agenda.

The paper is structured as follows. First, the issues facing LAs and the key features of current thinking about fraud, including FAS, are outlined. Second, the empirical research method for the survey is briefly described. Third, the findings of the survey are presented. The final section offers conclusions and implications.

The fraud challenge for LAs

Fraud

Fraud and corruption cost local government dear, taking many forms and occurring across a wide range of operations and sometimes targeted across multiple LAs. CIPFA, a professional association which is responsible for the training and accreditation of the majority of LA internal auditors, as well as providing a range of toolkits and services to LAs, undertakes an annual fraud survey. Its 2018 survey (CIPFA, 2018) indicates that:

- The total estimated value of fraud detected or prevented by LAs in 2017/18 was £302 million, £34 million less than the previous year's total.
- The number of frauds detected or prevented rose to 80,000 from the 75,000 cases found in 2016/17.
- The number of serious or organized crime cases doubled to 56 in 2017/18.
- The amount lost to business rates fraud increased significantly to £10.4 million in 2017/18 from £4.3 million in 2016/17.
- 'Blue Badge' fraud (relating to parking for disabled users) also increased by £3 million to an estimated value of £7.3 million for cases prevented/detected in 2017/18.
- The three greatest areas of perceived fraud risk are procurement, council tax single person discount (SPD) and adult social care.
- The four main types of fraud (by volume) that affect LAs are council tax, housing, Blue Badge fraud and business rates.

Indeed, it was the first iteration of the strategy for LAs—the 2011 Local Government Fraud Strategy—that warned that both opportunity and pressure were being intensified at local level:

Radical changes are underway to how local services are to be delivered. The next few years will see major reforms to the welfare system, policing and local government. The change of emphasis from local government being a provider to a commissioner of services changes the risk profile of fraud, as well as the control environment in which risk is managed. More arm's length delivery of services by third parties in the voluntary and not-for-profit sector and personal control of social care budgets, for example, will mean that more public money is entrusted to more actors, whilst the controls the local authority previously exercised are removed or reduced. Without new safeguards, preventing, detecting and investigating fraud will become more difficult. All of these changes are happening against a backdrop of depressed economic activity in which the general fraud risk tends to increase. Harder times tend to lead to an increased motivation to defraud by some clients, suppliers and employees who are feeling the squeeze (National Fraud Authority, 2011, p. 6).

Context and change

The concerns raised by the 2011 strategy came at a time of significant change. The localism agenda has had a significant impact in terms of driving down local government expenditure and requiring changes to the level and delivery of functions and services: 'local government reforms … emphasise local responsibility, the abolition of targets and reduction of planning powers. They cut budgets substantially and encourage private providers to contract for the whole range of local services' (Taylor-Gooby & Stoker, 2011, p. 9). The changes have increased subcontracting to the private sector, both for-profit and not-for-profit organizations, of many services traditionally provided by LAs themselves—a development that is typical of New Public Management (Alonso, Clifton, & Díaz-Fuentes, 2013). Procurement fraud is a major consequential risk:

It has been estimated that procurement fraud costs local government in the region of £876 million a year making it the largest single area of financial loss to fraud in local government. This is fraud—and other related criminal activity—that occurs in connection with the local authority supply chain. It occurs throughout the procurement cycle and is particularly prevalent in the contract management phase (LGA, 2015, p. 2).

Another major factor, which is increasing the number and size of fraud attacks on LAs, is digital technology. Many types of cybercrime are relatively easy to commit, but difficult to address (May & Bhardwa, 2018). Cyberfraud is a growing problem. Digital technology not only creates new points of vulnerability but, also, due to its rapidly-evolving nature, places great technical demands on in-house staff, who are hard-pressed to remain up to date. Moreover, organized crime has not been slow to take advantage of the opportunities that the shift to digital offers (May

& Bhardwa, 2018) and, as previously noted, the number of serious or organized crime cases doubled to 56 in 2017/18 according to CIPFA's annual fraud survey. Furthermore, although not all cyberfraud is across borders (Levi et al., 2017), international criminal groups have become seriously involved. Not only is there likely to be an imbalance between the sophistication of the criminal groups and the resources of the target, but the criminals are able to exploit the diffuseness and opaqueness of the Internet, as well as legislative and enforcement weaknesses in different jurisdictions, to evade punishment.

Nevertheless, although there can be practical challenges, both the 2011 and 2016 fraud strategies for local government promote the principle of addressing fraud *from cradle to grave*—prevent, detect, investigate and recover. The former argued:

> *Enforcement covers the investigation, punishment and recovery of assets and funds. Punishing fraudsters acts as a powerful deterrent. Where fraud is discovered the full range of sanctions should be deployed, including civil, disciplinary and criminal action. Effective enforcement requires that local authority investigators have the professional skills (operating within a professional code), appropriate powers and access to specialist support to undertake their duties* (National Fraud Authority, 2011, p. 27).

Much of that specialist support used to come from the Audit Commission—the public body which included the District Audit Service (DAS). The external audit regime began in 1844 (see Coombs & Jenkins, 2002), with national oversight and monitoring introduced by the Local Government Finance Act 1982 through the establishment of the Audit Commission. It took a continuing and proactive stance on the need to identify and address financial loss as well as ensure appropriate governance arrangements (see Public Audit Forum, 2001). It assumed responsibility for the existing statutory public external audit arrangements, which became its audit practice. DAS provided mandatory external audit services to LAs using in-house and contracted private sector firms, setting the standards for audits which included specific audit days to assess each council's arrangements to prevent and detect fraud and corruption.

The Audit Commission issued public interest reports (PIR; legally-privileged reports which commented on unacceptable or potentially illegal conduct). It funded and facilitated the Good Conduct and Counter Fraud Network, which promoted anti-fraud work among all council external auditors, including private sector firms. It was a designated body for whistleblowing under the Public Interest Disclosure Act (PIDA). It had mandated powers for the collection and publication of annual fraud and corruption data (published in the annual *Protecting the Public Purse* reports). It used its

powers to set up and lead a national annual data-mining and matching initiative—the National Fraud Initiative (NFI)—from information provided by both public and private sectors, whose results were sent as 'risk' matches to be reviewed as potential frauds, overpayments and errors in public expenditure. It issued guidance on areas such as governance, probity and working with private and voluntary sector partners, the outcomes of which it reviewed and monitored, often with prescriptive assessments of what should be done. Furthermore, its comprehensive performance assessment was intended to ensure robust procedures were delivered within what it termed the softer characteristics of leadership and standards.

Although the curtailment of the Audit Commission's roles had been signalled, as part of the government's localism agenda, in a 2008 Conservative Party paper which proposed a narrower focus in ensuring 'the propriety of local government's spending and to investigate complaints' (Conservative Party, 2008, p. 18), the 'decision to close the Commission outright was unanticipated' (Sandford, 2016, p. 15). Analysis of the closure announcement suggests that the nature and presentation of the decision to wind up the Audit Commission by 2014 quickly shifted the discourse from the Audit Commission's abolition to 'the low politics of technical debate about the new audit system' (Tonkiss & Skelcher, 2015, p. 875; see also Timmins & Gash, 2014), albeit offset by concerns about the lack of attention to future ownership of its anti-fraud responsibilities. These included warnings from the Association of Chartered Certified Accountants (ACCA) that different functions could risk 'potentially being fragmented across different bodies in an unco-ordinated and inconsistent way' (House of Commons Communities and Local Government Committee, 2011, Ev93) and those of the Committee on Standards in Public Life about the inherent robustness of the new arrangements (see Lawton & Macaulay, 2013, p. 78).

Under the Local Audit and Accountability Act 2014, councils may appoint their own external auditors, after a transitional period where contracts had been bid for and awarded to private sector firms by the Audit Commission. The contracts are managed through the Public Sector Audit Appointments Limited (PSAA), an independent company limited by guarantee incorporated by the Local Government Association in 2014. PSAA continued to be responsible for appointing most councils' auditors for the audit of the accounts for 2017/18 and, it was hoped—at least by the DCLG (Department for Communities and Local Government)—that councils would continue the existing arrangements from 2018/19 onward rather than secure their own arrangements.

Responses

This new context had been anticipated by the 2011 strategy: 'local authorities and central government will need to look to design new arrangements for the new conditions. That will most likely require the greater sharing of counter-fraud and audit resources, the creation of a new control framework and new institutional arrangements, building on the existing shared counter fraud infrastructure' (National Fraud Authority, 2011, p. 18). For LAs, the fraud challenge comprises not only mitigating the threat through strategies for prevention, but also how to respond through detection, investigation and recovery—especially with the reduction in policing resource for fraud (see Gannon & Doig, 2010). One response has been counter-fraud services (CFS), which originated within the NHS, though they have often been reported as under-resourced and 'more susceptible to cuts in their budgets' (Button, 2011, p. 254). However an LA's response to fraud is organized, it may comprise many possible elements, including developing an anti-fraud culture, understanding and measuring fraud risk, and managing and learning from incidents (see Samociuk, Iyer, & Doody, 2010). Various activities or stages are involved. As *Fighting Fraud* notes, to acknowledge the existence of fraud is a critical first step; and understanding fraud risks and committing support and resource are vital to a robust anti-fraud response. Steps need to be taken to prevent fraud, but with determined and ingenious fraudsters and an ever-evolving context, attempts must also be taken to detect fraud, perhaps by making better use of information technology. Once the possibility of a fraud has been identified, it is important to investigate and, if appropriate, to pursue the fraudsters with a view to recovering losses and seeking the perpetrators' punishment, in collaboration with the police—if they are willing to commit resources to this.

Thus, fraud may be tackled by in-house CFS in collaboration with the internal audit function, which itself may be provided in-house or outsourced in some way. However, LAs report that their staff do not always have the skills or training to tackle fraud (CIPFA, 2016) and, in a period of constrained resources, it is difficult for local government to build this capacity. Nor may it rely, as it did with the Audit Commission, on the capacity and terms of reference of the external auditor (see National Audit Office, 2019a; Sandford, 2019); at a time when the risk profiles of many LAs have increased, so have their concerns about the contribution of external audit (see National Audit Office, 2019b). Nevertheless, many of the firms that provide external audit to local government offer additional forensic accounting services (FAS), usually in a separate team. For example, the 'Big Four' audit firms list 'Forensic and financial crime team' (Deloitte), 'Forensic services' (PwC), 'Forensic and integrity services' (EY) and 'Forensic' (KPMG) on their websites. FAS could be—if affordable—a valuable source of further help to local government in tackling fraud, providing extra capacity and additional skills.

The role of FAS

The precise definition of FAS is still a matter for debate and, indeed, tends to depend on context (Huber & DiGabriele, 2014) and on a particular author's purpose and perspective, but Van Akkeren and Buckby's description is a good starting point:

> To investigate, resolve and minimise fraud, forensic accounting practitioners are consulted for their specific skills and expertise. Their work includes investigating financial inconsistencies, analysing evidence, interviewing potential suspects and preparing expert reports in their attempt to identify the person or persons responsible for the crime (Van Akkeren & Buckby, 2017, p. 384).

While the latter element of Van Akkeren and Buckby's description emphasizes detection and investigation, the idea of minimizing fraud also points to the role that forensic accountants can play in preventing fraud, as well as recovery. It should also be noted, as Apostolou and Crumbley (2005) highlight, that there are important differences between the role of a forensic accountant and an auditor: an auditor determines compliance with auditing standards and considers the possibility of fraud, whereas a forensic accountant has a single-minded focus on fraud and similar irregularities, as contracted with the client. Moreover, while the authors above use the term 'forensic *accounting*' (and we will continue to do so, in line with common practice), it is a multidimensional field of activity, less focused on accounting than might be suggested by its name. FAS teams tend to comprise individuals with complementary skills rather than a common base of specialist skills (Hegazy et al., 2017). Although the field in the UK is dominated by professionally-qualified accountants and many accounting firms offer FAS, such firms also employ staff with other qualifications and skills. Furthermore, some law firms also offer FAS, and there exist specialist firms too.

Forensic accounting is a growing area of practice that has come to the fore since the first years of the 21st century (Hegazy et al., 2017; Chew, 2017). The public sector in general is recognized as a major client for FAS providers (Hegazy et al., 2017). LAs certainly tend to be experienced in using consultancy services in general (Kipping & Saint-Martin, 2005), and the use of FAS might have a role to play in helping them meet the increasing threat of fraud. FAS can not only increase general capacity at critical times (perhaps when a major fraud is under investigation), but also provide expertise that is not possessed in-house. This paper therefore seeks to answer the following research questions:

- What is the current position regarding the use of forensic accounting services by local government?
- What are the prospects for the future use of forensic accounting services by local government?

These questions were addressed as part of a questionnaire survey of English LAs. The design and conduct of the survey are explained in the next section.

Survey design

The questionnaire was designed to address the objectives of a research framework developed from the academic and practitioner literature. Four of the questionnaire's 10 sections are utilized here: local authority characteristics; use of, and satisfaction with, FAS; perceptions about FAS; and intention to use FAS in the future. A pre-test of the questionnaire was given to academics (one with experience as a local authority finance director) and postgraduate students, and refined accordingly. A sample of 50 internal auditors, chief executives and internal auditors was used to pilot the questionnaire in April 2014. The responses received did not necessitate significant changes to the questionnaire and so are included in the final sample for analysis.

The survey was sent, with a subsequent reminder, from June to November 2014, to all 353 LAs in England. FAS were defined as 'services provided by an external party such as accounting firms that applies specialized investigative skills and techniques in detecting any existing fraud and proactively setting up fraud prevention systems'. In order to increase the response rate, the questionnaire was sent to a named person where possible. Since all LAs have an internal audit function, the head of internal audit was targeted. However, the name of only a third of heads of internal audit could be found on

websites (119 out of 353, or 33.7%), so questionnaires were also sent to chief executives and directors of finance, whose details were generally easier to discover. The composition of the sample and responses is shown in Table 1.

The response rates from different sorts of LA were broadly comparable, except that county councils were more responsive. There is no particular reason to suppose that their answers will be systematically different, but the difference in response rates should be noted. As might be expected, responses were most frequently from internal auditors (65.5% of responses), followed by directors of finance (16.5%) and CFS managers (11.5%). The latter category had not been directly addressed, so they must have been passed the questionnaire by someone else; there are a few similar cases in the 'other' response category in Table 1.

Sending to three categories increased the probability of obtaining a response from a particular LA but, because anonymity was promised to respondents in order to encourage their response and to discourage socially desirable response bias, it is not possible to know the extent to which multiple responses were received. The response rate therefore needs to be expressed as a possible range rather than a single figure. On the one hand, the overall return of all questionnaires was 13.1% (139/1059), but the response rate from internal auditors amounted to 25.8% (91/139). Although a higher response rate would have been welcome, this represents a very respectable outcome for a survey of this type. Nevertheless, any conclusions and recommendations will bear in mind that responses were received from a minority of LAs—about a quarter at most.

SURVEY FINDINGS

Overview

As background, the questionnaire asked about the provision of internal audit and CFS. Table 2 summarizes the responses.

Table 2 shows that three-fifths of internal audit services are maintained wholly in-house. However,

Table 1. Sample and responses.

Type of local authority	Number	Question-naires sent	Internal auditor (IA)	Counter-fraud manager	Director of finance	Other	Total	Overall (%)	IA (%)
English county	27	81	14	3	2	0	19	23.5	51.9
Metropolitan borough	36	108	11	0	1	0	12	11.1	30.6
English unitary	56	168	14	4	1	3	22	13.1	25.0
London borough	33	99	7	1	2	2	12	12.1	21.2
English district	201	603	45	8	17	4	74	12.3	22.4
Total	**353**	**1,059**	**91**	**16**	**23**	**9**	**139**	**13.1**	**25.8**

(Column group headers: "Completed questionnaires received" spans Internal auditor (IA), Counter-fraud manager, Director of finance, Other, Total; "Estimates of response rate[1]" spans Overall (%), IA (%).)

[1] Estimates of response rate: Overall = total responses divided by number of questionnaires sent; IA = number of responses received from internal auditors divided by the number of local authorities.

Table 2. Provision of internal audit and counter-fraud services.

	Number of LAs	%
Current provision of internal audit services		
Maintained in-house	82	59.0
Joint/shared services	27	19.4
Partially outsourced	8	5.8
Fully outsourced	22	15.8
Total	139	100.0
Current provision of in-house counter-fraud services (CFS)		
Has in-house CFS	98	70.5
No in-house CFS	41	29.5
Total	135	100.0

Table 4. Types of FAS used.

Type of forensic accounting service	Used in past year
Fraud risk management	8
Fraud detection	7
Asset tracing and recovery	7
Fraud investigations	7
Digital forensic including data mining, data imaging and recovery	6
Reviewing current counter-fraud procedures	5
Fraud prevention system	5
Fraud training	5
Assessing and improving internal control system	5
Developing regulatory compliance strategies	4
Litigation support and expert witness	2
Damage or loss quantification	2
Prosecution cases	2

this means that two-fifths involve some sort of external provision, which suggests that a significant proportion of LAs are comfortable with working with outsiders in this area—which might be of relevance to the provision of FAS. Dedicated CFS exist in more than two-thirds of LAs, but that still leaves almost a third that do not have such services and thus might be ripe for using FAS—although perhaps they are not taking fraud as seriously. Moreover, in the vast majority of cases where there is a CFS team, fewer than 10 members of staff are employed, which suggests limited capacity and is consistent with Button's (2011) comment that there tends to be at most a 'handful' of staff.

Experience of using FAS

Respondents were asked whether their LA had experience of using FAS. Table 3 summarizes the findings.

Table 3 shows that less than a fifth (18.7%) of the total respondents used FAS. English county councils and London borough councils were the most likely to use FAS. The relatively high usage by LBCs (but still only a third of them) might reflect a response to the number of public housing sector and benefit claimants—both high risk areas for fraud—or the capital's international links and hence accessibility to overseas criminals. Overall, usage of FAS does not appear to be widespread, especially if users are thought more likely to respond to the survey than non-users. Nevertheless, it is interesting to see what users do.

Respondents were asked what different types of FAS had been used within the last year. Complementing the earlier definitional discussion, the list of options was constructed from a desk-based review of FAS provider websites. Table 4 presents the responses of the 26 FAS users.

As can be seen from Table 4, no one service dominates, and none is used by more than a third of users—or less than 7% of the total respondents. There is a mix of interventions, from the strategic or preventative, through to investigation and prosecution. Some of these services are likely to complement what LAs, especially those with their own in-house CFS, can do to some extent themselves, while others are likely to bring more specialist input (for example training, digital work or expert witness).

Finally, it should be noted that FAS were sourced from a variety of providers. The 26 respondents who reported using FAS can be broken down as follows: eight used only Big Four accounting firms (KPMG, PwC, Deloitte and EY); 18 used only other firms; and four used both. Thus, the Big Four do not dominate the market.

To sum up, it appears that usage of FAS, whether provided by Big Four accounting firms or others, is not widespread. Various services are used, but no particular area of activity dominates.

However, while the level of usage is currently relatively low, the questionnaire attempted to gain an insight into possible future developments, given that FAS appear generally to be increasing in importance.

The future of FAS in LAs

In their study of forensic accounting providers, Hegazy et al. (2017) found that the market was expected to grow. This might suggest that the usage of FAS by LAs will build on the position indicated by the survey findings reported so far. However, any increase will likely be influenced by the intentions and attitudes of

Table 3. The use of FAS by LAs.

	English county		Metropolitan borough		English unitary		London borough		English district		Total	
	n	%	n	%	n	%	n	%	n	%	n	%
FAS	7	36.8	2	16.7	3	13.6	4	33.3	10	13.5	26	18.7
None	12	63.2	10	83.3	19	86.4	8	66.7	64	86.5	113	81.3
Total	19	100	12	100	22	100	12	100	74	100	139	100

Table 5. Future intentions regarding the use of FAS.

Future intention	Definite intent to use	Some intent to use	Don't know	Little intent to use	No intent to use	Total
LAs that have used FAS	2	13	7	3	1	26
LAs that have not used FAS	28	57	21	6	1	113
Total number of respondents	30	70	28	9	2	139

present users—currently only a minority of LAs. In the questionnaire survey, users of FAS were asked about whether they thought their LA would continue to do so. The first line of Table 5 summarizes their views.

Four respondents believed they had little or no intention of continuing to use FAS going forward, and only a small majority had some intention to do so (15/26 = 57.7%). Of course, this might just reflect a genuine lack of confidence in predicting the future, but it is not unreasonable to suggest that if the use of FAS had proved a resounding success, with users becoming convinced of their value and the likelihood of being able to make a convincing business case, some clearer indications of intention to use again might have been anticipated. Responses ($N =$ 26) to a question about satisfaction with FAS are illuminating in this respect; Table 6 summarizes the responses.

A basic Likert scale is not a precise measurement of the benefits, or net benefits, derived from the use of FAS, but again the findings suggest a lack of enthusiasm, at least towards Big Four firms, with only half of users being at least satisfied. This probably helps to account for the limited intention towards further use of FAS in Table 5. Although the numbers are small, it is interesting to note that in three of the four cases where definite dissatisfaction was registered, 'very dissatisfied' was the response, which suggests that some expectations had been severely disappointed (although whether these were unrealistic or they considered they had been led to expect more than they received, is unknown).

However, respondents whose LA had not used FAS were also asked about their intentions to do so in the future. Their responses were more favourable than those who had used FAS, with a significant majority (85/113 = 75.2%) indicating some possible intention to use (see Table 5). Although there might have been an element of socially desirable response bias on the part of respondents who had not used FAS, there are thus indications that there might be future growth in demand for FAS, which will need to happen if they are going to make a major contribution to helping LAs meet the fraud challenge.

Further insight is provided by Table 7, which summarizes the responses from all 139 respondents to questions about awareness, knowledge of benefits, knowledge of risks, and overall perception of FAS.

Overview

The 2016 *Fighting Fraud* strategy noted that its 2011 iteration had argued that a 'vital element of any effective counter-fraud strategy is the ability of the organization to call on competent, professionally accredited counter-fraud specialists trained to the highest possible professional standards to investigate suspected fraud' and yet it also noted that since 2011:

> Many local authority practitioners reported that the capacity to tackle fraud and corruption was likely to be reduced, or had already been reduced, as a result of austerity-related local authority funding reductions. In many cases practitioners also reported that the skilled investigation resource transferred to the Department for Work and Pensions Single Fraud Investigation Service (SFIS) had not been replaced, and some stated that after the SFIS transfer their authority would have no fraud team (CIPFA, 2016, p. 15).

In such circumstances, externally-sourced FAS could fill that gap, providing both extra capacity and specialist skills. While current external auditors tend to provide a basic, minimal service when compared to what the Audit Commission did, many of those firms also offer FAS—although they might not represent the best value for money and, notwithstanding the attempt to limit the scope of audit in relation to fraud, might find themselves facing a conflict of interest if involved in the investigation of fraud. However, with their knowledge of a particular LA's systems, they might be well placed to offer additional advice in relation to the prevention of fraud, which is often overlooked (Moore & Martin, 2017). Thus, whether provided by their existing auditors, another accounting firm, a law firm or a specialist FAS firm, FAS would seem to offer LAs a valuable complement to their existing, but limited and highly pressured, in-house capabilities. This is particularly the case in relation to digital fraud,

Table 6. Satisfaction with FAS.

Type of provider	Satisfaction level					
	Very dissatisfied	Dissatisfied	Uncertain	Satisfied	Very satisfied	Total
Big Four accounting firms (KPMG, PwC, Deloitte and EY)	1	1	3	3	2	10
Other providers	2	0	4	8	6	20
Total	3	1	7	10	8	30

Table 7. Overview of attitudes to FAS.

Statements	Extent of agreement (% of respondents)					
	Strongly disagree	Disagree	Neutral	Agree	Strongly agree	Total positive ('agree' or 'strongly agree')
My local authority is aware of the role of forensic accounting services in fraud detection and prevention	1.4	20.9	24.5	48.9	4.3	53.2
My local authority is knowledgeable about the benefits of using forensic accounting services	2.9	29.5	31.7	34.5	1.4	35.9
My local authority is knowledgeable about the risks of using forensic accounting services	2.9	29.5	36.7	29.5	1.4	30.9
Overall, my local authority's perception of forensic accounting services is positive	0.7	12.2	64.0	19.4	3.6	23.0

which is evolving rapidly and requires specialist skills, especially when the fraud is perpetrated by organized criminal groups.

However, Table 7 suggests that less than a quarter of LAs are really positive about FAS. To some extent, this reflects actual knowledge of FAS, acquired through experience in a limited proportion of cases, but it is striking that almost half of respondents do not agree that their LA is aware of the role of FAS in fraud detection and protection. (This might reflect, or be reflected in, the lack of consideration of FAS in either the 2011 or 2016 strategies.) Thus, while there is evidence of some usage of FAS in the local government sector, it is not unreasonable to suggest that the possible contribution of FAS is probably not something that has been widely considered and thought through. This perhaps reflects the funding pressure that local government is under, but both prevention and recovery offer the prospect of financial benefit, suggesting that carefully targeted and managed use of FAS might have something to offer.

Conclusions

Local government is reported to be under-resourced to tackle fraud. Staff have been lost; internal audit is no longer mandated to have fraud as part of planned work; and external auditors, who took over the Audit Commission's audit responsibilities (Tonkiss & Skelcher, 2015), are said to be uninterested in fraud and probity (Doig, 2018)—all at a time when fraud risks are increasing. The *Fighting Fraud* report (CIPFA, 2016) recognizes that fraud is a major challenge for LAs and makes some useful recommendations, but it does not consider the use of externally-sourced forensic accounting services (FAS), which have seen significant growth and promotion internationally in recent years (Hegazy et al., 2017). In the light of resources and embedded competence falling far short of national rhetoric about tackling public sector fraud in the UK for many years (Doig, 2018), this omission merited empirical examination.

Although the research data has some limitations, it provides a useful first snapshot of the situation. Indeed, following on from Hegazy et al. (2017), which claims to be the first study of FAS in the UK, but with

a focus on the provider side, our paper appears to be the first to examine systematically the use of FAS in *any* sector in the UK. To summarize the answers to the research questions on the current and future use of forensic accounting services by English LAs:

- There is some use of FAS by LAs, but—especially if users are more likely to respond to a survey than non-users—it is currently not widespread. Moreover, previous users seem, overall, to be somewhat ambivalent about the value of FAS. On the other hand, many non-users are probably unaware of what is available and how FAS might complement their existing capabilities.
- There does not seem to be a significant core of enthusiastic pioneers or early adopters that will champion the rapid take-up of FAS across the sector—which would presumably be needed in a period of austerity. While there is some evidence of interest in using FAS in the future, growth is likely to be held back by both limited awareness of FAS and continued financial constraints. This might mean that some 'invest to save' opportunities are missed.

Nevertheless, LAs face a significant threat of fraud, which—because of digital technology and organized crime—is likely to increase in both size and complexity. As *Fighting Fraud* emphasizes, a tougher response is required. The report also refers to the need for innovation, to keep ahead of fraudsters. However, it does not mention externally sourced FAS provided by professionals who are likely to have specialist expertise that is not necessarily possessed by LAs' in-house CFS team (if there is one) or internal audit staff. It would therefore seem unwise to dismiss the use of outsourced FAS *tout court*; they have something to offer, as appears to have been discovered by some LAs, according to our findings. In particular, the digital threat is likely to require particular expertise.

Indeed, the survey indicated that FAS had not been consciously rejected by many non-users. Perhaps what is needed now is awareness raising across the sector. There is some suggestion that one set of FAS providers—the private sector external auditors that took over from the Audit Commission—are not particularly interested, for whatever reason, in taking on wider roles in relation to fraud and probity (Doig, 2018), so they might not be a strong influence on awareness. However, the general rise in the profile of FAS is likely to have an effect (Hegazy et al., 2017). What would probably be most effective, though, is the development of a more detailed understanding of the ways in which specific FAS can be profitably employed by LAs; case studies or other accounts of successful implementation would seem to have a role to play here. This would help other LAs to come to a sensible decision about the use of FAS and, where appropriate, to make a satisfactory business case. However, it should be noted that making a business case is currently an area of challenge undermining the 'invest to save' approach to combatting fraud advocated in *Fighting Fraud*. It is especially difficult in an era of financial conformance (Ferry & Eckersley, 2015), when the principal focus is on spending alone. Nevertheless, if *Fighting Fraud* is updated or superseded in time, perhaps it could explicitly consider the case for various types of FAS and, if possible, include reports of successful implementation. While we do not advocate a wholesale rush to use externally-sourced FAS, greater awareness and a better understanding of what they have to offer would surely be a valuable contribution to helping LAs enhance their counter-fraud armoury and make informed decisions of how best to meet the increasingly complex fraud challenge.

Disclosure statement

No potential conflict of interest was reported by the author(s).

References

Alonso, J. M., Clifton, J., & Díaz-Fuentes, D. (2013). Did new public management matter? An empirical analysis of the outsourcing and decentralization effects on public sector size. *Public Management Review*, 17(5), 643–660.

Apostolou, N., & Crumbley, D. L. (2005). The expanding role of the forensic accountant. *The Forensic Examiner*, 3(9), 39–43.

Button, M. (2011). Fraud investigation and the "flawed architecture" of counter fraud entities in the united kingdom. *International Journal of Law, Crime and Justice*, 39(4), 249–265.

Chew, B.-L. (Ed.). (2017). *Forensic accounting and finance: Principles and practice*. Kogan Page.

CIPFA. (2016). *Fighting fraud & corruption locally: The local government counter fraud and corruption strategy, 2016-2019* (CIPFA). Retrieved from https://assets.publishing.service.gov.uk/government/uploads/system/uploads/attachment_data/file/503657/Fighting_fraud_and_corruption_locally_strategy.pdf

CIPFA. (2018). *CIPFA fraud and corruption tracker survey summary report 2018* (CIPFA). Retrieved from file:///C:/Users/sbuscjc/Downloads/CIPFA%20Fraud%20and%20Corruption%20Tracker%20Summary%20Report%202018.pdf

Conservative Party. (2008). *Control shift: Returning power to local communities*. Policy Green paper No. 9 (The Conservative Party).

Coombs, H. M., & Jenkins, D. E. (2002). *Public sector financial management*. Third Edition Thomson Learning.

Doig, A. (2018). Fraud: From national strategies to practice on the ground—A regional case study. *Public Money & Management*, 38(2), 147–156.

Ferry, L., & Eckersley, P. (2015). Budgeting and governing for deficit reduction in the UK public sector: act three 'accountability and audit arrangements'. *Public Money &Management*, 35(3), 203–210.

Gannon, R., & Doig, A. (2010). Ducking the answer? Fraud strategies and police resources. *Policing and Society*, 20(1), 39–60.

Hegazy, S., Sangster, A., & Kotb, A. (2017). Mapping forensic accounting in the UK. *Journal of International Accounting, Auditing and Taxation*, 28, 43–56.

Hood, C., & Dixon, R. (2016). Not what it said on the tin? Reflections on three decades of UK public management reform. *Financial Accountability & Management*, 32(4), 409–428.

House of Commons Communities and Local Government Committee. (2011). *Audit and inspection of local authorities*. 4th Report. HC 763 (House of Commons Communities and Local Government Committee).

Huber, D., & DiGabriele, J. A. (2014). Research in forensic accounting—what matters? *Journal of Theoretical Accounting Research*, 10(1), 40–70.

Kipping, M., & Saint-Martin, D. (2005). Between regulation, promotion and consumption: Government and management consultancy in Britain. *Business History*, 47(3), 449–465.

Lawton, A., & Macaulay, M. (2013). Localism in practice: investigating citizen participation and good governance in local government standards of conduct. *Public Administration Review*, 74(1), 75–83.

Levi, M. (2017). Assessing the trends, scale and nature of economic cybercrimes: Overview and issues. *Crime, Law and Social Change*, 67(1), 3–20.

Levi, M., & Burrows, J. (2008). Measuring the impact of fraud in the UK: A conceptual and empirical journey. *British Journal of Criminology*, 48(3), 293–318.

Levi, M., Doig, A., Gundur, R., Wall, D., & Williams, M. (2017). Cyberfraud and the implications for effective risk-based responses: Themes from UK research. *Crime, Law and Social Change*, 67(1), 77–96.

LGA. (2015). *Managing the risk of procurement fraud*. Local Government Association.

May, T., & Bhardwa, B. (2018). *Organised crime groups involved in fraud*. Palgrave Macmillan.

Moore, F. H., & Martin, S. (2017). The forensic accountant in practice. In B.-L. Chew (Ed.), *Forensic accounting and finance: Principles and practice* (pp. 1–17). Kogan Page.

National Audit Office. (2019a). *Local auditor reporting in England 2018*. HC 1864. National Audit Office.

National Audit Office. (2019b). *Local authority governance*. HC 1865. National Audit Office.

National Fraud Authority. (2011). *The local government fraud strategy*. National Fraud Authority.

Public Audit Forum. (2001). *Propriety and audit in the public sector*. National Audit Office.

Samociuk, M., Iyer, I., & Doody, H. (Eds.). (2010) *A short guide to fraud risk: Fraud resistance and detection*. Gower.

Sandford, M. (2016). *Local audit in England*. Briefing paper 06046. House of Commons Library.

Sandford, M. (2019). *Local audit in England*. Briefing paper 07240. House of Commons Library.

Taylor-Gooby, P., & Stoker, G. (2011). The coalition programme: A new vision for Britain or politics as usual? *The Political Quarterly, 82*(1), 4–15.

Timmins, N., & Gash, T. (2014). *Dying to improve. The demise of the audit commission and other improvement agencies.* Institute for Government.

Tonkiss, K., & Skelcher, C. (2015). Abolishing the audit commission: Framing, discourse coalitions and administrative reform. *Local Government Studies, 41*(6), 861–880.

Van Akkeren, J., & Buckby, S. (2017). Perceptions on the causes of individual and fraudulent co-offending: Views of forensic accountants. *Journal of Business Ethics, 146*(2), 383–404.

Local government ethics in England: how is local ownership working?

Alan Doig

With the abolition of the Audit Commission and the Standards Board for England, and the emphasis in the Localism Act 2011 on local ownership in England for standards, research was undertaken into a group of councils to assess their legislative compliance arrangements and the development of organizational ethical cultures. The research argues that the delivery of the former is a work-in-progress and that there is little evidence of the latter.

Introduction

The announcement in 2010 that the incoming government intended to abolish the Audit Commission was very much a political decision that seemed at variance with the roles of ensuring the propriety of local government spending and investigating complaints that were proposed by the Conservative Party's (2008) *Control Shift* policy document. The announcement was a surprise, unlike the fate of the Standards Board which had already been signalled as a candidate for abolition. Nevertheless, both bodies were criticised for being over prescriptive and opposed to the primacy of localism. For example the Committee on Standards in Public Life (CSPL) had argued that 'only by local ownership and involvement can issues of ethical organizational culture be properly addressed and the overall regulatory framework for standards in local government made proportionate and strategic' (CSPL, 2005; see also Department for Communities and Local Government, 2013), while the government's view was that the Audit Commission was a 'centrally imposed, bureaucratic and costly audit and inspection regime' (Lowther, 2013; see also Doig, 2014).

While any objection to the abolition of the Standards Board was muted, there was concern as to how the government would approach not only reforms to the existing legislative and procedural framework intended to address ethics at local level (see CSPL, 2011; Macaulay *et al.*, 2012), but also the preparedness of local councils to implement them: 'the question of whether local authorities and their leaders recognize a need for local action to support ethical cultures, whether they are willing and able to take these actions' (Greasley, 2007). Similarly, the partisan approach to remove the Audit Commission, including its audit practice component, was one strong on rhetoric and low on the more pertinent technical issues relating to public external audit and also to the Audit Commission's developing work on probity, governance and ethical standards (see Doig, 2014; Timmins and Gash, 2014; Tonkiss and Skelcher, 2015).

The Localism Act 2011

In the event, as well as employing their own external auditors (or at least having the power to do so individually—or more likely collectively—after the end of the transitional arrangements in 2018), the Localism Act places responsibility for public ethics entirely on local government. It has a dedicated section on standards whose premise is relatively simple, if vague: councils are required to promote and maintain high standards of conduct. To achieve this, the Act requires councils to have a code of conduct which, 'when viewed as a whole', should be 'consistent with' the seven principles devised by the first report of the CSPL, chaired by Lord Nolan (see figure 1).

Councils have to have 'arrangements' to investigate breaches of the code and decide what to do; but neither the 'arrangements' nor any possible sanctions are legislated for in the Act. The Act also requires the appointment of an 'independent person' whose mandatory responsibility is to have his or her views sought and taken into account—and no more than that—before a council makes its decision on an allegation that it is investigating; decisions on whether to investigate lie with the council. Councils have to have procedures for the registration and disclosure of financial and what the Act terms 'interests other than pecuniary interests'. The Act doesn't define either, although it indicates who may be included within the former, such as a spouse's pecuniary interests. The detail for pecuniary interests was provided in 2012 in *The Relevant Authorities (Disclosable Pecuniary Interests) Regulations* and later for interests in general (Department for Communities and Local Government, 2013). Failure to register and declare pecuniary interests, or to be misleading about the information that should be provided, are criminal offences.

The Localism Act's requirements drew attention on two issues:

- An immediate question of whether the requirements would resolve concerns being expressed by the CSPL. It described the abolition of the Standards Board as 'stripping back of the current structure to virtually nothing' (Kelly, 2010) and the consequence of abolishing both bodies as ensuring that 'the biggest regulatory gap is in relation to local government' (CSPL, 2012).
- How far the Act was about compliance frameworks, or how much it and local ownership would promote ethical organizational cultures. This distinction has been described as the route from the low road of compliance to the high road of public ethics where 'the low road leads further down the path of compliance, with the ethical framework limited to quantifiable performance measures such as the maintenance of registers of interest. The high road, on the other hand, is far more ambitious, leading to an ethical culture that permeates throughout the organization' (Lawton and Macaulay, 2004; see also Doig, 2104).

Figure 1. Nolan's seven principles of public life (CSPL, 1995).

Selflessness
Integrity
Objectivity
Accountability
Openness
Honesty
Leadership

Towards assessing local ownership in practice

Along with examining councils' online information, Freedom of Information requests were undertaken between January and May 2016 to make a preliminary assessment of local ownership in practice since the Act was passed among the 12 councils and three police forces that comprise England's North East region.

Criminal offences relating to financial interests
None of the three police forces had received any allegation or report of any breach of the criminal requirements on financial interests. In fact two of them stated that the offence in question was not a 'notifiable offence'. This means that, while the government may have announced in 2010 that 'serious misconduct' for personal gain would be a criminal act, the actual offences are classed as 'less serious' offences, alongside other similar offences such as anti-social behaviour, driving under the influence of alcohol, parking offences and TV licence evasion (see Office for National Statistics, 2015). One consequence is that such offences, if and when they occur, are excluded from the recorded crime collection; as one force responded, 'this is not something that the force would record…contact the local authority you are interested in'. No council reported any allegation being made to any of the three forces.

The code
All councils have codes. What comprises the code, however, varies from council to council. Given that 'since the passage of the 2011 Act, model codes of conduct have been produced by the Department for Communities and Local Government, the Local Government Association, and the National Association of Local Councils' (Sandford, 2016), it is hardly surprising that most councils offer an identikit code where the emphasis is on generic issues of bullying, impartiality, improper use of office for advantage, respect and disrepute. The codes' link to Nolan's seven principles is invariably offered as consistent with, underpinned by, or prepared in order to comply with, the principles. However, the seven principles themselves were not, as a number of councils noted, 'part of this code'. Only a minority incorporated the principles—in each case with additional principles—into their code as introductory general principles.

None appeared to rely on the Department for Communities and Local Government's own 'illustrative' code, which was firmly based on the original principles' focus on the overlaps between material benefits from, and conflicts of interest between, public office and personal or party benefit. Few councils had revised their codes in line with the CSPL's own revisions to the focus of the seven principles in 2013 (CSPL, 2013). On the other hand, this leaves most councils with codes which reflect the much more generic and generalized principles as defined by the CSPL, but which still have appended to them the original principles with their narrower focus.

Procedures

All of the councils in the North East had accessible online procedures and policies on complaints, acceptance criteria and investigations into allegations of breaches of the code. All councils had a committee or panel—not always called a 'standards committee'—to deal with allegations. All had an independent person (in some cases, two people) whose involvement in the process appeared in a number of councils to go beyond the statutory minimum, including:

- Participation in the standards committee, or equivalent.
- Advising on actions following complaints.
- Giving advice to members who were subject to a complaint.

Nevertheless, it was difficult from online information to identify what they actually did, and what comments or decisions they made, when and why. Similarly, while agendas and minutes from the committees or panels were also available online, they didn't always carry more than limited information (although cases taken through to a formal decision were published, with details).

Register of interests

All councils had a register; some were organized centrally but many were provided on individual councillors' websites. Only one council had a year-on-year record of each councillor's declared interests, while one council referred to an online register (which couldn't be found online), and yet another made its register available 'for inspection during office opening hours'. One council referred to the register as relating to 'disclosable pecuniary interests'. Most covered pecuniary and non-pecuniary interests, including gifts, hospitality and interests disclosed at meetings. The statutory requirements do not require the council to verify or confirm interests, and none appeared to do so.

Caseloads

The variations of responses to the Freedom of Information requests and the different periods over which data is recorded by councils do not lend themselves to an accurate quantitative analysis of the data, but the average number of allegations per council seems to be about 15 a year. Behind this figure, however, is a spectrum, from one council that reported zero allegations over the three years to one which had received an average of over 40 a year. A number of councils didn't record to which part of their code the allegation related. For the majority who did report this, most allegations were from members of the public and most involved the 'respect' or 'disrepute' catch-phrases that dominate many of the codes.

Councils named the councillor concerned when any formal report was issued. In terms of allegations, others reflected the response of one council that 'releasing details of individual complaints could lead to the identification of councillors and individuals, therefore, we refuse to release the information'.

Sanctions

The Act makes no provision for sanctions and thus councils are restricted to internal sanctions which range from 'formal censure' to recommendations to the council of removal from committees, or official posts on committees, removal from the cabinet or portfolio responsibilities, denial of access to information, and training. In most cases—and not all councils keep detailed records of outcomes—the sanctions were limited to 'censure' and 'informal resolutions' (although some councils had removed members from official positions, required training or issued 'guidance' to whole committees). Most allegations were recorded as 'no further action'. One case, where a councillor was alleged to have published legally-privileged information about a planning application, the council noted in its published report that the councillor knowingly disclosed the information, demonstrated no remorse, indicated his willingness to repeat his actions, and did not attend the committee meeting. The only recommendation in his case was to suggest that he be invited to confirm he would not repeat his actions and, if he refused, he would not receive any more confidential information.

Training, compliance, cultures and links to other initiatives

Councils are subject to other related agendas, including the UK Anti-Corruption Plan published in 2014 and the Local Government Counter Fraud and Corruption Strategy 2016–2019. Both encompass robust processes, transparency, prevention and ethical cultures. While the response to these—and the Local Government Transparency Code 2015 requires a council to publish some data annually on cases and costs—are often separate documents, collectively they draw attention to the need to maintain, at the least, 'a robust counter fraud and corruption culture with clear values and standards' (CIPFA, 2016).

The important point here is that there are a number of common themes, including that laid down by the Act, which are as much about ethical organizational cultures as they are with compliance with legal requirements. Through their retention of standards committees, or the equivalent, such as audit and governance committees, many councils continue to refer to their roles as including high standards of conduct, ethical standards, ethical governance and so on. Further, such roles in a number of cases also cover, for example whistleblowing, risk or probity aspects of audit and governance arrangements and encompassing staff, as well as members.

Nevertheless, their main roles appear more shaped by the Act alone, rather than appearing to encompass roles and responsibilities under the other initiatives, and thus concerned with what might be termed 'compliance arrangements', rather than what might be termed 'ethical organizational cultures'. In terms of available information, a handful of councils provided full details of councillors' training history, including induction and standards and refresher training but many did not. There appeared to be almost no information on integrated or council-wide training and associated reinforcement and monitoring arrangements. There was also little or no information on councils addressing continuing areas of concern, such post-retirement or post-resignation activities of members or staff, and lobbying (which was not addressed by the Transparency of Lobbying, Non-party Campaigning and Trade Union Administration Act 2014, as the then local government minister, Eric Pickles, had hoped).

Assessment

In terms of the requirements of the Localism Act and in terms of the appropriate (and accessible) procedures, the 12 councils were found to be compliant and, it could be argued, were satisfying their statutory obligations. It is also worth noting that councils had policies and procedures in place to address corruption and fraud. A number of councils were also involved in regional initiatives to explore issues relating to compliance arrangements.

On the other hand, the presence of the catch-all 'respect' and 'disrepute' clauses in most codes, and the absence of effective sanctions, do not provide evidence to demonstrate the proportionality or the effectiveness of the compliance arrangements, and whether they address the original focus of a number of the seven principles, the work on probity by the Audit Commission or the main areas of concerns addressed by the Standards Board (where allegations were more about members' interests than about respect and disrepute issues).

Looking at developments to date, two issues are particularly pertinent:

• Organizational ethical culture.
• Internal or external monitoring.

None of the council websites carried any detailed information on the promotion and monitoring of an ethical organizational culture. A limited amount of non-specific information was found is in some annual governance statements (one typical council simply claimed that it promoted: 'high standards of conduct and behaviour'). Few, if any, of the 12 councils published any information on their websites, either from the standards committee (or equivalent), from internal or external audit, or from the independent person(s), on effectiveness of the overall compliance framework and whether the latter was considered proportionate and strategic, let alone whether there was a functioning ethical organizational culture.

It could be argued that the journey toward, let alone along, the high road of organizational ethical cultures is a work in progress. It also has to be acknowledged that councils have limited access to resources and support. Nevertheless, and aside from the CSPL's recent concerns that 'changes to the Local Authority standards regime may result in ethical standards becoming less of a priority and less actively monitored' (CSPL, 2014), the gap between where councils are now and where they could (or should) be is illustrated by the proposals of the committee's December 2015 report on ethical standards for providers of public services.

According to this report, councils, as commissioners of such services, would be expected to work within a framework intended to support and embed high ethical standards in the provision of public services, 'based around principled leadership and governance including a code of conduct, a culture of dialogue and challenge, clarity of accountability and ethical capability and transparency' (CSPL, 2015). They are also expected to monitor providers of public services in terms of a series of measures that, first, could be 'expected of, implemented and embedded by providers of public services and monitored and evaluated by commissioners to provide assurance of ethical standards'. Second, this in turn would 'encourage not only commissioners to be explicit about their expectations on ethical standards, but also providers to reflect on their capacity and capability to meet those standards' (CSPL, 2015). Leaving aside the question of councils' own capacity and capability to undertake such evaluations, the issue here is whether councils have such a framework or have such measures in place in their own organizations, and who evaluates or monitors them now and in the future, to assure local ownership in practice and improvement?

References

CIPFA (2016), *Fighting Fraud and Corruption Locally: The Local Government Counter Fraud and Corruption Strategy* (CIPFA Counter Fraud Centre), p. 21.

CSPL (2005), *Getting the Balance Right: Implementing Standards of Conduct in Public Life Getting the Balance Right*, Cm 6407, p. 4.

CSPL (2011), *Submission to Public Bill Committee on the Localism Bill*.

CSPL (2012), *Response from the Committee on Standards in Public Life to the Issues and Question Paper Issued in Connection with its Triennial Review*

2012, p. 16.

CSPL (2013), *Standards Matter. A Review of Best Practice in Promoting Good Behaviour in Public Life*, Cm 8519.

CSPL (2014), *Ethics in Practice: Promoting Ethical Conduct in Public Life*, p. 24.

CSPL (2015), *Ethical Standards for Providers of Public Services—Guidance*, pp. 5 and 10.

Conservative Party (2008), *Control Shift. Returning Power to Local Communities. Responsibility Agenda: Policy Green Paper No. 9*.

Department for Communities and Local Government (2013), *Openness and Transparency on Personal Interests: A Guide for Councillors*.

Doig, A. (2014), Roadworks ahead? Addressing fraud, corruption and conflict of interest in English local government. *Local Government Studies, 40*, 5, pp. 670–686.

Greasley, S. (2007), Maintaining ethical cultures: self-regulation in English local government. *Local Government Studies, 33*, 3, p. 461.

Kelly, C. (2010), *Press Release: Public Confidence in Local Government Standards is at Risk* (Committee on Standards in Public Life).

Lawton, A. and Macaulay, M. (2004), Ethics at the crossroads? Developments in the ethical framework for local government. *Local Government Studies, 30*, 4, p. 625.

Lowther, E. (2013), See www.bbc.co.uk/news/uk-politics-21047426

Macaulay, M., Hickey, G. and Begum, N. (2012), *Preparing for the New Standards Regime in English Local Government* (University of Teesside).

Office for National Statistics (2015), *Information Paper: Quality and Methodology Information*.

Sandiford, M. (2016), *Local Government Standards: Briefing Paper Number 05707* (House of Commons Library), p. 6.

Timmins, N. and Gash, T. (2014), *Dying to Improve. The Demise of the Audit Commission and Other Improvement Agencies* (Institute for Government).

Tonkiss, K. and Skelcher, C. (2015), Abolishing the Audit Commission: framing, discourse coalitions and administrative reform. *Local Government Studies, 41*, 6, pp. 861–880.

IMPACT

While 'public ethics' and 'organizational ethical cultures' may seem nebulous terms, there have been a number of adverse reports involving unacceptable conduct and cultures in the public sector organizations. This article looks at how English local government has dealt with its statutory requirements to address 'high standards of conduct'. While councils have arrangements that address those requirements, the link between them and effective organizational ethical cultures is not made. There are lessons here for the public sector generally both in terms of basic compliance requirements but also the need to ensure that these are part of, and effective within, wider ethical cultural environments.

Councillor ethics: a review of the Committee on Standards in Public Life's 'Local Government Ethical Standards'

Jonathan Rose ⓘ and Colin Copus

ABSTRACT

The Committee on Standards in Public Life's (CSPL) 2019 report *Local Government Ethical Standards* presents a detailed review of local government ethics in England, aiming to highlight both best practice and areas for improvement. In so doing, it makes 26 recommendations ranging in importance. Likely to be one of the most important, and most controversial, is a recommendation to allow local authorities to suspend democratically-elected councillors for up to six months. This paper presents a review of the report and its recommendations, with a particular emphasis on the 'values-versus-compliance' distinction in ethical regulation.

IMPACT

Policy-makers and practitioners are often faced with difficult choices concerning ethical regulation, and attempts to improve ethical regulations can sometimes cause new and unexpected problems. The authors review the Committee on Standards in Public Life's report *Local Government Ethical Standards*, placing the ethical challenges and opportunities for unintended consequences into the values-vs-compliance framework. The paper will be useful for policy-makers and regulators concerned with local government in England, who may be charged with implementing aspects of this report, while the broader issues discussed about the challenges of ethical regulations and the limits of compliance-based policies will be useful in a wide range of contexts and countries.

Introduction

In January 2019, the Committee on Standards in Public life (CSPL) released the report *Local Government Ethical Standards*. The CSPL was established in 1994 by John Major, then prime minister, in a context of broad-based concerns about the integrity of those in public life. Since then, the CSPL has gone on to be one of the premier ethical ethical regulators in the country, with a broad mandate to promote the Seven Principles of Public Life:

- Selflessness.
- Integrity.
- Objectivity.
- Accountability.
- Openness.
- Honesty.
- Leadership.

The CSPL takes a broad view in their work, and aims to provide critical reviews of wide areas of public life, rather than serving as an investigative body. The 2019 report, which aims to evaluate and provide guidance to improve ethical standards in local government in England, again display the committee's comprehensive and coherent approach to standards across the public sector.

The 2019 report is not the first time the CSPL has explored the standards regime in local government. The third report of the committee, published in 1997, also examined the state of local government ethical standards. Similarly to the 2019 report, in 1997 it was found that the vast majority of councillors and officers maintained high standards of behaviour and that instances of corruption or poor behaviour were confined to a tiny minority. The recommendations of that report, most of which were included in the Local Government Act 2000, in one form or another, were based on the same compliance approach to ethical and behavioural standards that can be observed in the 2019 report. The 1997 recommendations included, *inter alia*: a nationally defined model code of conduct be created to provide a framework for local codes; each council to form a standards committee; a tribunal be created to act as independent arbiters on standards issue and hear appeals from councillors; and the replacement of surcharge (the ability of the courts to legally oblige individual councillors to pay for council spending judged to be illegal) with a new offence of misuse of public office. Interestingly, recommendation 23 of the 1997 report was that local standards committees should be able to recommend suspension of councillors for up to the three months. As will be seen later, in the intervening years between the two reports the suspension period recommendation has been doubled.

Much has changed in local government regulation since 2000. The Localism Act 2011 made several changes to the standards regime in local government, with the most important being the abolition of the national Standards Board and the localizing of codes of conduct by the abolition of the national model code of conduct. Under the Localism Act, however, councils are still legally expected to create and adopt local codes of conduct. Councils also need to appoint at least one 'independent person' from outside of the council, to assist the council in promoting and maintaining high standards of conduct. This independent person must be consulted by the council on decisions to investigate a complaint that the code of conduct may have been breached and before it makes a decision on that complaint.

While the changes since 2011 make a fresh look at local government standards useful, that the CSPL decided to take on this topic at this particular moment is both interesting and important. As the CSPL themselves note (2019, p. 20), this investigation was not undertaken because of any particular scandal but instead represents a conscious effort to improve standards generally. Reviewing systems before a crisis emerges is a positive starting point and indeed ideally should be normal, but the fact is that reform agendas are usually constructed in response to specific scandals (see, for example, Anechiarico & Jacobs, 1996, pp. 24–25; Hail, Tahoun, & Wang, 2018). Moreover, through the evidence gathering, the CSPL were keen to stress that their investigation was not in response to any perception that local government was rife with ethical and standards problems. A starting point that any review might strengthen what was already a reasonable system and encourage more engagement with the issue of ethics and ethical standards to avoid problems in the future is one which should be emulated elsewhere. Nonetheless, the absence of a specific scandal to which this report can be connected may make it less likely that the suggestions in the report will be implemented quickly, particularly in light of the Brexit issues which currently dominate political schedules and the parliamentary timetable.

Regardless of its likelihood to succeed in affecting change, however, the depth of the research and analysis provided by the report will undoubtedly make this one of the most important evaluations of local government ethics to have taken place since the wide-ranging changes to local government made in the Localism Act. It also points the way to overcoming some of the doubt caused by the localization of codes

of ethics by the Localism Act. As the report points o (CSPL, 2019, p. 10), following the Localism Act the has become 'considerable variation' in the codes conduct in existence. The report grapples with t difficult task of attempting to ensure a system which all local residents can expect a certain standa of behaviour from their councillors while also allowi for local concerns to be reflected in local coun standards regimes. In total, the report makes separate recommendations and identified 15 areas best practice. The recommendations vary in their sca Some are relatively minor, such as recommendatio for changes to legislation to ensure that councillors not have to report their home address publica (recommendation 2); or changes in legislation ensure that a council's code of conduct appl whenever a councillor claims to act, or gives t impression that they are acting, in their offic capacity (recommendation 4). Others are far mo important and serious, such as the recommendation allow councillors to be suspended for up to months without allowances (recommendation potentially leaving constituents without access democratic representation.

Notwithstanding the wisdom of the pro-active wo of the CSPL, it is somewhat ironic that while some the recommendations add clarity and cohesion to t system others appear to be operating with assumption that councillors are likely to be acting bad faith. As such, the report risks not reflecti strongly enough the realities and dynamics of lo government politics. Moreover, the report tends reinforce a legalistic approach to regulation and th recommends introducing important rule-bas standards where compliance will be assured throu sanctions; rather than attempting to reinforce value-based system within which councillors shou operate.

The context of the Local Government Ethical Standards report

The committee's report comes at an important time local government in the England. The role councillors is more complex than ever, particularly light of the broader political climate which h increasingly demanded new ways of working a greater degrees of collaboration between the pub and private sectors. Indeed, the fragment landscape of public sector provision leads to t need for councillors to draw together the activities a range of external bodies and, in many cases, either act as members of external boards a agencies or hold those same bodies to accou (Copus, Roberts, & Wall 2017). As councillors enga ever more with an array of public and non-pub bodies, whether as commissioners of services, or partners in joint enterprises such as local economic partnerships (LEPs), or as board members of public–private council service providers, the ethical environment in which individual councillors operate is becoming more complex (a point noted by the CSPL, 2019, p. 86). A councillor who serves on the board of a quasi-private enterprise will have an almost inherent conflict of interest whenever the goals of the organization are not perfectly aligned with those of the council or local residents or, indeed, of the party of which they may be a member.

Moreover, councillors serving on such boards are not acting as representative of their council, but are expected to act as board members and in the interests of the organization concerned. The CSPL are correct to view this as a substantive challenge to ethical norms, and there remain important questions about how such interactions ought to be managed and whether current approaches to conflicts of interest that can arise are sufficient. There is of course a role for the overview and scrutiny function of local government to hold not only these external bodies to account, but also the councillors who serve on them. Yet ethical standards are an issue which cuts across the work of scrutiny committees and which by its nature demands an overarching view—if not nationally then at least within individual councils—of what standards are, what is expected, how appropriate behaviour will be encouraged, and what sanctions will exist for breaches of the standards.

It is precisely because of the significance of these challenges, and the importance that this report will likely have, that it is worth considering the report as a whole in broader terms as well as the sum of its parts. In the context of the broad approach, it is important to consider the overarching framework in which the report's suggestions are grounded. Ethical regulations are often considered according to whether they are primarily 'values-based' or primarily 'compliance/rules-based' (for a discussion, see Webb, 2012; Scott & Leung, 2012; Heywood & Rose, 2016); that is to say that regulations can either attempt to control unethical behaviour by creating or encouraging pro-integrity values, or by banning corrupt behaviour. The values-vs-compliance framework both allows for a classification of regulations, but also for a more critical consideration of a suite of regulations. Moreover, each of these approaches have different benefits and limitations and so each approach is differentially helpful in different circumstances. Thus, the choice of an overarching approach is of particular consequence.

In general, the CSPL report follows a familiar compliance-based approach and the major regulatory changes suggested are primarily, although not exclusively, compliance focused. While the general compliance focus of the report is in many ways

expected given the general tenor of ethics reform at present, such reforms may paradoxically leave the local government sector less well prepared to deal with potential unethical behaviour. Indeed, we shall see later that there are some hidden temptations in the report for unethical political behaviour to be given a larger playground.

Values versus compliance in local government

The values-versus-compliance framework is useful for understanding the conceptual approach that underlies different systems of ethical regulation, and for appreciating the CSPL's report and recommendations. Of course, both the values and compliance approaches are ideal types; extant systems of regulation are almost always a mixture of both types and the evaluation is about where the emphasis is placed. Yet the relative balance between these different approaches helps to set the tone of ethical regulation within an area, can condition behaviour towards (or against) certain approaches to working and, moreover, provides an insight into the assumptions of regulators about those they are regulating.

The compliance approach, which relies on rules and legalistic or quasi-legalistic processes, does have some important advantages; including making clear what behaviours are forbidden, which therefore provides a clearer guide to officials as to what required actions are. Compliance-based systems are also usually clear about the penalties for breaking the rules, which can be set at levels sufficient to strongly deter unwanted behaviour. Nonetheless, to effectively set out a list of actions that are not permitted, compliance-based policies need to be quite specific about what behaviours are forbidden and provide robust and clear definitions of each prohibited behaviour. What is and is not permitted is even more important when the means of setting out the rule to be followed is through legislation; statutes are almost inherently specific, and the interpretation of statues by the courts provides the clearest possible guide of what is prohibited. Because of this, compliance-based systems often have a characteristic more like a blacklist of forbidden behaviours. Such a 'blacklist' approach is in general challenging, because the totality of potential behaviours that might need regulating needs to be considered before the regulation is implemented. Additional nuancing of the regulations often requires more serious interventions; a fact which is already apparent in the necessity for primary or secondary legislation to update some current local government ethical regulations in England (CSPL, 2019).

Yet as the role of councillors continues to develop, and new ways of working continue to emerge, it will become increasingly difficult to construct or maintain an adequate blacklist that covers all existing and potential ethical pitfalls. The rapidly changing role and work of councillors and the different types of councils on which they sit—county, district, borough, unitary and parish—means that an overarching system of rules and compliance will need to account for the way councillors conduct different roles in different settings and contexts, some of which are external to the council of which they are a member. Moreover, whenever updates to ethics regulations require legislative changes the ethical system becomes at the mercy of political timetables that are often dominated by other pressing issues; and this is particularly evident as Brexit dominates parliamentary concerns.

The increasing complexity of both council business and councillors' work, both within the council and when interacting with a wide range of external organizations, and the ethical challenges that will bring, is a point the CSPL themselves note repeatedly; including in their introductory letter to the prime minister (2019, p. 6). The CPSL does, however, stop short of exploring whether this means that the system of ethical regulation may need a more fundamental overhaul. One alternative is to move towards a greater focus on values-based regulations. Value-based regulations aim to appeal to the better natures of those being regulated; they aim to set out and reinforce shared principles of high standards and encourage people to act in accordance with those high standards. Values-based regulations are therefore much less prescriptive; they do not tend to use legalistic approaches in the first instance, but instead empower people to make ethical choices. Of course, this approach requires regulators to place much more trust in those they are regulating and the evidence received by the committee suggests such trust is lacking. Providing the space for people to proactively choose to do 'the right thing' inherently carries some element of vulnerability, as all relationships that are built on trust do. Indeed, the CSPL report starts with a display of the Seven Principles of Public Life (CPSL, 2019, p. 5) as a reminder to do the right thing, as it were, and such broad statements are exhortations to correct behaviour as a framework with which few could object. What is lacking, however, is the trust that councillors will act in accordance with those principles.

Because of the 'vulnerability' inherent in the values-based policies, this approach to regulation may actually be a less good choice in a context in which standards are very low and many people cannot be trusted. Yet, notwithstanding periodic examples of poor governance within individual councils, there are good reasons to believe that in general councillors and council workers are likely to be trustworthy. Indeed,

councillors are overwhelmingly motivated by commitment to public service. In a recent study the Local Government Association, by far the m popular reason given for becoming a councillor w 'to serve the community', with almost 85% councillors listing this as a motivation (LGA, 2019, 6). While more detailed research suggests that t reasons for councillors standing is complex a multifaceted (see, for example, Copus, 201 including party political factors, it remains the c that public service motivation is a recurring feature individual motivations. Combined with this is the f that monetary rewards for being a councillor often extremely low in relation to the time t people spend on council business. It is common councillors to spend more than 10 hours a week council business, and more than 40% of councill spend over 20 hours a week on council busin (LGA, 2019, p. 5), yet councillor positions will typic offer compensation less than an equivalent minim wage job. While the exact relationship betwe financial compensation and integrity is complex, a some research has suggested that increasing leads to a higher corruption (Foltz & Opo Agyemang, 2015), it seems unlikely that councill would invest the amount of time and effort that th clearly do if they were not primarily motivated non-material factors (see Copus, 2016). In total, t may not be perfect evidence that councillors actually trustworthy, but it certainly suggests that approach built on trust may be beneficial.

Not only might it make sense to assume that m councillors are trustworthy, ethical standards frequently maintained in practice solely because vast majority of councillors are indeed trustwort The CSPL rightly note that the regulatio surrounding disclosable pecuniary interests extremely weak (CSPL, 2019, p. 11). As Cornersto Barristers noted in their evidence submission (cited CSPL, 2019, p. 45), the current arrangements disclosable pecuniary interests contain 'manif omissions such as hospitality deriving from councillor's position, unpaid employment (includ directorships), interest in land outside of a counc area, pecuniary interests of close family memb who are not spouses, and memberships of lobby campaign groups'. In such a situation, the fact t local government standards are generally high h very little to do with the regulations, and everythi to do with the personal integrity of councillors.

Regardless of the evidence in favour of counci ethics, the CSPL report includes some significa compliance mechanisms that extend well beyo what currently exists in local government regulatio The most important of these is recommendation that: 'local authorities should be given the power suspend councillors, without allowances, for up to months' (2019, p. 73). The recommendation is prefaced by recommendation 10 which states: 'a local authority should only be able to suspend a councillor where the authority's independent person agrees both with the findings of a breach and that suspending the councillor would be a proportionate sanction' (2019, p. 57). That particular safeguard places too much responsibility in the hands of the independent person and relies on that person being just that: *independent*. In this role, an independent person must not only have no association with any political party or group, but must also be of the calibre to withstand what might be considerable pressure to agree with the council. The fatal flaw in this safeguard is that the independent person is appointed by the council, creating a further potential for ethical hazards.

The report also notes that it heard evidence of a 'small but significant number' (the figure is not quantified) of councillors 'who appeared to have no respect for a standards regime' (CSPL, 2019, p. 65) but, as with all reviews, the temptation is to legislate for the worst. The report notes that party group discipline has been used to fill the gap. Yet it cautions that party discipline is an internal affair and the underlying danger of relying on party procedures is that, if disciplining a member risks a group losing its majority on a council or committee, there may be reluctance in using it (CSPL, 2019, p. 68). However equally, the belief that a putatively independent process can be grafted on top of the existing system, and the suggestion that the process for suspending councillors could end up overseen by those who may have very strong interests in weakening a rival party group, has the potential to result in a problematic use of a new power. At worst, the recommendation may risk providing opportunities for enhancing party political conflict and damaging local democracy. The recommendation for suspension, which ultimately deprives local residents of their councillor, risks drawing out the worst of compliance regimes: situations in which the ethical course of action is disregarded in favour of following the preferred internal organizational style. Councillors who are strident in their defence of their local residents against a council who they perceive as negligent or even hostile, and thereby earn a reputation for being 'disruptive', may face the prospect of suspension even while fulfilling their democratic and ethical obligation to support their local residents.

Notwithstanding a very significant move towards new compliance mechanisms, the CSPL at the same time do reflect on the utility of values-based approaches, and some of their suggestions are based on supporting the integrity in local government through ethical cultures and training. Recommendation 25, to introduce a formal expectation of induction training, is both useful in itself as a practical measure but also provides the potential to create a space at the start of councillors' careers to make broader ethics questions salient and to consider how ethical dilemmas can be resolved (CSPL, 2019, p. 99). This approach is in line with that used in the past in The Netherlands Tax and Customs Administration, which was able to increase the salience of ethics while maintaining appropriate discretion for officials (see Van Blijswijk, Van Breukelen, Franklin, Raadschelders, & Slump, 2004). The recommendation may yet benefit from going even further: ethical discussions and reflections would ideally become a routine part of councillors' working lives. Unfortunately, compliance-based recommendations, like suspension, risks discouraging exactly these kinds of open discussion and critical reflections about ethical hazards (Heywood & Rose, 2015). This is at the heart of the tension between values-based and compliance-based regimes, a tension the CSPL acknowledged (2019, p. 65).

Although the starting point for the CSPL review and report was from a non-crisis point, it is important to remember that despite consistent evidence of material weaknesses in some regulations, notably including disclosable pecuniary interests, English local government has little corruption. That there is so little corruption is a testament to councillors, rather than the standards regime or the law.

Cultural change and political realities

The CSPL report recognizes that ethics and behaviour 'must be embedded in organizational culture' (2019, p. 65), yet regulating the behaviour of councillors must account for not only the council as an organization, but also the political party group (or independent group) of which councillors are members. The report (2019, p. 12) recognizes the importance that party groups play in maintaining an ethical culture and states that they are 'semi-formal' institutions with a complementary rather than parallel role in the ethical system. But the party group is not semi-formal; rather, it is a formal, organized and coherent body with its own rules and regulations and its own officers and leadership. Moreover, each political party has their own version of group standing orders and their own political culture when it comes to interpreting and employing those party rules, which vary between parties and across parties in different parts of the country. In a detailed study of political party groups, Copus (1999a and b and 2004; see also Leach 2006) defined party groups as formal organizations but which are also an informal part of the council structure. Copus (2004) and Leach (2006) explored the way party groups interpose themselves between councillors and the public (and officers) seeking to shape councillor behaviour for the benefit of the group and for the purposes of cohesion, unity and discipline. The call by the CSPL for party groups to be instrumental in a cultural change will, in part, depend on how the national parties continue to develop their standing orders to reflect ethical and behavioural issues, and then that national drive will then need to be accepted and interpreted by local groups to suit their own circumstances. The national Labour party has long attempted to control the organization and activities of its local party groups, while the Conservative party and Liberal Democrats have latterly followed suit, but with their own cultural approaches to local party groups (Copus, 2016).

Of course, while there is much that separates councillors from different parties, culturally there are shared and common experiences of being a councillor on which the CSPL call for cultural change can be built: the influence council membership has on councillors' work, private and social life; the time demands of council work; the need to forge working relationships between officers and councillors; the general image of councillors held by the public, the media and government; the need to balance political objectives with what can realistically be achieved through being a councillor; the desire to improve their areas and community well-being and the public spirit motivation that councillors display when seeking office; the frustrations generated by central control and regulations—to which the CSPL report will add; and, indeed, the relationships councillors have with their parties. Yet while all these common experiences do provide the ground for enhancing the ethical culture of local government, it must not be forgotten that English local government is heavily party politicized, with the May 2019 elections resulting in almost 89% of councillors in England coming from one of the three main parties—a slight drop on the 92% prior to the 2019 elections. The culture of political parties and how that is developed and displays itself in each council across England is part and parcel of the culture of local government and moves towards cultural change must recognize and cater for this fact.

Political culture shapes how councillors approach their activities and how they view the role of officers; and, as a consequence, how they develop working relationships with officers, seek to influence what they do, or to hold them to account. The latter is a vital part of the role of the councillor, but one which can pose challenges in officer-member relationships and relationships between back bench and leading councillors. There is a danger in evidence from officers and senior managers, or even from senior councillors closer to the bureaucratic organization, in that they could effectively attempt to protect the administrative machinery from too close an investigation from members. Any system of ethical or

behavioural sanctions must not play into the hands either managers seeking to prevent councillors fr holding up officers or the administrative machine justifiable public gaze and scrutiny, nor must th provide additional weapons for party political batt Again, this reinforces concerns about complian focused regulations that are much less present values-based approaches. Cultural change is of cou difficult, and attempts to introduce a more valu based culture in local authorities have often met sl progress (Doig, 2017). Yet the increasing complexity councillors' work, as we have argued, shows that we seeing the limits of compliance-focused approaches more radical approach aiming for broader cultu change among both the regulators and the regula may be necessary. The exact process by which su radical changes to ethical systems can be introduc remains an important open question that requi further research.

Beyond cultural issues, there still remain spec practical issues with the suggestion to allow suspension of councillors. The purpose of sanctio in the words of the CSPL (2019, p. 65). is: 'motivati observance of standards arrangements, deterri damaging behaviour, preventing further wrongdoi and maintaining public confidence'. Yet it debatable whether the power to suspend council vested in the council is needed to uphold the ideals. While the report discusses, and reje difficulties in this suggestion as possibly conflicti with ECHR article 6, it is less clear about how t process should work in practice, and seemingly re too heavily on the independent member as safeguard against misuse. Nonetheless, there rem significant dangers with the proposal. If the cour as an elected body or councillors sitting on standards committee are given the power to suspe councillors, then this potentially puts in the hands a majority group a weapon by which to silence th most assiduous and effective critics among ot council groups. Allowing councillors to suspend ot councillors may represent, particularly in coun with problematic cultures, too great a power and t great a temptation. It is one thing for councillors be able to remove a councillor from a group, it entirely another to allow them to be able to remo a councillor from the council for a given period time. Such a power would be open to influence mangers and senior officers who may also be subject of such a critic among elected members a seek to influence the use of the power to silence t critic.

We have highlighted this one recommendati because, unlike the others contained within t report, this recommendation strikes at the heart elected local democracy and the principle that o the voters can elect and through the electoral process remove their elected representatives. An option more in fitting with that principle would be to introduce into local government the right to recall councillors—within a similar legal framework to that used by MPs. Allowing councillors to suspend other councillors underestimates patterns of political and party political behaviour as they currently exist in English local government and the role of political parties in shaping that behaviour and the ethos and attitudes that lay behind them.

The weakness and danger in this one recommendation (the power to suspend councillors) does not, however, fatally undermine the report by any means. Indeed, many of the other recommendations go on to provide a sensible set of proposals for strengthening the regulatory framework within which councillors and, indeed, officers operate. However, reflecting on the nature of the report, it would be fair to observe that the evidence presented balances more towards that presented by officers, officer organizations and senior members—lacking is the wider voice of the councillor.

Conclusion

Given the evidence received by the CPSL during its inquiry, the report provides a set of recommendations that reflects current concerns of many operating in local government. It provides a way in which more coherence can be given to a localized system, additional clarity added to processes and procedures and a firmer link between the rules and the mechanism for compliance. Yet this compliance focus poses substantive challenges in its own right. Time will tell if the committee has got this part right.

Regardless of the specific critiques of the recommendations in the report, it is again important to highlight that the CSPL's decision to review local government ethics without needing a scandal to prompt the review is an example of best practice for regulation. Not working under a feverish atmosphere of political scandal provided the necessary space to investigate a large area in significant detail. Other public bodies concerned with the regulation of public life, both in the UK and beyond, ought to reflect on the wisdom of the approach taken by the CSPL.

Disclosure statement

No potential conflict of interest was reported by the author(s).

ORCID

Jonathan Rose ⓘ http://orcid.org/0000-0001-5187-3221

References

Anechiarico, F., & Jacobs, J. B. (1996). *The pursuit of absolute integrity: How corruption control makes government ineffective.* University of Chicago Press.

Committee on Standards in Public Life [CSPL]. (2019). *Local government ethical standards a review by the committee on standards in public life.* London: Committee on Standards in Public Life.

Copus, C. (1999a). The party group: A barrier to democratic renewal. *Local Government Studies (special edition), 25*(4), 77–98.

Copus, C. (1999b). The party group and modernising local democracy. *Representation, 36*(3), 243–250.

Copus, C. (2004). *Party politics and local government.* Manchester University Press.

Copus, C. (2016). *In defence of councillors.* Manchester University Press.

Copus, C., Roberts, M., & Wall, R. (2017). *Local government in England: Centralisation, autonomy and control.* Palgrave Macmillan.

Doig, A. (2017). New development: Local government ethics in England: How is local ownership working? *Public Money & Management, 37*(1), 63–68.

Foltz, J. D., & Opoku-Agyemang, K. A. (2015). Do higher salaries lower petty corruption? A policy experiment on West Africa's highways. *Unpublished Working Paper, University of Wisconsin-Madison and University of California, Berkeley.*

Hail, L., Tahoun, A., & Wang, C. (2018). Corporate scandals and regulation. *Journal of Accounting Research, 56*(2), 617–671.

Heywood, P. M., & Rose, J. (2015). Curbing corruption or promoting integrity? Probing the hidden conceptual challenge. In P. Hardi, P. M. Heywood, & D. Torsello (Eds.), *Debates of corruption and integrity* (pp. 102–119). London: Palgrave Macmillan.

Heywood, P. M., & Rose, J. (2016). The limits of rule governance. In A. Lawton, Z. van der Wal, & L. Huberts (Eds.), *Ethics in public policy and management: A global research companion* (pp. 181–196). London: Routledge.

Leach, S. (2006). *The changing role of local politics in Britain.* the Policy Press.

Local Government Association [LGA]. (2019). *National census of local authority councillors 2018.* London: Local Government Association.

Scott, I., & Leung, J. Y. (2012). Integrity management in post-1997 Hong Kong: Challenges for a rule-based system. *Crime, Law and Social Change, 58*(1), 39–52.

Van Blijswijk, J. A., Van Breukelen, R. C., Franklin, A. L., Raadschelders, J. C., & Slump, P. (2004). Beyond ethical codes: The management of integrity in the Netherlands tax and customs administration. *Public Administration Review, 64*(6), 718–727.

Webb, W. N. (2012). Ethical culture and the value-based approach to integrity management: A case study of the department of correctional services. *Public Administration and Development, 32*(1), 96–108.

Fraud: from national strategies to practice on the ground—a regional case study

Alan Doig

The intentions of a number of national strategies and other initiatives to address fraud are reviewed in the context of one UK region. This paper considers how far various agencies in that region have responded to fraud. It then discusses which factors appear to have influenced the role of the strategies and other initiatives as an anti-fraud framework or to deliver anti-fraud work.

Fraud: the context

Before the UK's 2006 Fraud Review

Prior to the Fraud Review, responsibility for preventing or investigating fraud lay with, whether in terms of approaches or resources committed by public sector bodies or by individual police forces, the organizations themselves. For a number of the organizations, external auditors at central and local levels—the National Audit Office (NAO) and the Audit Commission—undertook reviews to assess their arrangements (Doig, 1996; 2006). Fraud increasingly emerged on policy agendas because of concerns over the rising costs and pervasiveness of fraud, and reducing police resources. In 2000, a consultancy report (NERA, 2000) for the Home Office argued that discovered fraud could range from £5 billion to £9 billion and undiscovered fraud, additionally, from £5 billion to £9 billion (the Home Office estimated that the total cost of crime to England and Wales in 1999/2000 was around £60 billion [Brand and Price, 2000]). A year later, research on behalf of the National Working Group on Fraud, a committee representing police fraud squads, confirmed a general and continuing decline in policing resources dedicated to fraud investigation (Doig *et al.*, 2001).

On the other hand, reforms were already taking place at organizational and legislative levels, either because fraud was an inevitable aspect of the work of specific departments, concerns at levels of fraud, the demands of external auditors, the need for a more organized internal response, or reviews to update legislation. The Department for Work and Pensions (DWP) has long had significant prevention and deterrence resources integrated into its work. Its current strategy, first issued in 1998, revolves round implementing five main themes—prevent, detect, correct, punish and deter—and

measurable delivery. In 1998, the Department of Health (DH) announced a Directorate of Counter Fraud Service (NHSCFS) and published its 'overall strategic framework within which the new unit will meet its remit—our policy, aims and objectives together with the approach, tactics and standards we propose to adopt' (DH, 1998, p. 8). In 2002, the Proceeds of Crime Act added another criminal justice sanction that would allow the confiscation of any benefit from criminal activity, including fraud. In 2006, the first Fraud Act was enacted, simplifying offences and addressing weaknesses in the Theft Acts.

The Fraud Review and anti-fraud strategies

Nevertheless, against the perceived rise in the cost of fraud and the decline in police resources, most efforts to address fraud were increasingly considered to lack coherence, co-ordination, common approaches and a commitment of resources. However, the DH approach suggested a way forward. As the Interim Report of the Fraud Review noted: 'many government departments and agencies deal with particular aspects of fraud. The "map" is very complex. But no-one pulls it all together. There is duplication and overlap of activities and functions, and gaps with some problems going unaddressed. The next phase of the Fraud Review will include a project to design a National Fraud Strategy for the whole economy. It will be based upon a model that has already been developed and implemented successfully in the National Health Service' (Fraud Review, 2006a, p. 4).

The work of the Fraud Review (2006b) took a primarily, but not exclusively, criminal justice approach, making a range of thematic and institutional recommendations, including a comprehensive measurement of fraud, promotion of prevention good practice, fraud as a policing priority, and agencies to support delivery. Integral to the approach was the national strategy, which 'should take a "holistic" approach, focusing efforts and resources where they are likely to be most effective rather than most attention grabbing, and focusing on the causes of fraud as well as dealing with the effects. The strategy will not replace existing strategies but rather will help co-ordinate ongoing efforts. Such an approach is likely to emphasise upstream action to prevent and deter fraud, such as educating consumers and businesses on how to avoid becoming victims. Despite these efforts fraud will still happen and the strategy will have to set priorities for downstream investigations and effective ways of punishing fraudsters and obtaining justice for victims' (Fraud Review, 2006b, p. 6).

One of its recommendations, the National Fraud Strategic Authority (later the National Fraud Authority [NFA]), issued the national anti-fraud strategy three years later (NFSA, 2009). This proposed building and sharing knowledge about fraud, tackling the most serious and harmful fraud threats, disrupting and punishing more fraudsters, while improving support to victims and the nation's long-term capability to prevent fraud. In 2011, the NFA worked with an advisory group, the Fighting Fraud Locally Oversight Board (FFLOB), to produce a local government anti-fraud strategy. This proposed the protection of 'public funds through the creation of a positive incentive regime, the removal of barriers to information sharing and by conducting a review of the use of powers by local authorities' (FFLOB/NFA, 2011, p. 6).

The publication of the strategies was supplemented by further reviews of public sector fraud, again emphasising the need to quantify the cost of fraud, the role of intelligence, information-sharing and prevention, increased collaboration, and more public–private sector partnerships (see Doig and Levi, 2013). A final, over-arching strategy review was published by the NFA in 2011 to 'provide fresh impetus in our fight against fraud' (NFA, 2011, p. 4). While the proposals included an emphasis on awareness and prevention, and better use of intelligence, collaboration and cross-cutting initiatives, the main focus was on fraud involving organized crime and organized approaches to fraud, as well as a stronger institutional focus through the Economic Crime Command (ECC) of the new National Crime Agency (NCA). This would address constraints on police resources by developing 'innovative, partnership solutions working across police forces, the NCA and its Economic Crime Command, other law enforcement organizations and the public, private and voluntary sectors' (NFA, 2011, p. 20).

Post-2011 strategies and other initiatives

Ironically, the NFA's 2011 announcement about the proposed role for the NCA was revisited in December 2013 when the government announced the NFA's closure. While the government professed that the NFA had been successful in raising awareness of fraud and improving co-ordination, it believed there should be a single national focus on cutting economic crime as part of the government's approach to serious and organized crime through the NCA ECC. Some of the NFA's responsibilities became part of the City of London Police (CoLP), which had been proposed by the Fraud Review as the national lead force on fraud. Already responsible for the National Fraud Intelligence Bureau (NFIB), which triages allegations of fraud into intelligence packages for police investigation, CoLP also took over Action Fraud, the central fraud reporting body, from the NFA. The NFA's local government work was handed over to the Chartered Institute of Public Finance and Accountancy (CIPFA), which had also taken on a number of responsibilities for public sector fraud and corruption following the closure of the Audit Commission (Doig, 2014; 2017).

In 2015, the CoLP's Economic Crime Directorate developed a draft National Police Fraud strategy and a National Police 'Protect' strategy. ('Protect' is one of the 4 'Ps'—Pursue, Prevent, Protect and Prepare—that are the components of the implementation frameworks for the UK's strategies for terrorism, organized crime, and cybercrime.) These placed the emphasis on volume fraud and on organized crime or criminal networks; the latter would be addressed through intelligence, investigation and disruption by the NCA and regional police units. The approach to volume fraud would be largely determined at local level, although supported by national resources, support and co-ordination. It would be primarily victim-focused, intended to prevent individuals or organizations from becoming victims and supporting them if they did.

In 2011, the government introduced the Localism Act which, while not directly relating to fraud, mandated councils to promote and maintain high standards of conduct, as well as requiring councils to have a code of conduct and disclosure requirements for members' interests. In the same year it also introduced a Transparency Code with the intention of providing both mandatory and optional information, including categories relating to fraud, to help citizens hold their councils to account (see DCLG, 2011; Sandford, 2016). Between 2010 and 2014, the Department for Communities and Local Government (DCLG) made some £35 million available in two tranches for competitive anti-fraud project bids, including funding to the (renamed) Fighting Fraud and Corruption Locally Board (FFCLOB) to update the 2011 strategy in the light of developments such as the national Serious and Organized Crime Strategy and the first UK Anti-Corruption Plan.

Issued in 2016, this new strategy's recommendations included:

• Working groups to look for good practice and 'quick wins', as well as fraud and corruption enablers with a view to preventing more fraud and corruption.
• A focus on procurement fraud.
• DCLG support in promoting good practice and addressing housing fraud.
• A structured programme on fraud and corruption awareness for elected local council members and senior managers.

It recommended that councils ensure the provision of risk-assessed resources, work together on counter-fraud hubs, horizon-scan and explore new areas, for example cyber and identity issues, and explore new methods to detect fraud such as behavioural insights.

For central government departments with their own strategies, delivery continued to be the primary focus. For example, much of DWP's work entailed developing and updating strategy implementation through pilots, proof of concepts, and adapting approaches, within the context of the five themes, and bringing 'together fraud and error work that was spread across the department' (NAO, 2015, p. 9). The NHSCFS had a dedicated staff resource, comprising some 250 staff in nine directorates, one of which covered investigations with approximately 70 staff, including eight regional teams. It also accredited and liaised with local counter-fraud specialists (LCFS), which all NHS bodies had to appoint (although not necessarily on a full-time basis). The requirement for anti-fraud and anti-corruption arrangements—currently part of the NHS Standard Contract documentation (termed 'Standards for Providers') since 2013—resulted in all bodies having their own published policies and procedures. For other departments the NAO has continued a general monitoring role and, as a consequence of its parliamentary reporting arrangements, invites scrutiny by the Committee of Public Accounts, while other parliamentary committees also scrutinize departmental work; other parts of the public sector, such as the police, are also subject to external inspection.

A continuing cause for concern?

The concerns about fraud that led to the Review and the strategies continue. In terms of the cost of fraud, research in 2007 sponsored by the Association of Chief Police Officers estimated the overall cost of fraud in the UK at a minimum of £12.9 billion (Levi et al., 2007). The NFA, whose remit included annual estimates of fraud, produced its final report in 2013 with an estimated overall cost of fraud £52 billion; the costs within the public sector were £14 billion against the tax system, £2.6 billion against central government, £2.1 billion against local government, and £1.9 billion against the benefits and tax credits system (NFA, 2013). In 2016, a commercially-supported study estimated the figure to be £193 billion (Experian et al., 2016); public sector fraud accounted for £37.5 billion; NHS fraud was estimated at £2.47 billion; and local government fraud was estimated at £7.31 billion.

Within such estimated figures, the reality of reported losses is, however, lower but still significant. The NHS received some 5,000 reports of potential fraud and corruption in 2015/16; the total value of fraud, bribery and corruption identified by NHS Protect and local investigators following the successful conclusion of investigations in that period was £6.5 million and a further potential £25 millions' worth of losses were under investigation. In its final report, in 2013/14, the Audit Commission stated that the number of detected cases fell by 3% to just over 104,000, while their value increased by 6% to over £188 million; £129 million of which was housing benefit and council tax benefit fraud (a 2014/15 report prepared by former Audit Commission staff stated that the £188 million figure had risen to over £207 million). The National Fraud Initiative* (NFI) reported that, between 2014 and 2016, identified fraud overpayments and errors amounted to £198 million. In terms of benefits fraud where the DWP has been under continuous pressure to improve its methodology, in 2015/16 around £1.6 billion was overpaid due to fraud. In 2017, the Cabinet Office reported that central

---

*Formerly run by the Audit Commission and now housed in the Cabinet Office, the NFI is a data-matching exercise from both public and private sector sources, sent as 'risk' matches to public bodies to be reviewed as potential frauds, overpayments and errors in public expenditure.

government departments detected fraud worth £73.6 million, and prevented fraud losses of £33 million, in 2015/16 (Cabinet Office, 2017, p. 6).

If the cost of fraud was rising, then there were also continuing concerns over public sector responses. In 2016, the NAO noted that, for central government departments, levels of fraud were often unknown and, without incentives or resources, there was poor reporting with gaps and inconsistencies in information collection. There were unreported or undetected losses and losses that were not being adequately addressed, government departments were relied on to manage fraud but had mixed capacity and capability 'to understand and address fraud risks', and there were limited means to evaluate 'success' (NAO, 2016a, p. 7).

Levels of police resource remained low (Button *et al.*, 2014), as did the use of joined-up anti-fraud working between departments (Doig and Levi, 2009). Elsewhere it was argued that the NHS anti-fraud work in some areas may not have led to any statistically significant drop in levels of fraud (Tickner, 2015). In 2013, a DCLG minister told the House of Commons Communities and Local Government Committee that 'the large majority of detected fraud had been identified by only a small proportion of councils and that 100 councils had detected no fraud at all' (Communities and Local Government Committee, 2014, p. 42).

Public sector fraud in practice: a regional perspective

Given that fraud is, in terms of cost, persistence and patchy responses, a continuing issue, and that there have been—and are—a number of strategies and other initiatives to address it, this paper reviews how far fraud is being addressed within the contexts of national and other strategies by a number of public bodies and local government in the north east region.

The research comprised desk reviews of official reports and academic publications, freedom of information requests and semi-structured interviews with personnel from the north east police forces, internal auditors and investigators working in the NHS and local councils, and senior DWP management.

The Department for Work and Pensions
The DWP operates a national remit in a dynamic benefits environment, in terms of both the volume of claims, and the interdependence of claims, as well as the impact of wider government policy, such as the introduction of Universal Credit (UC) to streamline and integrate the payment of benefits. The DWP's fraud-prevention approach

is integrated into its general matching system across its datasets. These are continuously tested through adaptive operating rules reflecting levels of risk (by, for example, claimant type, claim type, and level, type, newness and history of claims). Testing datasets and sharing datasets is undertaken both for fraud and for general application, both within the DWP and with other agencies, such as HM Revenues & Customs (HMRC). All staff undergo fraud-awareness training and all work computers include a referrals portal.

The DWP has three inter-connected and fraud approaches: the Fraud and Error Prevention Service (FEPS), the Local Service Investigation (LSI) and the Central Crime, Intelligence and Investigative Service (CCIS). FEPS and CCIS are national services. LSI is divided into two areas, north and south (north ranges from Wales to the north east of England), and further organized into geographic groups (for example London and the home counties) and then districts, which are largely coterminous with local authority areas. The staffing of the national services are, in the case of FEPS, approximately 1,500 staff located in four regional hubs. There are some 900 CCIS staff based regionally and locally, often located with LSI whose 2,000 staff is geographically located across numerous sites, working in teams of around 10–12. Nationally, some 5,000 personnel deal with around 1.2 million cases annually, 10% of which lead to criminal investigation and approximately 4,500 lead to prosecutions by the CPS; more local north east figures are not externally published and, in any case, casework may be allocated around the country where and when necessary.

All cases, whether staff referrals, hotline allegations from the public, referrals from other agencies, or matches across the DWP databases, are managed through Central Referrals where they are enhanced (through, for example, social media and internal sources) and triaged toward four outcomes—no further action (around 20% of cases); to FEPS to ensure compliance because there is no specific evidence of deliberate abuse or criminality; to LSI for investigation (although cases may be moved between it and FEPS depending on initial findings); or to CCIS if there is evidence of serious or organized criminality. Cases are distributed through FRAIMS—the Fraud Referral and Intervention Management System—a single, nationally-networked IT system that captures all fraud and compliance cases and their outcomes on one system and allocates cases. The databases are enhanced by real-time information from HMRC on earnings and other income sources.

Apart from HMRC and specialist links between CCIS, the police and the NCA ECC, the main sector with which DWP is engaged is local government. The proposal for UC includes housing benefit, triggering off a plan for a Single Fraud Investigation Service (SFIS), a project where the 'single' referred to the merger of council investigators and DWP's existing LSI; the former were some 1,800 investigators working for local authorities to prevent or investigate fraud associated with the administration of housing benefit. While councils will continue to process claims and administer housing benefit until UC is fully implemented nationally, by late 2016 around half had transferred over. Councils also receive funding under FERIS (the Fraud and Error Reduction Incentive Scheme), which offers financial rewards to local authorities who reduce fraud and error in their housing benefit cases by a range of initiatives, including publicity, intra-council collaboration and data use or encouraging reporting of change of circumstances. A further fund is available for demonstrable results in reducing fraud and error, but the amounts involved in both instances are not significant (and unlikely to continue if UC is rolled out nationally).

Local government
The establishment of SFIS has invariably impacted on councils' capacity to undertake fraud work because the staffing resource provided councils with an inhouse investigative capacity which, the Audit Commission estimated, was dealing with up to 40% non-benefit fraud by 2010/11 (see Doig, 2014). Nearly 50% of the DCLG competitive project funds had originally been earmarked for replacement staff (see Communities and Local Government Committee, 2014, p. 42). The decision to use it, and the other funding, for fixed-term initiatives led to numerous projects involving data-sharing, often between neighbouring councils. Unfortunately, few of the councils in the north east were recipients, and nor has the DCLG undertaken any review from which they could benefit in terms of shared good practice elsewhere.

The 12 north east councils mentioned the 2011 FFL strategy, but none have appeared to use the strategy or the associated checklist as an overall framework (although many delivered on a number of the proposals in the checklist). None reported on how—or if—the council was delivering the strategy. Hardly any mentioned the 2016 strategy. While all councils had a fraud and corruption strategy or policy, a lesser number had a related investigation or response plan and an anti money laundering policy. While a number reported annually on fraud-related outputs, few published monitoring or evaluation reports on implementation of a strategy. All referenced the NFI and all encouraged reporting of concerns, benefit frauds and so on, by the public; most, but not all, had a published whistle-blowing policy. Councils looked to CIPFA for risk, fraud and corruption guidance and training. Many councils were members of NAFN (the not-for-profit National Anti-Fraud Network, which provides specialist services) and hold meetings with DWP, while housing benefits responsibilities rest with councils pending the full roll-out of UC and because DWP data was relevant to council decisions on, for example, council tax reduction payments.

In relation to the Transparency Code, five of the councils appeared to have no online reference to counter-fraud work among their Transparency Code information and, of the seven who did, only two had 2016 information and two were undated. Not all information was presented to a standard format, but it would appear that less than 40 (or about 20 full-time equivalent [FTE]) staff were involved in fraud work at an estimated cost of approximately £1 million annually. Only two councils provided the optional information.

In terms of those councils studied in more depth for operational issues, it was clear that the departure of staff under SFIS had a significant impact on staff resource. They were also adversely affected by changes to the work of internal audit, where fraud is no longer necessarily a mandated part of planned audit work. This was added to by the general disinterest of the private sector external auditors who had taken over the Audit Commission's audit responsibilities, but not its wider roles in relation to fraud and probity arrangements. Two councils, losing 26 staff between them, have or are in the process of establishing corporate fraud units with four staff in each, based in or linked to the internal audit function as a central resource to co-ordinate fraud work across departments (here fraud work has been hampered by the presence of multiple internal processes and by specific departments, such as social services and parking management, adopting their own audit and enforcement approaches where evidence of fraud or recovery of funds may not necessarily be the main focus of their work).

The police
At the regional level, the police approach to organized fraud reflects the delivery of a number of strategic objectives through the establishment

of regional organized crime units focused on Level 2 (cross-force) organized crime, including fraud. In the north east, the unit has about 100 officers drawn from the three local forces; five form the fraud team. Their cases come from one of the three local forces or internally, followed by a formal management-tasking process that manages both workload and criteria. The latter reflect the unit's focus: offenders or inquiries involve cross-force work, complexity in terms of networks involved and financial structures, an organized crime element, harm caused and/or vulnerable victims (in terms of the seriousness or persistence of the crimes or methods used), and where the investigation of organized criminals may be best pursued through their fraud-related activity because it presents 'their principal vulnerability from a law enforcement perspective' (HMIC, 2015a, p. 60).

Among the three local forces, the approaches have been, as the policing strategies to combat fraud proposed, dependent on local policing priorities. One force had abolished its fraud squad some five years ago, but has now re-established a fraud squad within a newly-formed cybercrime investigation unit. One has a long-standing economic and cybercrime unit located within the specialist crime department. The third force has a fraud unit located in the force's major crime sub-department within the special operations department. Together they have less than 25 fraud investigators. Each approaches NFIB packages differently—both in terms of intake, acceptance and reporting back, as well as who investigates cases within the force. Cases investigated include internal or management frauds, including book-keeping, mandate fraud, election fraud, public sector corruption, GP practices' funds frauds, probate, carer and invoice diversion fraud, romance scams, investment fraud, and abuse of position of trust.

Only one force works primarily within the CoLP Protect strategy; it will only take on one or two cases a year after a serious case review for which the main criterion is complexity in terms of, for example, multiple victims or accounts. It has developed its own fraud and problem-solving plan around the Protect strategy and focuses its work on support to divisions. The unit also works with banks, community support officers, the probation service and Trading Standards, to protect vulnerable, elderly and other victims and potential victims.

None of the forces has significant joint working arrangements with or resourcing from the national level. Apart from operational matters, there is limited partnership working at the local level with other public bodies.

The National Health Service (NHS)

A review into both the extent of NHS Protect responsibilities and perceptions of a continuing uneven relationship between NHS Protect, and the DH and the NHS, resulted in several changes. In recognizing the absence of a counter-fraud presence within the department, the establishment of a DH Anti-Fraud Unit (AFU) is underway. This will investigate fraud within the department and arms-length bodies outside NHS Protect's remit, as well as agreeing workplans and priorities for the department in terms of addressing fraud across the NHS. NHS Protect has lost responsibility for security, which will become the responsibility of individual trusts, and has ended its roles in learning support and training, and at regional and local levels (consequentially also losing a number of staff).

As of November 2017, NHS Protect has been relaunched as the NHS Counter Fraud Authority, accountable to the AFU. Assessing fraud to be over £1 billion, the Authority has also launched a new three-year strategy that will see it acting as an intelligence-led organization providing a national overview of fraud, as well as focusing on complex cases, including those involving bribery and senior management (FIRST, its case management system, will be used by a Tasking and Coordinating Group to allocate cases). It will continue to receive NHS bodies' reporting on anti-fraud and anti-corruption arrangements under the Standards for Providers (part of the NHS Standard Contract) and now also the Standards for Commissioners (such as Clinical Commissioning Groups—CCG—which are responsible for overseeing providers' counter-fraud arrangements). It will undertake general fraud awareness and risk work, provide LCFSs with more intelligence, and information on trends, as well as working with them to improve performance through formulating strategies, collaboration and partnership, and benchmarking and assessing local initiatives.

One consequence will see trusts and other agencies taking more responsibility for local fraud and also the increasing employment of LCFSs by NHS internal audit providers, many of whom have combined into regional consortia to provide economies of scale, but also to service a range of trusts and other health services. They will also have to respond as healthcare provision becomes complex and complicated (for example, a local CCG, the main budget allocator, might have hundreds of providers, from public, private and the third sectors) and where the accountable agency—for example a local authority—may fall outside the NHS framework.

The major north east NHS internal audit consortium covers at least three counties, comprises six offices and 65 FTE staff, including six FTE LCFSs (and a newly-appointed head of fraud) providing internal audit services to its member organizations and, where these have client organizations, as an inhouse client service, to more than 20 trusts and CCGs, with a combined annual expenditure of over £7 billion. The standard audit service days are purchased according to the organization's annual audit plan (the days vary by organization) while anti-fraud is purchased separately and based largely on the Standards for Providers requirements, with days allocated according to its core components such as prevention and sanctions. The inclusion of an anti-fraud capacity within a single organization will mean a shift in focus and direction for both LCFSs and the consortium, not least because the FIRST-derived profiles (for the second half of 2015 the more significant case types were sickness, often involving working elsewhere; overtime; avoiding charges by overseas patients; double working; travel and subsistence) in triggering expectations, particularly by trust audit committees, of the need to develop a more coherent and proactive local response.

From strategy to practice on the ground: an assessment

In 2008, the National Strategic Fraud Authority's national fraud strategy—proposing a better knowledge of fraud, targeting the most serious fraud threats, improved capability for prevention, and measurement—was intended 'to take forward the Government's response to fraud' for which it claimed to be establishing 'a radical overhaul of the Government's delivery framework on fraud' (NFSA, 2009, pp. 10, 14). The 2011 refreshment of the national strategy, sponsored by a number of central government departments, including the Cabinet Office, emphasised the 'four priorities' agreed by the government's Fraud, Error and Debt Taskforce: collaboration; assessment of risk and measurement of losses; prevention; and zero tolerance (see NFA, 2011, p. 21). In 2016, the NAO was reporting that 'the government lacks a clear understanding of the scale of the fraud problem and departments vary in their ability to identify and address the risk of fraud' (NAO, 2016a, p. 32). In 2017, the Cabinet Office was proposing that central government departments have a counter-fraud strategy, a fraud risk assessment, a fraud policy and response plan, an annual action plan, fraud detection work, access

to trained investigators and fraud awareness training, and measurable indicators (Cabinet Office, 2017, p. 25).

This illustration focuses attention on three questions concerning strategies and practice on the ground: why there appears to have been little progress on the recommendations of past strategies and initiatives; why are some sectors returning to implement recommendations proposed some years ago or implementing recommendations already delivered in other sectors but with no assessment as to their effectiveness; and why generally there is a gap between strategic objectives and the practice on the ground.

The NAO provides two generally-applicable answers that may be drawn from, first, its review of central government department plans in terms of managing their overall activities and, second, from its review of central government departments' approach to fraud. In the first the NAO stated that: 'problems in the delivery of public services can be traced back to the way government makes decisions about how to implement policy...the current approach amounts to a collection of top-down, set-piece processes and guidance...and not the overarching integrated framework for strategic business planning and management that government needs' (NAO, 2016b, pp. 6 and 10). For the second, also in 2016, it noted that, while the Cabinet Office was the policy lead for fraud, it did 'not have strong levers to direct actions as even "mandates" have to be negotiated and agreed' (NAO, 2016a, p. 35).

The answers may also concern current permutations of, and delivery of, levers, co-ordination and leadership. The Home Office's Joint Fraud Taskforce continues to 'encourage' the prioritization of fraud within police forces, as well as working on awareness and developing fraud networks, while the Cabinet Office has published counter-fraud organizational and investigation standards. CIPFA's Counter Fraud Centre states it leads and co-ordinates the fight against fraud and corruption across local and central government, the health, education and charity sectors while HMIC noted in 2016 that the NCA's leadership function in terms of the quality of its strategic action plans had, in the case of the 'identified' threat area of public sector fraud, yet to be achieved (HMIC, 2016, p. 24). Further, the absence of a strategic cross-sector or national perspective perpetuates, as the chair of Committee of Public Accounts noted, more generally (2016, p. 10), a compartmentalized system that 'seems impervious to attempts to break down the walls of the silos from which public services emanate' (see also Doig and Levi, 2009). Part of the answer must also relate to resourcing strategies. In the case of local government, they 'are dealing with unprecedented "budget gaps"—that is, a massive shortfall in resources resultant from the combination of funding reductions and cost pressures' (Hastings *et al.*, 2015, p. 602) and, in the case of the police, 'the scale of these cuts was unprecedented and has required police services to reconsider their priorities' (Millie, 2014, p. 52).

Finally, part of the answer may lie within the NAO's proposals for an appropriate anti-fraud framework, including 'clear strategies and governance; an effective, well implemented control environment; and an ability to measure and evaluate performance' (NAO, 2016a, p. 5). Organizations, especially in the absence of firm or strong levers and in the current climate of budget restraints and competing policy agendas, may opt for limited, specific technical or control responses rather than wider governance arrangements to develop an organizational anti-fraud culture; 'specific anti-fraud activity is augmented by all-embracing governance contributions for risk management, internal audit, information governance, ethical standards and corporate governance, which are all elements towards the creation and maintenance of an antifraud culture' (Marks and Melville, 2012, p. 78; see also Doig, 2014; 2017). Taken together, the answers to the questions may not only highlight the various inhibitors and facilitators that explain differential responses across sectors but also the likelihood of a continuing gap between strategies and practice and whether current responses will, belatedly, begin to bridge the gap.

At the level where local discretion and decision-making are paramount in terms of implementation, there is often a noticeable divergence between strategy intention and practice as a consequence of individual organizations determining their own approach or interpretation. For example, to achieve the police fraud strategies at local level, the National Police Co-ordinator for Economic Crime had advised all police forces in 2015 that they should have, among other requirements, an identified lead at senior management team level; and an accountable chief officer to monitor and manage performance (see HMIC, 2015b, p. 73). The HMIC review noted, however, that many forces failed to assess the impact of fraud within their force strategic assessments and that 'there was an absence of strategic leadership and direction,

which resulted in a lack of performance management and priority setting in relation to the reporting and investigation of fraud' (HMIC, 2015b, p. 67).

In the case of local government, the abolition of the Audit Commission, the one—and central—firm lever for anti-fraud work, prompted the 2011 FFL strategy to suggest that 'local authorities and central government will need to look to design new arrangements for the new conditions. That will most likely require the greater sharing of counter fraud and audit resources, the creation of a new control framework and new institutional arrangements, building on the existing shared counter fraud infrastructure' (FFLOB/NFA, 2011, p. 18). By 2016, however, the next iteration of the strategy was already noting that 'the capacity to tackle fraud and corruption was likely to be reduced, or had already been reduced, as a result of austerity-related local authority funding reductions'. In terms of the expectations of the 2011 strategy, it reported that inter-organizational collaboration and data-sharing was making slow progress because counter-fraud work was not consistently prioritized and there was a lack of financial incentives to make the business case, because of a lack of understanding of data protection rules, and because of a lack of funding. Also, with staff resources reducing, there were no funds to train new staff, while 'senior managers were finding it difficult to dedicate sufficient time to demonstrate their support for counter-fraud activities due to the focus being on other priorities such as meeting budget savings targets and maintaining key services to residents' (FFCLOB/CIPFA, 2016, p. 15).

At the next level, those with existing sector strategies but subject to continuing change to the implementation context, including the reduction of resources, such as the NHS, the commitment to the resourcing of anti-fraud work, particularly at local level, has been diminished but may be mitigated with the integration of that work within audit arrangements. The proposed changes at the DH and NHS Protect remain in progress although a 2017 police review of the latter's investigations has already warned of the need for a much more directional role across a range of operational areas at local level in support of the national strategic objectives. In addition, the capacity and commitment of CCGs to oversee the anti-fraud, bribery and corruption arrangements in place within providers has also yet to be tested. Further, the increasing autonomy of NHS foundation trusts means that fraud compliance and enforcement capability may increasingly influence a trust's risk appetite to address fraud which, in turn, may sit uneasily with the primacy of patient care and the work of professional staff (in a way that is not reflected in, for example, HMRC or DWP in terms of the active pursuit of tax or benefits fraud).

Finally, those with organizational strategies and with enduring oversight (and where the NAO applies generally-applicable baseline criteria such as those used for its fraud stocktake reviews) appear to have the potential for deliverable or successful implementation. In its 2015 fraud and error stocktake for HMRC and DWP, the NAO noted that both had a joint strategy which identified a common approach and overlapping areas, as well as pursuing their own programmes and targets. Both had strengthened their governance arrangements and were using data to improve their understanding of the causes of fraud and of targeted interventions, but both had still to improve delivery of their strategies, design fraud and error responses into core processes and strengthen measurement of performance (NAO, 2015).

The possible explanations for, and consequences of, the divergence between national strategies and initiatives and practice on the ground should not deny many examples of local and regional interventions. On the other hand, they do emphasise not only the differential approaches but also that the resolution of the gap may, in terms of sector or organizational priorities and especially resources, be difficult to reconcile in the short term. In many ways the current situation reflects the issues that prompted the establishment of the 2006 Fraud Review and a number of its recommendations, and in particular the establishment of the NSFA/NFA and the strategies. Here the value lay not just with the strategic objectives but also with the role to review and report at six-monthly intervals on activities and the progress made against the strategic priorities, adapting the strategy to meet emerging challenges and evolving threats, and measure and analyse the national incidence and impact of fraud to help to shape initiatives and measure success (NSFA, 2009, p. 12). Closing the current gaps may therefore require a reconsideration of the need for strategic guidance, firm levers, commensurate resourcing, facilitation of joined-up thinking and information-sharing and continuing (and informed) oversight at national level.

Conclusion

The findings from the research suggest that, since 2006, the strategic approaches can only be considered in terms of practice on the ground as a work-in-progress, providing guidance rather than an enduring framework, with different organizations adopting specific components for specific purposes, rather than using the framework for a joined-up and coherent approach to fraud, internally and externally. This is further exacerbated by the absence of additional resources, and by national leadership or oversight on rolling out good practice, or ensuring the more cultural and governance arrangements to facilitate an anti-fraud organizational environment.

For fraud prevention in the UK, the interplay between national strategies and organizational priorities, within a context of budget reductions and other, often competing, agendas, remains an unending story. Both the rhetoric and the recommendations of the strategies in place may be—or are—necessary, but there are not yet the necessary or sufficient conditions for actual operational implementation work, and certainly not where gap-closing features noted above are absent. There is also a continuing absence of co-ordination between reforms at central/local levels, and continuing mismatches between the potential for fraud at local level and the institutional arrangements to address them.

Despite the best intentions of fraud strategies and policy initiatives in the UK, and while there is much *ad hoc* partnership working, joint working and information-sharing, there is a general identifiable dis-connectedness and potential dysfunctionality at national level as a consequence of the absence of resources, clarity of priorities and leadership or oversight that can be translated into institutional, procedural and resourcing implementation on the ground that effectively addresses a persistent and costly area of concern.

References

Brand, S. and Price, R. (2000), *The Economic and Social Costs of Crime* (Home Office).

Button, M., Blackbourne, D. and Tunley, M. (2015), 'The not so thin blue line after all?' Investigative resources dedicated to fighting fraud/economic crime in the UK. *Policing*, 9, 2, pp. 129–142.

Cabinet Office (2017), *Cross-Government Fraud Landscape Annual Report*.

Committee of Public Accounts (2016), *Protecting the Public's Money: First Annual Report from Chair of Committee of Public Accounts*. HC 835.

Communities and Local Government Committee (2014), *Local Government Procurement*. HC 712.

DCLG (2011), *The Code of Recommended Practice for*

IMPACT

This paper has universal applicability in reviewing the objectives of anti-fraud strategies drawn up at national level, and the practice on the ground, using a bottom-up perspective to assess how national approaches are—or are not—implemented. It highlights the questions of continuing ownership of the strategy, sector or organizational frameworks, other priorities and agendas, budgets and resourcing and measurement of progress before asking the effect those aspects have on implementation. It uses a UK region as a case study in the context of the 2006 UK Fraud Review and the various consequential anti-fraud strategies and initiatives for national and local levels. Noting the continuing concerns over the costs and pervasiveness of fraud since 2006, as well as over differential responses to the implementation of strategies, the research for the paper provides insights from below into the commitment to the strategies and initiatives, organizational discretion, availability of resources, evidence of progress, and the impact of other agendas and issues, such as austerity and what the National Audit Office called 'firm levers'. The paper suggests that the interplay between the aspects, concerns and insights noted go some way to explaining why much of the intention of the Fraud Review and its recommendations has yet to be realized. It also underlines more generally the need for strategic oversight, the importance of resources, implementation frameworks, and performance and progress measures, without which any strategy is unlikely to succeed.

Local Authorities on Data Transparency.

DH (1998), *Countering Fraud in the NHS.*

Doig, A. (1996), Public sector audit: the first and last defence against fraud? In Wilson, J. (Ed), *Current Issues in Accounting and Auditing* (Tudor Business Publishing/Hodder & Stoughton).

Doig, A. (2006), *Fraud* (Willan Publishers).

Doig, A. (2014), Roadworks ahead? Addressing fraud, corruption and conflict of interest in English local government. *Local Government Studies, 40*, 5, pp. 670–686.

Doig, A. (2017), Local government ethics in England: how is local ownership working? *Public Money & Management, 37*, 1, pp. 63–68.

Doig, A., Johnson, S. and Levi, M. (2001), Old populism or new public management? Policing fraud in the UK. *Public Policy and Administration, 16*, 1, pp. 91–113.

Doig, A. and Levi, M. (2009), Inter-agency work and the UK public sector investigation of fraud 1996– 2006: joined-up rhetoric and disjointed reality. *Policing and Society, 19*, 3, pp. 199–215.

Doig, A. and Levi, M. (2013), A case of arrested development? Delivering the UK national fraud strategy within competing policing policy priorities. *Public Money & Management, 33*, 2, pp. 145–152.

Experian/PKF Littlejohn/Centre for Counter Fraud Studies (2016), *Annual Fraud Indicator 2016* (University of Portsmouth).

FFCLOB/CIPFA (2016), *The Local Government Counter Fraud and Corruption Strategy.*

FFLOB/NFA (2011), *The Local Government Fraud Strategy.*

Fraud Review (2006a), *Interim Report* (www.lslo.gov.uk).

Fraud Review (2006b), *Report* (www.lslo.gov.uk).

Hastings, A. et al. (2015), Coping with the cuts? The management of the worst financial settlement in living memory. *Local Government Studies, 41*, 4, pp. 601–621.

HMIC (2015a), *Regional Organized Crime Units. A Review of Capability and Effectiveness* (Home Office).

HMIC (2015b), *Real Lives, Real Crimes. A Study of Digital Crime and Policing* (Home Office).

HMIC (2016), *An Inspection of the National Crime Agency's Progress against Outstanding Recommendations made by HMIC and Areas for Improvement* (Home Office).

Levi, M. et al. (2007), *The Nature, Extent and Economic Impact of Fraud in the UK* (ACPO).

Marks, G. and Melville, D. (2012), The evolution of fraud and anti-fraud activity in local authorities. In Morales, C. and Boardman, F. (Eds), (2012), *Public Service Reform in the UK: Revolutionary or Evolutionary?* (PMPA).

Millie, A. (2014), What are the police for? Re-thinking policing post-austerity. In Brown, J. M. (Ed), *The Future of Policing* (Routledge).

NAO (2015), *Fraud and Error Stocktake.* HC 267, Session 2015–16.

NAO (2016a), *Fraud Landscape Review.* HC 850, Session 2015–16.

NAO (2016b), *Government's Management of its Performance: Progress with Single Departmental Plans.* HC 872.

NERA (2000), *The Economic Cost of Fraud.*

NFA (2011), *Fighting Fraud Together.*

NFA (2013), *Annual Fraud Indicator.*

NFSA (2009), *The National Fraud Strategy. A New Approach to Combating Fraud.*

Sandford, M. (2016), *Local Government Transparency in England.* Briefing Paper 06046 (House of Commons Library).

Tickner, P. (2015), *Fraud and Corruption in Public Services* (Routledge).

Index

Page numbers in **bold** refer to tables and those in *italic* refer to figures.

For Product Safety Concerns and Information please contact our
EU representative GPSR@taylorandfrancis.com Taylor & Francis
Verlag GmbH, Kaufingerstraße 24, 80331 München, Germany